Sin and Its Remedy in Paul

Contours of Pauline Theology

Series editors, NIJAY K. GUPTA and JOHN K. GOODRICH

The Contours of Pauline Theology book series engages the thought of the Apostle Paul, exploring key texts and crucial topics pertaining to Paul's theology and their explication in modern scholarship. These stimulating volumes bring together a diverse line up of leading voices in Pauline studies to probe important concepts that permeate Paul's theological vision and deserve nuanced conversations. The volumes are innovative and yet accessible enough for students and scholars alike.

Sin and Its Remedy in Paul

EDITED BY
Nijay K. Gupta
AND
John K. Goodrich

CASCADE Books · Eugene, Oregon

SIN AND ITS REMEDY IN PAUL

Contours of Pauline Theology

Copyright © 2020 Wipf and Stock Publishers. All rights reserved. Except for brief quotations in critical publications or reviews, no part of this book may be reproduced in any manner without prior written permission from the publisher. Write: Permissions, Wipf and Stock Publishers, 199 W. 8th Ave., Suite 3, Eugene, OR 97401.

Cascade Books
An Imprint of Wipf and Stock Publishers
199 W. 8th Ave., Suite 3
Eugene, OR 97401

www.wipfandstock.com

PAPERBACK ISBN: 978-1-5326-8956-7
HARDCOVER ISBN: 978-1-5326-8957-4
EBOOK ISBN: 978-1-5326-8958-1

Cataloguing-in-Publication data:

Names: Gupta, Nijay K., editor | Goodrich, John K., editor
Title: Sin and its remedy in Paul / edited by Nijay K. Gupta and John K. Goodrich.
Description: Eugene, OR: Cascade Books, 2020. | Series: Contours of Pauline Theology | Includes index.
Identifiers: ISBN 978-1-5326-8956-7 (paperback) | ISBN 978-1-5326-8957-4 (hardcover) | ISBN 978-1-5326-8958-1 (ebook)
Subjects: LCSH: Paul, the Apostle, Saint. | Bible. Epistles of Paul—Criticism, interpretation, etc. | Sin—Biblical teaching.
Classification: BS2650.52 S56 2020 (print) | BS2650.52 (ebook)

Manufactured in the U.S.A.   NOVEMBER 2, 2020

For Ben Blackwell
Frater Dunelmensis

Contents

Contributors ix
Preface xi
Abbreviations xiii

1. Sin in Context: Ἁμαρτία in Greco-Roman and Jewish Literature
—*Nijay K. Gupta* 1

2. Sin and Soteriology in Romans
—*Martinus C. de Boer* 14

3. Sin and the Sovereignty of God in Romans
—*Bruce W. Longenecker* 33

4. Models for Relating Sin as a Power to Human Activity
in Romans 5:12–21—*A. Andrew Das* 49

5. Letters from the Battlefield: Cosmic Sin and Captive Sinners
in 1 Corinthians—*Alexandra R. Brown* 63

6. Divine Generosity in the Midst of Conflict: Sin and Its Remedy
in 2 Corinthians—*Dominika Kurek-Chomycz* 81

7. Sin, Slavery, Sacrifice, and the Spirit: The Human Problem
and Divine Solution in Galatians—*David A. deSilva* 99

8. Dead in Your Trespasses: Sin as Infraction and Sphere
of Power in Colossians and Ephesians—*John K. Goodrich* 114

9. "But I Never Intended . . .": Implicit Hamartiology
in the Thessalonian Correspondence—*Andy Johnson* 130

10. Re-Ordering the Household: Misalignment and Realignment
to God's οἰκονομία in 1 Timothy—*George M. Wieland* 147

Index of Modern Authors 163
Index of Ancient Documents 167

Contributors

Alexandra R. Brown (PhD, Union Theological Seminary, New York) is Fletcher Otey Thomas Professor in Bible at Washington and Lee University, Virginia.

A. Andrew Das (PhD, Union Theological Seminary, Virginia) is Professor of Religious Studies and Assistant Dean of the Faculty for Assessment and Accreditation at Elmhurst College, Illinois.

Martinus C. de Boer (PhD, Union Theological Seminary, New York) is Professor of New Testament at Vrije Universiteit, Amsterdam.

David A. deSilva (PhD, Princeton Theological Seminary) is Trustees' Distinguished Professor of New Testament and Greek at Ashland Theological Seminary, Ohio.

John K. Goodrich (PhD, University of Durham) is Professor of Bible at Moody Bible Institute, Illinois.

Nijay K. Gupta (PhD, University of Durham) is Professor of New Testament at Northern Seminary, Illinois.

Andy Johnson (PhD, Luther Seminary) is Professor of New Testament at Nazarene Theological Seminary, Missouri.

Dominika Kurek-Chomycz (PhD, Katholieke Universiteit Leuven) is Senior Lecturer in New Testament Studies at Liverpool Hope University, United Kingdom.

Bruce W. Longenecker (PhD, University of Durham) is Professor of Christian Origins and W. W. Melton Chair of Religion at Baylor University, Texas.

George M. Wieland (PhD, University of Aberdeen) is Director of Mission Research and Training at Carey Baptist College, New Zealand.

Preface

THIS INAUGURAL VOLUME IN the Contours of Pauline Theology series began as a set of conference papers presented at the Pauline Theology research group of the Institute for Biblical Research. During the group's 2017 and 2018 meetings, six leading Pauline theologians were invited to read papers on the theme of "sin and its remedy in Paul." In 2017, three papers were presented on Romans, and in 2018 one paper each was presented on 1 Corinthians, 2 Corinthians, and Galatians. The aim of the two-year study was to seek to answer the following questions: How does Paul conceptualize sin? Does he primarily regard sin as disobedience, or as an enslaving power? If both, is there a model or perspective that best accounts for these multiple conceptualities? And what do the answers to these questions suggest about the christological and pneumatological remedies to the problem of sin as Paul conceives of them?

Both of the sessions were excellent, and we are grateful to all six of our presenters for their participation in the annual meetings, for expanding their original papers into chapter length studies, and for allowing us the privilege of publishing their essays together in this collection. Realizing, however, that a volume devoted only to four Pauline letters could hardly do justice to the topic under examination, we have chosen to supplement these initial studies on the *Hauptbriefe* with four additional chapters: an essay that targets the usage of sin language in extrabiblical Greco-Roman and Jewish literature, as well as essays on Colossians and Ephesians, 1 and 2 Thessalonians, and 1 Timothy, respectively. The result, we hope, is a volume that will both guide and stimulate students, teachers, and scholars to consider and appreciate more deeply the complexity of Paul's theology of sin and salvation.

It has been a pleasure to work with each of the contributors to this project, whose essays we genuinely appreciate. We also wish to thank our families for their support, Holly Dunaway for her keen editorial eye and assistance with the indices, as well as Michael Thomson of Cascade Books for his interest in this project and in the new series. Finally, we dedicate this volume to Ben Blackwell, whose friendship during and since our postgraduate years at Durham University has been a constant source of joy. The relationships forged in the Bailey Room are among our most cherished takeaways from our time in Durham. Ben, we are thankful to have been fellow travelers with you on the Dunelm Road.

Nijay K. Gupta
John K. Goodrich
January 7, 2020

Abbreviations

AB	Anchor Bible
ABD	*Anchor Bible Dictionary.* Edited by David Noel Freedman. 6 vols. New York: Doubleday, 1992.
AnBib	Analecta Biblica
ANTC	Abingdon New Testament Commentary
ATR	*Anglican Theological Review*
AYBC	*Anchor Yale Bible Commentary*
BBR	*Bulletin for Biblical Research*
BECNT	Baker Exegetical Commentary on the New Testament
BETL	Bibliotheca Ephemeridum Theologicarum Lovaniensium
BGU	*Aegyptische Urkunden aus den Königlichen Staatlichen Museen zu Berlin, Griechische Urkunden.* 15 vols. Berlin: Weidmann, 1895–1937.
BNTC	Blacks New Testament Commentary
BTCB	Brazos Theological Commentary on the Bible
BTS	Biblical Tools and Studies
CBQ	*Catholic Biblical Quarterly*
CRINT	Compendia Rerum Iudaicarum ad Novum Testamentum
HTR	*Harvard Theological Review*
ICC	International Critical Commentary
Int	*Interpretation*
IVPNTC	IVP New Testament Commentary

JAJSup	Journal of Ancient Judaism Supplements
JSHRZ	*Jüdische Schriften aus hellenistisch-römischer Zeit*
JSNTSup	Journal for the Study of the New Testament Supplements Series
JSPSup	Journal for the Study of the Pseudepigrapha Supplements Series
JTI	*Journal of Theological Interpretation*
JTS	*Journal of Theological Studies*
KJV	King James Version
LCL	Loeb Classical Library
LNTS	Library of New Testament Studies
LSJ	Liddell, Henry George, Robert Scott, Henry Stuart Jones. *A Greek-English Lexicon*. 9th ed. with revised supplement. Oxford: Clarendon, 1996.
MTSR	*Method and Theory in the Study of Religion*
NA28	*Novum Testamentum Graece,* Nestle-Aland, 28th ed.
NABRE	New American Bible, Revised Edition
NCBC	New Century Bible Commentary
NETS	New English Translation of the Septuagint
NIBC	New International Biblical Commentary
NICNT	New International Commentary on the New Testament
NIDNTT	*New International Dictionary of New Testament Theology*. Edited by Colin Brown. 4 vols. Grand Rapids: Zondervan, 1975–1978.
NIDNTTE	*New International Dictionary of New Testament Theology and Exegesis*, 2nd ed. Edited by Moisés Silva. 5 vols. Grand Rapids: Zondervan Academic, 2014.
NIGTC	New International Greek Testament Commentary
NIV	New International Version
NovT	*Novum Testamentum*
NovTSup	Supplements to Novum Testamentum

NRSV	New Revised Standard Version
NTL	New Testament Library
NTS	*New Testament Studies*
NTT	New Testament Theology
PNTC	Pillar New Testament Commentary
RSV	Revised Standard Version
SBL	Studies in Biblical Literature
SSEJC	Studies in Scripture in Early Judaism and Christianity
SNTSMS	Society for New Testament Studies Monograph Series
SNTW	Studies of the New Testament and Its World
STJ	*Scottish Journal of Theology*
TDNT	*Theological Dictionary of the New Testament.* Edited by Gerhard Kittel and Gerhard Friedrich. Translated by Geoffrey W. Bromiley. 10 vols. Grand Rapids: Eerdmans, 1964–1976.
THNTC	Two Horizons New Testament Commentary
TPINTC	TPI New Testament Commentaries
TynBul	*Tyndale Bulletin*
USFISFCJ	University of South Florida International Studies in Formative Christianity and Judaism
WBC	Word Biblical Commentary
WMANT	Wissenschaftliche Monographien zum Alten und Neuen Testament
WUNT	Wissenschaftliche Untersuchungen zum Neuen Testament
ZECNT	Zondervan Exegetical Commentary on the New Testament

1

Sin in Context: Ἁμαρτία in Greco-Roman and Jewish Literature

Nijay K. Gupta

This book focuses in large part on sin language in Paul's letters with an interest in the apostle's theology of sin, redemption, and salvation. But before engaging directly with the occurrences and usage of this language in Paul, it is helpful to take a step back and look more broadly at how the language of "sin," in particular the Greek word ἁμαρτία+,[1] was used in pagan and Jewish literature in the Greco-Roman world. This is a crucial preliminary study because modern readers of the Bible are tempted to think about the word "sin" only in relation to Christian religion. But the fact of the matter is that this terminology was widely employed in Jewish communities as well as in Greco-Roman literature, although New Testament writers, like Paul, certainly talked about "sin" in a very particular way (which we will discover and discuss in the other essays in this book).

We will commence with ἁμαρτία+ language in a variety of pagan Greek texts to understand how this terminology was used more widely in Greco-Roman society. Paul would have been fully aware of these uses, but also we can imagine that his (majority) gentile readers would have had certain assumptions about what this language means (from cultural usage) even while Paul was communicating his own conceptualization of "sin."

---

1. The (+) here will be used throughout the essay to refer to cognates of ἁμαρτία including ἁμαρτάνω and ἁμαρτωλός, as well as other root-related terms.

Then we will turn to give attention to sin language in Jewish literature with special interest in ἁμαρτία+ in the Hellenistic Jewish literature of the Second Temple period.

Ἁμαρτία in Greco-Roman Literature

In Aristotle's *Nicomachean Ethics* book 5, the famed philosopher addresses the question of what it means to be "just" in relation to lawfulness and fairness in society. Aristotle outlines three types of injury that befall someone and how one might become liable to fault. First, we have ἀτύχημα—an accidental injury (or harm to the other) that could not be reasonably avoided or foreseen. Then, Aristotle says, we have ἁμάρτημα (related to ἁμαρτία), an offense that was not intentional or malicious, but demonstrates negligence on the part of the perpetrator.[2] And, thirdly, Aristotle refers to ἀδίκημα—a wrongdoing committed with harmful intent (*Eth. nic.* 1135b).

It does not appear to be the case that everyone in Hellenistic society followed Aristotle's injustice taxonomy as a rule; rather, different writers had small variations on their use of ἁμαρτία+. But what is helpful to know at the outset of this discussion is that *no one* treated this as religious language at all. Rather, ἁμαρτία+ was used when a writer wished to discuss some error, mistake, or deviation from what is known to be right or proper. This might pertain to actual civil laws, but it was also employed for all manner of issues including social matters, accidents, and personal mistakes.[3] Below we will examine six hellenophone writers (Herodotus, Aristotle, Polybius, Strabo, Plutarch, and Arrian) on their usage of ἁμαρτία+. But we must keep in mind that these writers by and large represent the language of elite society. So, we might just say a word here about what we learn from the Greek papyri, which tends to represent language use across all social and economic sectors in personal notes, business dealings, contracts, etc. In a certain personal correspondence (13/14 BCE), a freedman appeals to his patron that he should not be mistreated because he has not done anything wrong (ἡμάρτηκά) (BGU 4 1141). In another private letter, Antonius Longus begs forgiveness from his mother, confessing "I know that I have sinned [οἶδα ὅτι ἡμάρτηκά]" (BGU 3 846).

---

2. This is often the case in American law with "involuntary manslaughter."
3. See "ἁμαρτία," *NIDNTTE*, 1:255–63, at 263; also Guy Kendall, "The Sin of Oedipus," *The Classical Review* 25.7 (1911) 195–97.

In Herodotus's *Histories*, ἁμαρτία+ appears about nine times. Three times it relates to the sins or wrongdoings of a person (1.19.1, 6; 1.119.1). We learn that the Agyllaeans consult the oracle of Delphi in order to discern how they might lift a curse, such that they could heal (ἀκέομαι) an offense (ἁμαρτία) made by their mistreatment of the Phocaeans (*Hist.* 1.167.2). We see the same kind of language in book 7, where Herodotus addresses the concern King Xerxes had with one of his corrupt judges, Sandoces. As a punishment, Xerxes had Sandoces hung on a cross. But he changed his mind and spared the life of Sandoces, judging (λογιζόμενος) that his good deeds (ἀγαθά) outweighed his offenses (τῶν ἁμαρτημάτων, 7.194.3). Here we see how broad is the meaning of a word like ἁμάρτημα. While it can carry the general meaning of fault or error, in the case of Sandoces the problem is a bribe (amongst other bad behaviors), a moral failure that is clear and intentional.

Later, in a speech by Alexander (son of Amyntas), Herodotus recounts these words: "I forgive [μεθίημι] the Athenians all the offenses [ἁμαρτάς]⁴ which they committed against me" (8.140.1.1). It was actually Alexander who had stolen and destroyed the Athenians' land, but here he makes an attempt to pacify them so they could make a treaty.

We already briefly mentioned Aristotle above. Here we can add his use of ἁμαρτία+ as it is found in his *Politics*. He can talk about fault committed in relationship to the mistakes of legislators (1269a.15-19), willful bad decisions (1270a.5-9), and any and all activities that operate outside of what is expected or normal (1320b.35-39; 1336a.1-4; 1338b.10-14). Sometimes it is helpful to understand how an author uses ἁμαρτία based on how the word is paired with synonyms or antonyms. At one point, Aristotle sets ἁμαρτία side by side with παρέκβασις, which means "deviation(s)" from a norm (1310b.5-9).

Polybius has over twenty uses of ἁμαρτία+ in his own *Histories*. Overall in this work, Polybius acts as more than a disinterested reporter of historical events. He has a rather transparent and keen interest in whether or not various leaders and pivotal figures made good or bad choices. That is not to say his use of ἁμαρτία+ is one dimensional. On several occasions ἁμαρτία+ refers to acts that may be nothing more than mistakes or errors (e.g., 5.11.7; 5.21.1)—for example, he notes "inaccuracies" (ἁμαρτίας) in

---

4. The noun ἁμαρτάς is the Ionic Greek equivalent to ἁμαρτία in Attic and Koine Greek.

city records (12.11.1). But at other times, he uses ἁμαρτία+ in reference to intentional (moral) offenses (such as treachery, 1.10.4; cf. 30.31.3).

One of my favorite aspects of Polybius's writings is the way he unabashedly critiques other historians. For example, he notes that Phylarchus goes too far in detailing the faults of the Mantineans, especially highlighting their "criminal acts" (τάς παρανόμους τῶν πράξεων, 2.61.1), while neglecting completely any of their noble deeds, "as if it were rather the proper function of history to chronicle the commission of sins [ἁμαρτίας] than to call attention to right and honorable actions [τὰ καλὰ καὶ δίκαια τῶν ἔργων], or as if readers of his memoirs would be improved less by account of good conduct which we should emulate than by criminal conduct which we should shun" (2.61.2–3).

Similarly, in a later part of Polybius's *Histories*, he makes mention of some writers who comment on the activities of Philip V, but leaves out the situation in Messene (see 8.8). Polybius does not shy away from recounting that Philip destroyed the country "like an enemy acting from passion rather than from reason" (8.8.1, LCL). What upsets Polybius in the other accounts of Philip's activity is when some act in fear or admiration of such kings and fail to treat their behavior (ἀσέβειαν ... παρανομίαν) as a mistake (ἐν ἁμαρτίᾳ); even more so they portray their behavior as noble (ἐν ἐπαίνῳ, 8.8.4). Polybius definitively states his view on the matter as follows: "My own opinion is that we should neither revile nor extol kings falsely, as has so often been done, but always give an account of them consistent with our previous statements and in accord with the character of each" (8.8.7, LCL).

A few more sections from Polybius deserve our attention. In the twelfth book he addresses again the matter of poor or sloppy historians. Timaeus, he explains, offers the guise of precision, but suffers from all-corrupting bias (12.26.3). Polybius is more than happy to diagnose Timaeus's errors (ἁμάρτημα) and faults (ἁμαρτία): "He seems to me to have acquired both a talent for detailed research and a competence based on inquiry, and in fact generally speaking to have approached the task of writing history in a painstaking spirit, but in some matters we know of no author of repute who seems to have been less experienced and less painstaking" (12.26.4). By this, Polybius goes on to explain that Timaeus put all his efforts into collecting data from books, but failed to interview witnesses (12.27.4).

A last section from Polybius worth noting is from book 16. Again, Polybius critiques academics who do sloppy work. He attacks the work of Zeno, especially on topography. He refers to Zeno's errors as "mistakes" (παράπτωσιν) and "faults" (ἁμαρτίας) (16.20.6). He mentions that he (Polybius) wrote to Zeno to correct him. Zeno wrote back and expressed his regret that he had made such mistakes, but also that the work had already been published. Rather than gloating, Polybius "begged" his readers to review his own work looking for mistakes and problems. If he misled others *intentionally*, he ought to be censured relentlessly, and if he erred by mistake of ignorance, he ought to correct him graciously (16.20.7–8). Before concluding our discussion of Polybius, it bears repeating that this last statement reveals that Polybius used ἁμαρτία+ in a broad sense of "error," without assuming malice, laziness, or any other motivational flaw.

Now we turn to Strabo's *Geography*, where we find a half dozen occurrences of ἁμαρτία+. Overall Strabo draws attention to others who have made historical or geographical "mistakes." For example, Strabo points out some writers who say that Homer was not familiar with the isthmus that lies between the Egyptian Sea and the Arabian gulf (1.2.24; cf. 1.2.38; 4.1.5; 7.7.12; 13.1.54).

Plutarch's use of ἁμαρτία+ in his *On Moral Virtue* is more like that of Aristotle. He addresses the relationship between emotion and reason. He observes that some philosophers treat *every* emotion as a mistake (ἁμαρτία). But Plutarch counter-argues that not all emotions are equal in their origin and effect. Emotions are not always wanton outbursts of passion. Often they come from some kind of internal reaction, and when the logic behind the reaction is well-reasoned, the emotion might also be reasonable. Thus, Plutarch gives the example of Plato's grief over the death of Socrates (10). Plutarch does not deny that emotions can become unbridled. And when they are, it is appropriate to see this as ἁμαρτία.

Finally we come to Arrian's *Anabasis*. Arrian uses ἁμαρτία in reference to a strategic mistake of a Macedonian troop (4.5.8). He can call ἁμαρτία the matter of "fault" in a disagreement (4.8.9), and similarly for a miscalculation in a combat strategy (5.4.5). Arrian's most interesting use of ἁμαρτία+ appears in his seventh book of *Anabasis*. Here he gives an extended defense of the behavior of Alexander the Great. Arrian admits that Alexander was known for many unusual or extreme behaviors, such as the unusual way that he dressed, his lavish drinking parties, and his frequent fits of rage. Arrian confesses that these are not perfect actions, but can be labeled rightly as "errors" (ἐπλημμελήθη). What sets Alexander apart from other ancient rulers is not that he was perfect—he was not—but, Arrian explains, he "was the only one . . . who, from nobility of character, repented of the errors which he had committed [μεταγνῶναί γε ἐφ' οἷς ἐπλημμέλησε]" (7.29.1). Most other people justify their wrongdoing (ἁμαρτία) with some excuse. But "it seems to me that the only cure for sin [ἁμαρτίας] is for the sinner [ἁμαρτόντα] to confess it, and to be visibly repentant [μεταγιγνώσκοντα] in regard to it" (7.29.2). Obviously Arrian believed Alexander to be just such a penitent man!

Our survey of Greco-Roman literature has been mostly descriptive, but permit me now to make a few analytical notes. First, we must be quick to observe that ἁμαρτία+ is *not* religious language in extant pagan discourse. It was not viewed as a "sin" against god or the divine realm. Most often the terminology pertains to any sort of error, mistake, or offense, with no assumption about motive. We might think of ἁμαρτία+ as a deviation from some standard or expectation, whether it is something malicious like murder or theft, or something innocuous like taking a wrong turn on a trip. We can also say that this was not terribly dominant language in society. It is not especially common in the Greek papyri, nor in literary sources. There are less than 200 occurrences of ἁμαρτία in pagan Greek literature. The New Testament all by itself comes close to that number (173), the Septuagint more than doubles it (525), and the OT Pseudepigrapha isn't far behind (108). Now we turn to how ἁμαρτία+ was used in Jewish literature before and during the time of Paul.

Sin Language in Jewish Literature

Before we look at ἁμαρτία+ in Hellenistic Jewish literature directly, it is wise to take the preliminary step of briefly discussing the language of "sin" in the Hebrew Bible (HB). In the HB there are a cluster of terms used in reference to sin, namely, מְרִי, עָוֹן, פֶּשַׁע, חַטָּאת, and רַע. Each of these has its own set of nuances, but they all relate to deviations from divine expectation or command to some degree. Rather than parse out the semantic distinctions of each of these words, I think it wise to take the approach of Joseph Lam, who considers four common metaphors used in relation to sin and covenantal transgression in the HB.[5] The first metaphor he identifies is that of *burden*, like carrying a heavy object. This relates, then, to the weight of guilt and punishment due to sin. For example, in Gen 18:20, the sin of Sodom and Gomorrah is referred to as "very heavy." Another image used in

---

5. See Joseph Lam, *Patterns of Sin in the Hebrew Bible* (Oxford: Oxford University Press, 2016).

the HB for sin is that of *accounting*, of debt and payment, where God stands as judge and ruler of his covenantal people. This is where we can place concepts like God "blotting out" transgressions" (Isa 43:25) and "erasing" iniquities (Ps 51:9). We will return to this metaphor later.

A third metaphor category that Lam identifies is that of *road* or *path* and involves *walking*. Lam notes Jer 18:11 ("Turn now, all of you from your evil way, and amend your ways and your doings"[6]) and the famous Suffering Servant text, where the prophet confesses, "All we like sheep have gone astray; we have all turned to our own way, and the LORD has laid on him the iniquity of us all" (Isa 53:6). Lastly, Lam offers the common HB image of sin as a stain, blemish, or contaminant, that is, whatever threatens purity and wholeness. So we could turn in illustration to a text like Prov 20:9: "Who can say, 'I have made my heart clean; I am pure from my sin?'"

Beyond these four metaphors, what else can we say about the concept of sin in the HB? Mark Boda has done substantial work on this subject. He echoes Wyschogrod in saying that the Hebrew people understood sin as "violation of the command of God."[7] It is not just a mistake or accident, but rather, "Sin is possible only when the transgression is a violation of the command of the divine lawgiver."[8] For Boda, it is essential to understand that the HB does not portray sin as primarily a legal category, where sin is an injustice against the society of people or against the state. Rather, it is a religious category, an act of rebellion against the authority of God. To break a covenantal command is "to blaspheme Him, to reject His authority, and to rebel against His rule."[9] The Pentateuch portrays sin not primarily as a personal choice, but as an "external condition that must be mastered" (Gen 4:7).[10] And it presents itself as "a dynamic force that has invaded humanity's inner being and produces an earth filled with violence."[11] Throughout the rest of the Pentateuch it remains a force that threatens the presence of God among his people.[12] This conception is repeated regularly throughout

---

6. Translations from the English Bible are NRSV unless otherwise noted.

7. Mark Boda, *A Severe Mercy: Sin and Its Remedy in the Old Testament* (Winona Lake, IN: Eisenbrauns, 2009), 104.

8. Boda, *Severe Mercy*, 104.

9. Boda, *Severe Mercy*, 109, citing Michael Wyschogrod, *Abraham's Promise* (Grand Rapids, MI: Eerdmans, 2004), 59.

10. Boda, *Severe Mercy*, 117.

11. Boda, *Severe Mercy*, 117.

12. Boda, *Severe Mercy*, 119.

the historical books and the writings. In the prophetic literature there is a strong emphasis on the sin of idolatry and Israel's failure to respect YHWH, demonstrated in their covenantal rebellion.[13]

When it comes to developments in the Jewish conception of sin into the Second Temple period, Gary Anderson has argued that, while a number of various guiding metaphors continue to exist, the idea of sin as *burden* becomes dominant.[14] This is supported by Lam as well.[15] We will not detail how the Septuagint handles sin language except to say that in many cases the translators attempted to find equivalent Greek terms for the Hebrew counterparts. However, in some places there is more variance, such as in LXX Proverbs where there is a tendency to talk about "sin" in terms of "impiety" (ἀσεβής; see, e.g., Prov 13:22), or LXX Job where we find occasions where the HB talks about "sin" but the translator renders this as thinking evil thoughts (e.g., ἐν τῇ διανοίᾳ αὐτῶν κακὰ ἐνενόησαν, LXX Job 1:5). But we will begin with the OT Apocrypha.

Tobit offers a very useful window into Jewish piety in the Second Temple period. At the beginning of chapter 3, Tobit laments over the state of Israel in exile and prays for divine mercy and grace.

> You are righteous, O Lord, and all your deeds are righteous, and all your ways are mercy and truth; you judge the age. And now you, O Lord, remember me, and look down. And do not punish me for my sins and for my unwitting offenses and those of my ancestors; they sinned before you, and they disobeyed your commandments. And you gave us over to plunder and exile and death and for an illustration and byword and reproach among all the nations among which you have scattered us. And now your many judgments are true in doing with me according to my sins, because we did not keep your commandments and did not walk truthfully before you. (Tob 3:1–5 NETS).

Tobit acknowledges God as judge and Israel as sinful and deserving of punishment (including plunder, exile, and scattering). Not only is "sin" (ἁμαρτία, 3:3) mentioned here, but also acts borne out of ignorance (ἀγνόημα, 3:3). Sin seems to involve (or at least sometimes include)

---

13. See especially Mark Boda, "Prophets," in *The T&T Clark Companion to the Doctrine of Sin* (eds. K. L. Johnson and D. Lauber; London: T. & T. Clark, 2016), 27–44.

14. See Gary Anderson, *Sin: A History* (New Haven: Yale University Press, 2010).

15. Lam, *Patterns of Sin*, 211.

intentional and willful wrongdoing, because Tobit confesses Israel's conscious disobedience in 3:4–5.

First Maccabees is remarkably different in its orientation to and use of sin language. The tendency is for this author to name as sinful Israel's *enemies*. For example, Antiochus Epiphanes is said to have come from a sinful root (ῥίζα ἁμαρτωλός, 1:10). Mattathias and his comrades are portrayed as banding together and striking down "sinners" (ἁμαρτωλός) and "lawless men" (ἄνδρας ἀνόμους, 2:44). It seems that 1 Maccabees lumps together both apostate Jews *and* gentiles in the term "sinners"—anyone who opposes the Law of God (cf. 2:48, 62).

Sin language appears frequently in the Wisdom of Solomon. As one might expect, the author portrays wisdom as the agent that can rescue from sin (10:13; 12:2). Sin is considered to be something mortals choose (1:4), but it can also become an obsession and overwhelm the sinner (Wis 11:15–16). The perspective overall on sin demonstrated in Wisdom of Solomon is well represented by this verse: "For even if we sin, we are yours, knowing your might, but knowing we are considered yours, we will not sin" (15:2 NETS). For the writer to say "we are yours" reinforces the grace of God; but the verse ends with the firm statement that human will can choose to refrain from sin.

Sirach, unsurprisingly, also frequently talks about sin in the context of wise living. Sin and obedience are regularly identified as personal (free will) choices (14:1). God is considered merciful and patient (2:11). And pious behavior can atone for wrongdoing (3:3). Indeed, he repeats that charity (ἐλεημοσύνη) atones for sin (ἁμαρτία) (3:14, 30).

Sirach offers two major warnings when it comes to sin. First, do not underestimate the problem of sin. One must "flee from sin" as if it were a snake (21:2a). It is dangerous: "its teeth are lion's teeth, destroying people's lives" (21:2b–c). The second caution is not to take the mercy of God for granted. Do not go on sinning, as if it were a simple or light thing for God to forgive (5:4–5): "for mercy and wrath are with him, and upon sinners will his anger rest. Do not wait to turn back to the Lord, and do not postpone it day after day; for suddenly the wrath of the Lord will go forth, and and in the time of punishment you will perish" (5:6–7 NETS; cf. 28:1).

Turning now to the OT Pseudepigrapha, we will look at Psalms of Solomon chapter 14. It is worth quoting the entire psalm.

> [1] A Hymn. Pertaining to Salomon. Faithful is the Lord to those who love him in truth, to those who endure his discipline,

> ² to those who walk in the righteousness of his ordinances, in the law which he commanded us that we might live.
>
> ³ The devout of the Lord shall live by it forever; the orchard of the Lord, the trees of life, are his devout.
>
> ⁴ Their planting is rooted forever; they shall not be pulled up all the days of heaven;
>
> ⁵ for the portion and the inheritance of God is Israel.
>
> ⁶ But not so are the sinners and transgressors of the law, who loved a day in the companionship of their sin.
>
> ⁷ Their desire was for the briefness of corruption, and they have not remembered God.
>
> ⁸ For the ways of human beings are known before him at all times, and he knows the storerooms of the heart before they come to pass.
>
> ⁹ Therefore their inheritance is Hades and darkness and destruction, and they shall not be found in the day when the righteous obtain pity.
>
> ¹⁰ But the devout of the Lord shall inherit life with joy. (Pss. Sol. 14:1–10 NETS)

This hymn first describes the devout who are blessed (14:1–5). Then it turns to the way of sinners (14:6–9), and ends again with the pious (14:10). Note how "sinners" (ἁμαρτωλοί) are associated with those who break the Law (14:6). Their transgression is described like a fleeting love affair with sin that brings little true satisfaction, but causes great harm (14:6b–7). Perhaps with poetic hyperbole the hymn consigns them to complete damnation—Hades, darkness, *and* destruction (14:9a)!

In the OT Pseudepigrapha the most extensive material related to sin language appears in the Testament of the Twelve Patriarchs. In the Testament of Judah, this wise father warns his children against greed and idolatry (19.1–2). Judah personalizes his advice by referring to his own struggles with greed, which would have destroyed his family had it not been for his "repentance from [his] flesh [ἡ μετάνοια σαρκός μου]" (19.2). While Judah does not shy away from acknowledging his own culpability for his sin, he (as in many other Jewish texts) appeals to his thoughtlessness and ignorance (ἄγνοια, 19.3). Furthermore, he partially blames "the prince of deceit" who takes advantage of his weak flesh and capitalizes on his pride (19.4).

Remarkably—even astonishingly—the Testament of Issachar takes an opposite perspective. While Judah humbly confesses his weakness, failure, greed, and gullibility, Issachar claims that he is without conscious sin (T. Iss. 7.1). He boasts of marital fidelity, sexual purity, sobriety, and material modesty (7.2-3). He never lied or deceived, he cared for his neighbors, he gave alms to the poor; in short, "I accomplished godliness and truth in all my days" (7.5).

He goes on to say he loved the Lord completely, and loved every neighbor as well (7.6). In his fatherly advice, he calls his kin to imitate him, so that "every deed of evil people will not rule over you, and you will subdue every wild beast, having with you the God of heaven and earth walking amongst people in generosity of heart" (7.7).

With these remarks from Judah and Issachar, we have two different perspectives on sin in Jewish literature. It is important that we not see these as diametrically opposed or contradictory; rather, they are two strands that are included within and intertwined with the Jewish piety of the Second Temple period. Jews could, at the same time, express remorse, humility, and penitence over sin, calling upon the mercy of God; and *also* they could express confidence in a commitment to holy and righteous living. They are, perhaps, taken to an extreme in this text, but both sides of this are well represented across Jewish literature.[16]

As far as Josephus is concerned, we see an interesting mix of ἁμαρτία+ usage. In the sections of *Antiquities* that relate to the story of Israel as seen in the OT, by and large Josephus's sin language corresponds to the language in the Septuagint (e.g., *Ant.* book 3). When we see Josephus move into postexilic history and the events closer to his time, he seems to reflect broader Greco-Roman (pagan) usage of ἁμαρτία+ (e.g., *Ant.* 16.159), where this language typically stands for offenses, mistakes, and deviations from a social, political, or legal norm (e.g., *J.W.* 3.75; 7.298). Later in *Antiquities*, for example, he uses ἁμαρτάνω in relation to betrayal of a friendship (18.164), though God could be betrayed as well (cf. *Ant.* 19.315). Also, as with many of the other writers we have considered, pagan or Jewish, Josephus treats "sins" as faults that occur both intentionally and unintentionally (*Ag. Ap.* 2.174).

The last author we will consider is Philo of Alexandria. Overall, Philo was more interested in using the philosophical language of virtue and vice

---

16. See G. W. E. Nickelsburg and M. E. Stone, ed., *Early Judaism: Texts and Documents on Faith and Piety* (Minneapolis: Fortress, 2009), 93-115.

than he was sin and righteousness. Nevertheless, he did use ἁμαρτία+ language. Of course we find it in his *Special Laws* when he discusses the meaning(s) of the various sacrificial laws and the nature of atonement. On one occasion he explains why the priests eat the meat of the sin-offering in one day (versus over a longer period of time): "the flesh of the sin-offering is consumed in a single day, showing that in sin we should procrastinate and be slow and dilatory in approaching it, but when the achievement of righteousness is our goal, act with speed and promptitude" (*Spec.* 1.243).

On a few occasions, Philo discusses the nature of sin. In *On Sobriety*, he uses Gen 4:7 to explain that sinful action (ἁμαρτάνω) is the outworking of vice in the heart (*Sobr.* 50; cf. *Leg.* 2.78). In his tractate *That the Worse is Wont to Attack the Better*, Philo breaks down the sinfulness of Cain in detail. Philo argues that his murderous actions are not the only wrong he is guilty of. He had already sinned by desiring the death of his brother, "since the purpose is as important as the completed action" (97). Now, Philo adds, it is possible to have passing feelings of malice that do not form into intention, and this is not sinful, because we can dispel these passions and they are often involuntary. But when the will has latched onto hatred with intent to harm, "the very planning involves guilt, for the deliberateness of the offence is the chief point made evident by its execution" (98). Though Philo is clear here about sin being an act of the mind and will, does he ever treat ἁμαρτία+ in relation to errors or misdeeds that are accidental? I believe so. In *On Flight and Finding*, Philo also addresses the sin of Cain. He suggests that we must treat our premeditated sinful actions as personal guilt. But if we accidentally cause some problem, we ought not to suffer from a guilty conscience, but assume that divine providence is at work (65). But Philo is also quick to note that we must never attribute our own conscious and willful sin to divine action (65).

Summary

Now that we have offered a selective survey of ἁμαρτία+ language in Hellenistic literature, we can now consider patterns and distinctive usage. Perhaps the first thing to say is that pagan Greek writers did not associate ἁμαρτία+ with morality *per se*. The typical use of ἁμαρτία+ is better understood as error or mistake, and there is all manner of occasions where such issues are unintentional, harmless, or both. What ἁμαρτία+ often reflects is some deviation from a standard or expectation. There are, of course, many situations where ἁμαρτία+ is seen as an offense against a person, law, or norm. We see this in various Greco-Roman histories as relational breeches or legal/political transgressions. It should also be clear that in the pagan Greco-Roman literature, ἁμαρτία+ is *not* religious terminology. That is because Greek and Roman religion did not focus on morality. One did not "sin" against the gods, unless someone actually offended a deity directly.

When it comes to Judaism and Jewish literature, ἁμαρτία+ is used in many different ways. Josephus often offers what seems like a conventional use of ἁμαρτία+ in relation to various political and legal errors. But by and large Jewish writers are heavily influenced by the use of sin language in the HB and the Septuagint. "Sin" is viewed as error, rebellion, evil intention, and behavior that disrespects YHWH, and it is especially indicative of behavior that breaches the covenantal Law. Some texts, like 1 Maccabees, focus on outsiders (apostate Jews and pagans) as "sinners," particularly when they stand against Ἰουδαϊσμός (the Jewish way of life). There are also texts that emphasize the need for Jews themselves to repent of sin and turn to God for mercy (e.g., Tobit). Wisdom texts (like Sirach, Wisdom of Solomon, Psalms of Solomon) and more philosophical writers like Philo dig deeper into the question of sin and human and divine agency.[17]

With the apostle Paul in view, we can say that he seems to have a narrower view of the nature and agency of ἁμαρτία. Some of his statements correspond closely to the kinds of penitential Jewish piety we have noted above (see Rom 4:7-8; Gal 2:15). An average Jewish or gentile reader, though, would find Paul's statements about sin quite philosophical (Gal 3:22; Rom 5-6; 14:23). Often he writes about ἁμαρτία in a way that Jews would not recognize or validate (Rom 3:9). His reference to sin against a brother or sister as a sin against *Christ* would be blasphemous (1 Cor 8:12). So too would the notion that the crucified Christ died to redeem Jews and gentiles from their sins (Gal 1:4; 1 Cor 15:3).

---

17. On this subject, see Miryam Brand, *Evil within and Without: The Source of Sin and Its Nature as Portrayed in Second Temple Literature* (JAJSup 9; Göttingen: Vandenhoeck & Ruprecht, 2013).

2

Sin and Soteriology in Romans

Martinus C. de Boer

As is well known, Paul tends to use the noun ἁμαρτία in the singular in Romans, where it occurs some 45 times.[1] There are only four such instances in his other undisputed letters.[2] By contrast, the plural occurs only three times in Romans (4:7; 7:5; 11:27) of which two are in OT quotations (4:7; 11:27). The remaining undisputed letters contain but four more instances of the plural.[3] It is clear from the raw data that the singular can be regarded as Paul's characteristic usage, certainly in Romans.

Also relevant is the fact that aside from the forty-five uses of the singular noun ἁμαρτία in Romans there are only twelve instances of cognate terms: the verb ἁμαρτάνω, "to sin" (Rom 2:12 [2x]; 3:23; 5:12, 14, 16; 6:15),[4] the noun (or adjective), ἁμαρτωλός, "sinner (sinful)" (Rom 3:7; 5:8 pl.; 5:19 pl.; 7:13),[5] and the noun ἁμάρτημα, "sinful deed" (Rom 3:25 pl.).[6] The noun

---

1. 3:9, 20; 4:8; 5:12 [2x], 13[2x], 20, 21; 6:1, 2, 6[2x], 7, 10, 11, 12, 13, 14, 16, 17, 18, 20, 22, 23; 7:7[2x], 8[2x], 9, 11, 13[2x], 14, 17, 20, 23, 25; 8:2, 3[3x], 10; 14:23.

2. Gal 2:17; 3:22; 1 Cor 15:56; 2 Cor 11:7.

3. 1 Cor 15:3, 17; Gal 1:4; and 1 Thess 2:16. The instance in 1 Cor 15:3 ("Christ died for our sins") is clearly part of a tradition that Paul is citing and that is probably the case in Gal 1:4 as well ("having given himself for our sins").

4. There are only six more instances in the remaining undisputed letters: 1 Cor 6:18; 7:28, 36; 8:12, 12; 15:34.

5. Also Gal 2:15 pl.; 2:17 pl.

6. Also 1 Cor 6:18. There are also conceptually related words, such as παράβασις,

ἁμαρτία in the singular dominates Paul's discourse on sin and does so particularly in Romans.[7]

Sin as a Cosmic Power in Romans[8]

The first occurrence of the term ἁμαρτία in Romans occurs in 3:9. In this verse Paul arguably sums up (much of) his previous argument,[9] which began in 1:18, by writing how he has established that all people, "both Jews and Greeks" are "under sin," ὑφ' ἁμαρτίαν. Joseph A. Fitzmyer writes that Paul here "personifies it [sin] as a master [κύριος] who dominates a slave; it holds human beings in bondage to it."[10] Fitzmyer thus paraphrases the phrase "under sin" as "under *the power* of sin," as do many other commentators and translations (e.g., NRSV).[11] It is this personification of ἁμαρτία

"transgression" (Rom 2:23; 4:15; 5:14; cf. Gal 3:19 pl.), παράπτωμα, "trespass" (Rom 5:15, 15, 16 pl., 17, 18, 20; 11:11, 12; cf. Gal 6:1; 2 Cor 5:19 pl.), ἀνομία, "iniquity / lawlessness" (Rom 4:7 pl. OT quotation; 6:19; cf. 2 Cor 6:14), ἀδικία, "wickedness / unrighteousness" (Rom 1:18, 29; 2:8; 3:5; 6:13; 9:14; cf. 1 Cor 13:6; 2 Cor 12:13), ἀκαθαρσία, "impurity" (1:24; 6:19; cf. 2 Cor 12:21; Gal 5:19; 1 Thess 2:3; 4:7), and ἀσέβεια, "ungodliness" (Rom 1:18; 11:26 OT quotation; cf. ἀσεβής, "ungodly," in Rom 4:5; 5:6).

7. Simon Gathercole's recent attempt to minimize the significance of Paul's use of the singular and to shift the emphasis to the plural goes against the evidence: Gathercole, *Defending Substitution: An Essay on Atonement in Paul* (Grand Rapids: Baker Academic, 2015), 48–50; and Gathercole, "'Sins' in Paul," *NTS* 64 (2018) 143–61.

8. This essay is primarily exegetical. For particularly helpful treatments that go beyond exegesis, see Beverly Roberts Gaventa, "The Cosmic Power of Sin in Paul's Letter to the Romans," in *Our Mother Saint Paul* (Louisville: Westminster John Knox, 2007), 125–36; Susan Grove Eastman, *Paul and the Person: Reframing Paul's Anthropology* (Grand Rapids: Eerdmans, 2017); Matthew Croasmun, *The Emergence of Sin: The Cosmic Tyrant in Romans* (Oxford: Oxford University Press, 2017).

9. John M. G. Barclay has recently argued that 1:18—3:20 is not to be construed as a unit "whose *single* theme is the sinfulness of all humanity" (*Paul and the Gift* [Grand Rapids: Eerdmans, 2015], 466), since there are also passages (2:7–10, 14–15, 26–29 in particular) that concern believers, both gentile and Jewish, who "have been *transformed* in their inmost being ('the hidden things' of 'the heart') by divine power" (467). Emphasis original in both quotations. For a critical survey of previous scholarship on this issue and a different treatment of the evidence, see Marcus A. Mininger, *Uncovering the Theme of Revelation in Romans 1:16—3:26* (WUNT 2/445; Tübingen: Mohr Siebeck, 2017).

10. Joseph A. Fitzmyer, *Romans: A New Translation with Introduction and Commentary* (AYBC; New York: Doubleday, 1993), 331.

11. Paul has used the expression "under Sin" earlier, in Gal 3:22. It was, therefore, already part of his thinking. He did not come up with the notion in composing Romans, which can be read as a further articulation of his thinking on this score. Indeed,

as an enslaving power that characterizes Paul's use of the singular—for which reason the English translation is normally capitalized: Sin. Though perhaps not every singular in Romans can be regarded as a personification of ἁμαρτία as an enslaving power (cf. 3:20; 4:8; 14:23),[12] that does appear to be the case regularly and consistently in Rom 5–8: forty-one of the forty-five instances of the singular in Romans are to be found in these chapters, beginning at 5:12 and extending to 8:10.[13]

In Rom 5–8, the personification of ἁμαρτία as an evil power introduced in 3:9 is further developed and emphasized. That is true quantitatively (there are a large number of instances) but also qualitatively (its nature and significance come to the fore in various ways). In 5:12, Paul writes that "through one human being [identified as Adam in 5:14], Sin came into the world [κόσμον]." At the beginning of time, we could say, Sin came into the human world as an intruder and as an alien force, conquering territory that belonged to someone else (God). Sin invaded and, like an ancient potentate, came to "reign/rule" (5:21; cf. 6:12: βασιλεύειν) or "lord it" (6:14: κυριεύειν) over the human world in all its dimensions, individual as well as social. It is thus not only a lord/master (κύριος) of slaves but also a ruler (βασιλεύς) with a domain. The residents who make up this domain, the world (κόσμος) under Sin, are expected to be obedient (6:16) to their lord and king, and thus to do what it[14] requires and demands.[15] In fact, as slaves

---

according to Mininger, the force of the verb προῃτιασάμεθα ("we have already established") in Rom 3:9 "is best understood, not with respect to what Paul has said previously in this letter, but with respect to what he has previously in his ministry in general, the very ministry which was just assailed in 3:8" (*Uncovering*, 320). Surprisingly, Mininger does not support this claim with a reference to Gal 3:22.

12. Mininger argues strongly for regarding the instance in 3:20 as a reference to Sin as a power (*Uncovering*, 310–12). It is in any event also the case that where Sin (as a power) is mentioned, sinning (as a human activity) is implied. Sin does not exist apart from sinning (see further on this point below).

13. Aside from the instance in 3:9, the remaining instances of the singular are to be found in 3:20; 4:8 (an OT quotation), and 14:23.

14. Given the fact that the Greek noun ἁμαρτία is grammatically feminine, the feminine personal pronoun "she" could be appropriate here. But the grammatical gender of the term seems to play no evident role in Paul's exposition any more than the grammatically masculine gender of the Greek term for death, θάνατος, does.

15. See 6:13 ("yielding our members[μέλη] to Sin as instruments of wickedness"), 6:19 ("yielding your members [μέλη] as slaves to impurity and increased iniquity"), and 6:12 ("obeying the desires [ἐπιθυμίαι]" of "our mortal body"; cf. 7:5 [παθήματα], 8 [ἐπιθυμία]; 8:13 [πράξεις]). For Paul, "our old human being" (ὁ παλαιὸς ἡμῶν ἄνθρωπος) and "the body of sin" (τὸ σῶμα τῆς ἁμαρτίας) (6:6) are characterizations of human beings, both

and thus as part of a given and fixed hierarchical structure of relationships, they have little or no choice. Perhaps in theory they have some choice but not in actual fact, not in practice, any more than slaves (in the ordinary, social sense of the term) did in the ancient world. Disobedience was theoretically *possible* but in practice *impossible*—a possible impossibility, as it were.

Hence, apart from Christ, human beings are, as Paul twice puts it in Rom 6, "slaves of Sin," δοῦλοι τῆς ἁμαρτίας (6:17, 20). In 7:14, he describes the (Adamic[16]) self as "sold [like a slave] under [the power of] Sin," πεπραμένος ὑπὸ τὴν ἁμαρτίαν. It does not belong to itself, but to something else. Sin has control; it has the power and the hegemony. In 7:16-17, Paul writes: "if I do what I do not want . . . it is no longer I that do it, but Sin which dwells within me." He uses the same language in 7:20. Sin causes someone to do what they do not want to do. Sin, then, is evidently not to be identified with the human self who wills to do what is good (as stipulated and determined by the Law) but cannot achieve it (7:18b). Sin is evidently not something intrinsic to the being and identity of human beings. The descendants of Adam are here being portrayed as the victims and pawns of an alien force that compels them to do things that they know they should not do.[17] As a power, Sin causes or effects "sinful deeds" (ἁμαρτήματα, 3:25), turning human beings into "sinners" (5:8, 19)[18] who actively "commit sin" (2:12; 3:23; 5:12; 6:15).[19] Sin is here understood to be an alien force that has invaded the individual human being with, as 5:12 suggests, an enormous and deleterious impact on the collective or social world of human beings, i.e., on interpersonal relationships.[20]

---

individually and collectively, under the power of Sin.

16. Cf. Martinus C. de Boer, *The Defeat of Death: Apocalyptic Eschatology in 1 Corinthians 15 and Romans 5* (JSNTSup 22; Sheffield: JSOT, 1988), 242n66; Paul W. Meyer, "The Worm at the Core of the Apple: Exegetical Reflections on Romans 7," in *The Word in This World: Essays in New Testament Exegesis and Theology* (ed. J. T. Carroll; NTL; Westminster John Knox, 2004 [1990]), 57-77.

17. See further on Rom 7: Eastman, *Paul and the Person*, 109-25.

18 The personification of Sin as inimical power cannot be dismissed as a merely metaphorical, literary, or rhetorical device. See Gaventa, "Cosmic Power," 133-34; Croasmun, *Emergence*, 8-11 and *passim*. The personification reflects something about reality as experienced by human beings.

19. Sin (as a power) thus always implies sinning (a human activity). Gathercole's critique ("'Sins' in Paul") that those who highlight Sin as a power in Paul's theology thereby neglect sins (sinful human actions) is thus misplaced. There is no Sin without sinning.

20. Cf. Eastman, *Paul and the Person*, 121: "There is no freestanding self capable of watching itself; it is already invaded by a personified power that radically compromises

As a ruler, Sin has a domain that can be understood as an orb or sphere into which every human being is born—which means that every human being has entered (and enters) at birth a world in which Sin already reigns or rules. For this reason, each and every human being is born a slave to Sin and will as a matter of course behave in a way that reflects this situation, which is one of bondage requiring conformity to the wishes of the master.[21] Or as Paul puts it: "all sinned" in 5:12, and earlier in 3:23: "all sinned and [for that reason] fall short of the glory of God." Using the past tense in both cases (an aorist in Greek: ἥμαρτον), Paul looks at the history of the world retrospectively, as it were, from the eschatological Christ event. In 3:9, where, as I noted earlier, he has written that both Jews and Greeks, in other words "all people," are "under Sin," he cites from Scripture to illustrate the concrete implications: "for it stands written: 'no one is righteous, no not one'" (3:10; cf. Gal 3:22). No one meets God's standard of what is good and right ("righteousness"). Paul goes on to cite a whole list of similar passages to drive the point home (3:11–18).[22] The domain of Sin is our collective destiny. And this domain is a *factual* reality, whatever the explanation of its origin may be.[23]

---

its agency."

21. The offspring of a slave in the ancient world was also a slave. On slavery in the Greco-Roman world, see the helpful overview of S. Scott Bartchy, "Slavery (New Testament)," *ABD* 6 (1992) 65–73.

22. See the discussion of Mininger, *Uncovering*, 305–9.

23. The traditional explanation of its origin is the notion of "original sin" in the sense attributed to or associated with Augustine: sin as a genetic defect that beginning with Adam has been transmitted from one human being to another through "concupiscence" (sexual desire and union), as if the propensity to sin were an inherited condition. See the critical review in Croasmun, *Emergence*, 133–37, who also discusses the common alternative, namely the *social* transmission of sin (attributed to Friedrich Schleiermacher, Albert Ritschl, Walter Rauschenbusch, and "liberationist" theologians). He cites in this connection the words of Monika Hellwig as a good summary of this explanation: "The complex structures of our societies set limits to what we can see, understand, and choose to do. We are caught in a web of relationships, expectations, economies, cultural activities, acculturation to particular contexts political and administrative arrangements which seem to take on a life of their own, larger, more enduring, and more resistant than the efforts of any individual or group of individuals to change or act in opposition to such forces. Here, then, is the concrete presence of original sin or the sin of Adam, the force of evil that precedes the choices of those who appear to be choosing, preempts the actions of those who appear to be acting, and tends to crush out of existence any who persist in acting in critical opposition" (from Croasmun, *Emergence*, 135). Croasmun sees value in both theories of transmission and himself adds to them "a theory of *mythological* transmission" (*Emergence*, 136; emphasis added), which is that of Paul: "Generation

Sin and Death

The ineluctable result of the rule of Sin is deliverance to the realm of Death.[24] When Sin came into the world, Death did too: "through the one human being, Sin came into the world and through Sin Death [came into the world]. And so Death [subsequently] spread to all people because [of course, as the evidence indicates][25] all people sinned."

Death too is personified by Paul as a cosmic power. Even though Paul does not use the expression "under Death," nevertheless, Death, like Sin, has "reigned" (βασιλεύειν; 5:13, 17) and "lorded it" (κυριεύειν; 6:9) over the world, over all humanity. It too, like Sin, is as an orb, realm, or domain. The inextricable link between Sin and Death is given expression repeatedly in the chapters 6–8 (cf. 6:16, 21; 7:5, 9–11, 13, 23, 24; 8:6, 10–11). Where there is Sin, there is also Death. Or as Paul puts in 5:21: "Sin reigned in Death." Death is the distinguishing mark, and result, of Sin's reign.

A comparison with 1 Cor 15, Paul's treatise on the resurrection of the dead, i.e., of those who have physically died, would suggest that θάνατος in Rom 5:12–21 concerns physical, bodily demise, what we could call natural or biological death: "through a human being death . . . in Adam all die" (1

---

after generation is bound to sin because each generation is bound—that is, enslaved—to Sin. It is the dominion of this cosmic tyrant that accounts for the persistence of human sin" (*Emergence*, 136; emphasis original). Croasmun writes that "we can make sense of Paul's language about Sin as a cosmic power by understanding Sin as a mythological person emergent from a complex system of human transgressions" (*Emergence*, 177), both individual and social (*Emergence*, 105). That could also, according to Croasmun, be said for Satan, for which reason Sin and Satan might in fact be different names for "the same entity" (*Emergence*, 189). For Croasmun, the mythological explanation does not mean that such transmission is any less biological or social. In his view "the tyrant, Sin, owes its longevity through the ages to the stability of its biological and social bases." In other words, "the sinful sociocultural environment shapes the bodies of individuals" and together allow Sin as a cosmic tyrant to emerge and persist (*Emergence*, 136). It takes on a life of its own, as it were. Along similar lines Eastman writes that "Paul narrates sin as both external and internal, and as both environmental and agential: human beings are 'in sin' and 'under sin' as a kind of relation environment, yet also indwelt by sin personified as an agent acting in and through the self" (*Paul and the Person*, 122). According to Eastman, "Sin is not a decision made by self-determining individuals, but rather a socially mediated power greater than human beings yet operative through human thought, words, and deeds" (*Paul and the Person*, 177).

24. This receives too little attention in the works of Barclay, Croasmun, and Eastman and its significance is therefore missed. See de Boer, *Defeat of Death*, 143–44.

25. This represents my interpretation of the debated subordinating conjunction ἐφ' ᾧ. See de Boer, *Defeat of Death*, 158, 161, 236–37n42.

Cor 15:21-22; cf. Gen 2:17; 3:3-4, 19; 4 Ezra; 2 Bar.). That understanding of death can certainly not be excluded here, given the references to the Christ's resurrection from the dead in the opening verses of chapter 6 (6:4, 5, 9) or the subsequent references to the "mortal body" (6:12) and the "mortal bodies" (8:12) of human beings (cf. 7:24; 8:10, 13, 23; 1 Cor 15:35-44). But in contrast to 1 Cor 15, physical death is surely not where Paul's focus lies in Rom 5:12-21 or in the three chapters that follow. Paul here uses the term θάνατος primarily in a metaphorical sense to signify the irremediable separation of human beings from God and thus their removal from life, i.e., life in God's presence and in accordance with the divine will. This metaphorical understanding of θάνατος as separation from God applies also to those who are still physically alive but find themselves "under the power of Sin," as all human beings do. Death thus has a profoundly theological significance for Paul since it indicates something about the relationship of human beings to God, namely, *the end and the absence* of such a relationship.[26] When Paul refers to θάνατος as "the wages" of Sin (6:23), he has this primary theological significance of death in view. Death is the total absence of life, life before God in particular, and it thus signifies the end of all human possibilities and hopes. And that in turn means that prior to or apart from God's intervention in Christ, there was and is no remedy for the human plight since to be "under Sin" is also to be in the realm of Death, the realm of absolute and (from a human point of view) irremediable separation from God. It is only God who can bring life out of θάνατος, something out of nothing (cf. Rom 4:17b). Only God can undo the ineluctable and utterly disastrous effect of Sin, that effect being θάνατος (total separation from God and from life before God).

The reign and the realm of Sin completely coincide with the reign and the realm of Death, for where the one rules the other rules as well. Since that is the case, it is also the case that God in doing something about Death must do (and does do) something about Sin. A moral appeal to change one's ways (to repent) seems to make no sense in this context, and Paul

---

26. Barclay unfortunately for all intents and purposes reduces Paul's discourse concerning death in Rom 5-8 to physical demise: "It is not for nothing that Paul emphasizes several times in these chapters the mortality of the body . . . new creation life begins" in the case of believers "not on the other side, but on this side of death," which is "a residue of their Adamic heritage"; "they are dead to sin (6:11), but not to death," i.e., physical demise (*Paul and the Gift*, 501; cf. 502-3). The nuanced analysis Barclay applies to χάρις is absent from his discussion of θάνατος. See also further below on the distinction maintained by Paul between mortality and actual physical dying, a distinction that is also absent from Barclay's analysis.

does not make such an appeal.[27] Only God can rectify this situation (and, of course, Paul believes God has done so).

Sin and the Law

Much of Romans seems to be concerned with making plain that the Law cannot be regarded as God's remedy for Sin.[28] According to 5:20, the Law "came in alongside" a situation determined not by willful, autonomous human transgression but by the twin powers of Sin and Death. The Law's effect was not to ameliorate that situation but to make it worse: the Law came in alongside "so that the trespass might increase." And that means that "Sin increased," which is to say, intensified and solidified its Death-dealing grip over human beings.[29] Paul continues along this line in chapter 7 of Romans. As "the Law of God" (7:22), the Law itself is "holy" and "spiritual" (7:12, 14) and thus not the culprit (Paul thereby *exonerates* the Law from all blame), but it is also an instrument of the power of Sin. Sin uses the Law or "the commandment," which is "holy and righteous and good" (7:12), as its "base of operations" (ἀφορμή; 7:8-11), and does so to lethal effect. As the instrument of Sin, the Law not only cannot (cf. 8:3; Gal 3:21) deliver the righteousness and thus the eternal life it promises, it ironically also brought about what it was meant to overcome and prevent, namely, Death understood as permanent separation from God and thus from life. Sin perverted the Law's promise of life (7:10) by turning it into an instrument, perhaps more accurately, *the* instrument of Sin's Death-dealing hegemony (7:5, 8-10). To emphasize the point, Paul can go so far as to say here that "apart from the Law, Sin is dead" (7:8) and that the "coming" of the Law

---

27. The single reference to repentance in Rom 2:4 is not an appeal to repent but part of Paul's indictment of the human being for presuming on "the riches and the forbearance and the patience" of God in the face of wrongdoing: Paul points out that "God's kindness" is supposed to "lead" someone "to repentance [εἰς μετάνοιαν]," which alas it has not done. Paul uses the Greek noun (μετάνοια) or verb (μετανοέω) elsewhere in his genuine letters only in 2 Cor 7:9-10 (noun) and 2 Cor 12:11 (verb). By contrast these two terms occur some twenty-five times in Luke-Acts, for which repentance is thus a key theme. That is not the case in Paul's letters.

28. See now also Udo Schnelle, "Die kosmische Auseinandersetzung zwischen Christus und die Sünde nach dem Römerbrief," in *Paulus und Petrus: Geschichte—Theologie—Rezeption* (eds. H. Omerzu and E. D. Schmidt; Arbeiten zur Bibel und ihrer Geschichte; Leipzig: 2016) 79-100, esp. 86, 92-93.

29. Cf. already 3:20: "through the Law comes knowledge of Sin." See Mininger, *Uncovering*, 314-17.

(the commandment) caused Sin to "come to life" (7:9).[30] For this reason, to be "under (the) Law" (6:14–15) is tantamount to being "under Sin" (3:9; 7:14).[31] That implicit equation seems to underlie much of the argument found beginning at 6:1 and extending into chapter 7. The Law, regrettably and lamentably, constitutes a dead end.

A presupposition of this argument about the inefficacy or weakness of the Law (8:3a) is that Sin is not a matter of the Law's transgression. Paul divorces Sin (and thus sinning) from the matter of Law observance. A transgression concerns a willful breaking (lit. a stepping over) of a given and recognized commandment. Transgression is what Paul calls "transgression *of the Law*," in 2:24. That in turn means that "where there is no law there is no transgression" either (4:15). Adam himself transgressed a specific divine commandment, as the account in Genesis indicates (Gen 2:16–17; 3:11), and for this reason Paul refers to "the transgression of Adam" (Rom 5:14). According to 5:13–14, however, "Death reigned from Adam to Moses"—thus, as Paul says, "*prior* to the Law"—because, as he continues, "Sin was in the world" during that time too. That means that those who lived in the pre-Mosaic period ("prior to the Law") had no divine commandment to transgress. By asserting that Sin was in the world prior to the giving of the Law, Paul in effect indicates that Sin is not a matter of the willful transgression of the Sinaitic Law. Because Sin was in the world prior to Moses, Death also reigned "even [καί] over those who did not sin" in the same way that Adam did (5:14), that is, by transgressing a given divine commandment.[32] The human condition is much more dire in Paul's view than the limitation of Sin/sinning to the transgression of God's Law would imply.

The Primal Sin and its Consequences

How then is Sin, and the sinning which results, to be regarded?[33] If not transgression of the Law, or of God's commandment, what then?

---

30. This passage shows how Paul can play with the terms life and death. Sin's "coming to life" actually effects "death" for human beings.

31. The phrase "under (the) Law," also used by Paul in Gal 3:23; 4:4–5, 21; 5:18, implies that just like Sin the Law is an enslaving power. See Mininger, *Uncovering*, 314–17 (on Rom 3:20).

32. Note that in 2:12, Paul refers to gentiles "sinning" outside of the Law or apart from the Law.

33. There is no Sin without sinning for Paul. See notes 12 and 19 above.

It is significant, I think, that Paul avoids the term "transgression" after 5:14 when referring to Adam and his descendants.[34] Instead, he resorts to the term "trespass" (παράπτωμα). Παράπτωμα signifies a falling away (cf. παραπίπτειν)—a falling away from God is evidently in view (cf. 1:19–23). The real sin of Adam in transgressing God's commandment in Eden was that it constituted a *trespass*, a term used in Wis 10:1 in connection with Adam's fall.[35] The trespass of Adam, his signature "disobedience" (5:19), is a falling away from God, i.e., his rejection and repudiation of God. This is the sin, in the sense of "sinful deed" (cf. 3:25), that was and is repeated by each and every human being in turn, including those who lived before Moses and thus before the Law could "register" it. "All sinned" (3:23; 5:12d) and "fall short of the glory of God" (3:23) because all *trespassed*, thereby producing the aggregate "many trespasses" referred to in 5:16. According to 4:25, where Paul cites what appears to be a traditional formulation, Christ died for this cosmic accumulation of trespasses by Adam's descendants: he "was handed over on account of our trespasses" (cf. 2 Cor 5:19; Col 2:13; Eph 1:7; 2:1, 5). In 5:20, the statement that "the trespass increased" is interpreted to mean that "Sin increased." Paul's point appears here to be that the vast increase or accumulation of trespasses led to the increase or wide extension of Sin's hegemony: Sin reigned in the universal domain of Death. And "so Death spread to all people, because all sinned," that is, because all repudiated God. This is the primary sin that characterizes and informs all subsequent misbehavior. Sin is the failure to acknowledge God, a failure with disastrous consequences for human life on earth (1:18ff.)[36]

One issue about which Paul is not as clear as we might wish is whether Adam's trespass and its repetition by each of his descendants is being regarded as the *result* or as the *cause* of Sin's hegemony. "Through one human being, Sin came into the world" (5:12a). Does Paul mean that the rule of Sin is the result of Adam's trespass? Or that the trespass itself was caused by Sin? And what would be the answer for Adam's descendants who repeat his trespass: Is the rule of Sin the result of their trespasses or are their trespasses the result of Sin's hegemony?[37] This dilemma reflects the old debate between

34. See de Boer, *Defeat of Death*, 165–67.

35. NRSV, e.g., unfortunately translates the term here as "transgression."

36. See Ernst Käsemann, "God's Image and Sinners," in *On Being a Disciple of the Crucified Nazarene* (Grand Rapids: Eerdmans, 2010) 108–19, esp. 114–15 ("Idol worship is original sin").

37. Elsewhere, I have written: "The power of Death came upon all people, since all, by being under the power of Sin, sinned. Sinning is not the result and the mark of a

corporate destiny and individual responsibility, between determinism and free will. Put otherwise: are human beings merely victims of powers beyond their control or can they (also) be held accountable for what they do?[38] Paul's answer seems ultimately to be both-and rather than either-or.

Some would read 5:12 as Paul's correction of the idea of corporate destiny in the first half of the verse with the notion of individual responsibility in the second. Adam's transgression caused the fatality of death to come upon all people (cf. 1 Cor 15:21-22) but since "all sinned" all are actually individually responsible for their own deaths. That is one notable way of reading 5:12.[39] A comparison with the appeals to Adam in such Jewish apocalyptic texts as 4 Ezra and 2 Baruch shows that this interpretation is unlikely. To cite from 2 Baruch: "Adam sinned and death was decreed against those who were to be born" (23:4); "when he [Adam] transgressed, untimely death came into being" (56:6; cf. Gen 2:17; 3:19). Along such passages, there are others, however: "Adam is . . . not the cause, except for himself, but each of us has become our own Adam" (54:15). Similar passages are found in 4 Ezra. In these Jewish apocalyptic works Adam functions both as a corporate personality whose trespass determines all subsequent human destiny (all die because of Adam's fall) *and* as the paradigmatic human being whose sinful deed sets the pattern for his descendants (all die because all repeated Adam's fall). That seems logically inconsistent, to us at any rate, but Paul seems to adopt it in Rom 5:12. As in 4 Ezra and 2 Baruch, Adam's two functions go together.[40] Where Paul deviates from the

---

choice made by an autonomous individual; it is the result and the mark of a cosmological force that has come into the world and has reigned over human beings since the time of Adam, bringing Death in its wake" (Martinus C. de Boer, "Paul's Mythologizing Program in Romans 5-8," in *Apocalyptic Paul: Cosmos and Anthropos in Romans 5-8* [ed. B. R. Gaventa; Waco, TX: Baylor University Press, 2013], 1-20, at 14). See also earlier de Boer, *Defeat of Death*, 161, and on Rom 5:12d, Schnelle, "Auseinandersetzung," 88-89 (Sin leads to or causes sinning). While this interpretation may on the whole be a correct reading of 5:12-21 insofar as this passage provides a description of the *factual* situation apart from Christ, I now think that this formulation may need some nuancing in light of the fact in view of Paul's total argument. See further below on the primal sin of Adam and subsequent humanity.

38. Bultmann's wrestles with this issue in *Theology*, I, 249-58, as does Croasmun, *Emergence*.

39. See in particular, Rudolf Bultmann, "Adam and Christ According to Romans 5," in *Current Issues in New Testament Interpretation: Essays in Honor of Otto A. Piper* (eds. W. Klassen and G. F. Snyder; New York: Harper & Brothers, 1962), 143-65. See also Bultmann, *Theology*, 1:249-58.

40. Cf. de Boer, *Defeat of Death*, 161. Also noted by A. J. M. Wedderburn, "The

treatment of Adam as found in 2 Baruch and 4 Ezra is in his conception of Sin and Death as cosmic tyrants that reign and rule over human beings whereby the Law, which is the God-given solution to the problem of Adam's fall in 4 Ezra and 2 Baruch (and in Jewish thought generally), is excluded by Paul as the remedy. It is merely a tool in the hands of Sin and brings death (Death) rather than life.

Looking back at chapter 1 of Romans we see that Paul reproaches humanity for having "exchanged the glory of the immortal God" for idols (1:23). They are, however, "without excuse" since "what can be known about God is plain to them.... Ever since the creation of the world his invisible nature, namely, his eternal power and deity, has been clearly perceived in the things that have been made" (1:19-20). It is "because they exchanged the truth about God for a lie and worshiped and served the creature rather than the Creator" (1:25) that God "gave them up [παρέδωκεν] in the lust of their hearts to impurity" (1:24) and also "gave them up [παρέδωκεν] to dishonorable passions" (1:26). God's handing over of humanity to such forms of sinful behavior is evidently the revelation of God's wrath mentioned in 1:18. Paul goes on to repeat the point a third time: "since they did not see fit to acknowledge God, God gave them up [παρέδωκεν] to a base mind and improper conduct" (1:28), which are catalogued in 1:29-31. Those who do such awful things are "worthy of death" he concludes (1:32). Death here again means eternal separation from God and from life, but now clearly as a punishment for sinful behavior (cf. 2 Baruch; 4 Ezra). Eternal death so understood will be their lot "on the day of wrath when God's righteous judgment will be revealed" (2:5).[41]

One could thus say that as a result of repudiating God and exchanging God for idols — which, I have suggested, is the trespass (or primal sin) referred to in chapter 5:12-21 — God handed the human world over to Sin's reign (and thus Death's as well). The terrible human condition is the result

---

Theological Structure of Romans V.12," *NTS* 19 (1972-1973) 339-54, citing a number of texts, including 4 Ezra 3:7-11; 7:116-119, and 2 Bar. 48:42-47; 54:14, and concluding that "the balance of an apparent determinism with a stress on individual responsibility and guilt is a pattern of thought well attested in Judaism" (p. 439); Ernst Käsemann, *Commentary on Romans* (Grand Rapids: Eerdmans, 1980), 148, citing 2 Bar. 54:15, 19.

41. See the further references to "wrath" in 1:18; 2:8; 3:5; 4:15; 5:9 (cf. 9:22; 12:19; 13:4-5). Evidently Paul sees a distinction between God's present wrath and his future wrath. See Mininger, *Uncovering*, 175: "Taking 1:18 and 2:5 together, one can therefore say that Paul describes a two stage unfolding of the display of God's wrath, *now* upon some who have already been handed over and *not yet* upon hypocrites presently experiencing God's temporary patience" (emphasis original).

of an initial human act, Adam's trespass, which is also repeated by each and every human being after him. This trespass is the conscious, deliberate repudiation of God and the result is a world ruled by Sin and Death. The joint rule of Sin and Death constitutes the realm of the repudiation of God, on the one hand, and irremediable separation from God, on the other. These two go hand in hand. The first leads ineluctably to the second. When Paul illustrates (or supports) his claim in 3:9 that all people are under Sin with scriptural citations, his catena of passages from Scripture concludes in 3:18 with a slightly modified citation from Ps 36: "There is no fear of God before their eyes" (LXX Ps 35:2, which has "his eyes"). They have rejected and repudiated God (cf. Deut 6:5-6). That is the basic problem (godlessness), the basic sin that leads to the hegemony of Sin (and thus Death) over the human world, causing all sorts of iniquity, wickedness, and impurity. It seems, therefore, that the hegemony of Sin is the result of the original, primal sinful act of rejecting or repudiating God, i.e., exchanging God for false gods, exchanging the truth for a lie.[42] Every human being repeats this primal sin, thereby becoming a slave of Sin with its terrible consequences for human life, which for this reason ends in Death (the realm of definitive and irremediable separation from God and from life before God). Or as Bultmann famously put it: "sin came into the world by sinning."[43]

We see something similar in Romans 7, Paul can here say that he was "once alive apart from the Law, but when the commandment came, sin came to life and I died" (7:9). Paul evidently here suggests with polemical intent that the situation of Adam's descendants to whom the universally applicable Law came is analogous to the situation of Adam to whom the commandment came (the "I" is probably Paul playing the role of the Adamic self, looked at from the vantage point of Christ).[44] Paul evidently thinks that "the commandment" of the Mosaic Law functioned in a way similar to the commandment given to Adam. The commandment caused Sin to come to life and thus paradoxically to bring about the fatal result it sought to

---

42. See Gaventa, "Sin," 233: "Paul's depiction of humankind opens with an action taken by humanity rather than by another power . . . humanity's refusal of God's lordship meant that God conceded humanity for a time to the lordship of another."

43. Bultmann, *Theology*, 1:251. On the one hand, Bultmann writes, "the sin of humanity after Adam is attributed to Adam's sin and . . . it therefore appears as the consequence of a curse for which mankind is not itself responsible"; on the other hand, while the human situation is one of "an enslavement to powers," it is nevertheless one for which the human being "is himself responsible" (*Theology*, 1:257).

44. See note 16 above.

prevent (7:9-10). It "deceived me," Paul writes, with a clear allusion to the story of Adam, and "it killed me" (7:11). This way of looking at the matter of the coming of the Law seemingly cannot be logically reconciled with 5:13-14 where Sin and Death are in the world prior to the coming of the Law. According to chapter 7, when the Law came, the result was the same as when the commandment not to eat of a certain tree came to Adam: Sin came into the picture, intensified its grip on human beings, bringing Death in its wake.

From what I have sketched, then, one could argue that for Paul human beings *in principle* had and have the ability not to sin, i.e., not to repudiate God (cf. Augustine's *posse non peccare*, able not to sin), but also that *in actual fact* they were, and are, *unable* not to sin (*non posse non peccare*).[45] The principle (able not to sin) makes it possible to call human beings to account for their sinful actions, their complicity in (the establishment and ongoing reality of) the reigns of Sin and Death,[46] whereas the *factual* reality of enslavement to Sin's power (not able not to sin) makes divine intervention necessary, or better, explains why God has indeed invaded the world under the dominion Sin and Death in order to replace their reign with the reign of his Grace as revealed and made effective in Christ.

The issue is then this *factual* reality and why it is what it is and why (ever since Adam) it is inevitable.

The Weakness of the Flesh

In Rom 5:6-10, Paul summarizes in passing the human condition under Sin. Paul here lists those for whom Christ died: the ungodly (5:6), sinners

---

45. Augustine, "Nature and Grace," in *Three Anti-pelagian Treatises of St. Augustine* (trans. and ed. F. H. Woods and J.O. Johnston; London: David Nutt), 137-38 (par. 57).

46. Eastman, *Paul and the Person*, 111: "Within this situation human actors are not simply passive victims, but rather are both captive and complicit," so that it is possible to speak of "humanity's collusion" with Sin. See also the extensive analysis of Croasmun on this point (*Emergence*, 109-11, 137-39, 175-77). His book is an attempt "to synthesize Rudolf Bultmann's account of personal responsibility for sin, Ernst Käsemann's account of Sin's tyranny, and the liberationist phenomenology of unjust structural coercion" (176). See further on the notion of complicity, J. Louis Martyn, "Afterword: The Human Moral Drama," in *Apocalyptic Paul: Cosmos and Anthropos in Romans 5-8* (ed. B. R. Gaventa; Waco, TX: Baylor University, 2013), 157-66 (163). Philip Ziegler, *Militant Grace: The Apocalyptic Turn and the Future of Christian Theology* (Grand Rapids: Baker Academic, 2018), xv, xvii, 59 ("women and men subjected to Sin are not merely its passive victims; they also become its active servants," summarizing the work of Käsemann).

(5:8), and enemies (5:10). The ungodly, sinners, and enemies—these are descriptions of Adamic human beings, i.e., those who have repudiated God and thus come to be slaves of Sin. (That is probably the reason why "ungodly" is the first term used). Christ dies for them, i.e, "for us," and did so "while we were weak." This phrase, which stands at the beginning of 5:6, is not to be construed as a reproach but as a neutral description of human beings as created beings. Weakness is closely associated with life "in the flesh," something that is picked up in chapters 7 and 8.[47] So Paul refers to "the weakness of your flesh" as a given in 6:19 (the first time Paul refers to the flesh in chapters 5–8). That weakness of the flesh makes it an easy prey for Sin: "I am fleshly, sold under Sin" (7:14; cf. 7:5).[48]

When Paul remarks that "Sin dwells in me" in 7:17, he goes on to say, "I know that nothing good dwells in me, that is, in my flesh" (7:18). It is Sin that dwells in his flesh. Indeed, in 8:3, he refers to "Sin in the flesh" and can even virtually equate the two when he writes here of "the flesh of Sin." To "walk" or "live according to the flesh" (8:4, 12–13) then describes life under the power of Sin, with as result a "mindset of the flesh" (τὸ φρόνημα τῆς σαρκός) that "is hostile to God" (8:7). It is for this reason, then, that "those who are in the flesh *cannot* [as a matter of fact] please God" (8:8).

If the weakness of the flesh makes human beings an easy prey for Sin, that then also counts for Death. Here the terms "mortal body" (6:12) and "mortal bodies" (8:11) are relevant. "Mortal" does not mean "dead" but "subject to Death" or, perhaps more accurately, "susceptible or vulnerable to Death," for that is what the human body as weak, i.e., as fleshly, is.[49] The body is "the body of Death" (7:24), the body that is "dead [νεκρόν] on

---

47. See Eastman, *Paul and the Person*, 121: "Sin is here [7:14] depicted as something that takes over ownership of the ego through its fleshly existence." The self is "invaded by a personified power that radically compromises its agency," which means that "the porous fleshly body, understood both as individual and as communal corporeal existence, is taken over by sin." Along similar lines, Croasmun, *Emergence*, 112–24.

48. See Will N. Timmins, *Romans 7 and Christian Identity* (SNTSMS 170; Cambridge: Cambridge University Press, 2017), 88: "'The weakness of the flesh' is an anthropological condition, linked to the present age determined by Adam, with its characteristic corruption and moral impotency. In a context dominated by both implicit and explicit references to the body, this is the most plausible understanding of the term."

49. See de Boer, *Defeat of Death*, 132 (on 1 Cor 15:50–57). Paul's uses term "body" (σῶμα) in two, overlapping ways, to designate the mortal, fleshly body of an individual human being and the collective social body. It is not always possible, or perhaps necessary, to distinguish them (e.g., "the body of Sin" in 6:6 or "the body of Death" in 7:24). Cf. Eastman, *Paul and the Person*, 120–25; Croasmun, *Emergence*, 112–22.

account of Sin" (8:10), for which reason it can also be called "the body of Sin" (6:6), i.e., the body ruled by Sin. The mortal body has inherent desires (ἐπιθυμίαι) that are exploited by Sin (6:12; cf. 7:8: "Sin wrought in me all desire"). The "members" (μέλη) of the body can be co-opted by Sin to serve as "weapons of wickedness" (6:13), thereby becoming "slaves to impurity and iniquity" (6:19), what Paul in 8:13 summarizes as "the practices/deeds [πράξεις] of the body" (cf. 7:5).

So to return to 5:6: "while we were weak," i.e., while we were "in the flesh," while we were in our "mortal bodies," and thus vulnerable to the dual rule of Sin and Death, with the result that we became "ungodly," "sinners," and "enemies of God," Christ died "for us."

God's Remedy

Particularly as God's enemies, human beings need peace or reconciliation with God. And that is what they receive through the death of Christ "for us" (5:8): "we have peace with God" (5:1), "we have now received reconciliation" (5:10). On the basis of faith, through the justifying death of Christ (5:1, 9), believers are given the righteousness (Christ's) that makes them (morally) acceptable to God (5:15-21). They are no longer regarded by God as ungodly people, as sinners (in the primal sense of the term: repudiators of God), or as enemies of God. Through faith they have come to acknowledge God's claim on their lives and attention spans.

These stirring assertions would perhaps not amount to much if Christ's death did not also involve deliverance from Sin's deadly rule, which is the realm of the rejection and repudiation of God. That is the theme of the opening paragraphs of chapter 6. Here Christ's death is spoken of not in terms of "dying for us," but in another way, which is to be found in 6:10: "the death he died he died to Sin." Paul here uses the expression "to die to something." This metaphorical expression means "to become completely separated from something." Christ quite literally died of course, but in so dying "he died to Sin" (cf. 6:2, 11; 7:6), i.e., Christ became completely separated from the power of Sin. He was "under Sin," like the rest of humanity, but he did not commit sin, did not succumb to Sin's hegemony (cf. 8:3; 2 Cor 5:21; Phil 2:6-11). He refused to be complicit in Sin's hegemony but remained faithful to God to the very end, the very bitter end. And that was his victory, one validated by his resurrection. For this reason, it can also be said that "Death no longer lords it over him" (6:9). At one level, this claim is understood quite literally, in terms of "Christ having being raised from the dead" (6:9; also 6:4) and his "resurrection" (6:5), but at another level it is also understood metaphorically to signify that he no longer abides, as does Adamic humanity before and apart from Christ, in the realm of separation from God, which is what Death signifies. Because Christ died to Sin, he lived and lives to God (6:10; cf. Gal 2:19).

Believers share in Christ's death to Sin (6:2); that is what Paul wants to emphasize here with his rhetorical question: "How can we *who died to Sin* still live in it?" (6:1b). He uses the tradition and language of baptismal initiation, a bodily event, as a way of giving expression to participation in Christ's death to Sin: "all of us who have been baptized into Christ Jesus, have been baptized into his death," that is, his death to Sin. "Our old human being was crucified with him," i.e., was put to death, metaphorically speaking, so that "the body of Sin," which is the body ruled by Sin, "might be destroyed," and that means that it is "no longer a slave of Sin" (6:6). "For someone who has died [with Christ to Sin], has been freed [lit. justified, δεδικαίωται] from Sin" (6:7), a claim which Paul repeats in 6:18 and 22, using the expression ἐλευθεροῦν ἀπό, to set free or liberate from (cf. 6:20; 7:3; 8:2, 21). Slaves need to be freed or liberated and that is what has happened to those who have been baptized into Christ. On the other side of that death to Sin lies "newness of life" (6:4), which is a participation in Christ's resurrection life, not just in the future but also now, and is characterized by righteousness, the polar opposite of sin.[50] Believers are to consider themselves "dead to Sin and living to God in Christ Jesus" (6:11). "If Christ is in you, [although] the body is dead (νεκρόν, a corpse) on account of Sin, the Spirit is life on account of righteousness" (8:10).[51]

It is then as liberated human beings, living by the power of God's grace (5:21; 6:14 15), that Paul exhorts the believers in Rome: "Let not Sin therefore reign in your [pl.] mortal body so that you obey its desires" (6:12). It is Christ's liberating action that for the first time makes the human being truly morally addressable and accountable. "Do not yield your members [i.e., limbs, organs] to Sin as instruments of wickedness, but yield

---

50. Cf. Eastman, *Paul and the Person*, 177: "Redemption is therefore . . . a matter . . . of liberation from one realm of power to another, from the rule of sin and death to life in Christ. In both cases, the person is constituted by participation in realities larger than the self or than merely human relationships."

51. Cf. Käsemann, *Romans*, 224: "in the context of the antithesis δικαιοσύνη cannot refer to the sentence of justification. . . . It is rather walking by the Spirit in bodily service in a way which is pleasing to God."

yourselves to God as people who have been brought from death to life, and your members as weapons of righteousness. For Sin will not rule over you, since you are not under Law but under grace" (6:13-14).[52] Believers in other words have been brought into the sphere of God's powerful, redemptive grace (5:2, 21; cf. 3:24). They are "under Grace," rather than "under (the) Law" (6:14-15) where Sin can exert its lethal control. If to be under Law is tantamount to being under Sin, to be under Grace is tantamount to being under Righteousness, here also personified as a power and a name for God (6:18, 19, 20). Believers are now, paradoxically, "slaves of Righteousness" (6:18; cf. 6:13), which is to say "enslaved to God" (6:22; cf. 6:13). They are not free in the sense of people who have no accountability to God; they are not autonomous, i.e., free to do whatever they want. Rather, they find their freedom in the reign and realm of God's powerful, redemptive Grace. In obedience (6:16) to God, believers are given back their true humanity, for they have been liberated from Sin and from Death, being given righteousness and thus life in their stead. This new life is "the impossible possibility" (Barth) created by God's intervention in Christ.

If Sin leads to or brings Death, God's redemptive Righteousness leads to or grants Life, not just in the future but also now, whenever believers stop being complicit in Sin's lethal reign and yield themselves to God (5:21; 6:8, 11, 22, 23). After all, as Ernst Käsemann has emphasized, baptism marks a change of lordship.

Conclusion

Paul's position can perhaps be summed up as follows: Though victims of Sin, human beings cannot entirely escape responsibility for the wrong that they do (cf. 1:20: "they are without excuse"),[53] and if they become believers who put their trust in Christ, they cannot claim full credit for the good that they may subsequently do, for they cannot achieve or do what is right without the Spirit which "dwells" in them (8:9, 11; cf. 8:10, 13, 14). In human action before and apart from Christ, there is another actor besides human

---

52 J. Louis Martyn, "Epilogue: An Essay in Pauline Meta-Ethics," in *Divine and Human Agency in Paul and his Cultural Environment* (eds. J. M. G. Barclay and S. J. Gathercole; London: T. & T. Clark, 2007), 173-83 (180-81).

53 See Martyn, "The Human Moral Drama," 157-66, esp. 163: "Paul emphasizes his apocalyptic view of Sin as an enslaving power without altogether eclipsing his view of sin as a human act."

beings, namely, Sin. By the same token, for believers in Christ there is another actor who cannot be ignored, namely, the Spirit of God and Christ.[54] If sinful deeds are never simply actions by autonomous human beings for Paul (Sin as an alien power with a domain must also be taken into account), the good works of believers are never simply the achievements of human beings autonomously deciding to do what is right (the role of the Spirit must also be acknowledged).

---

54. Cf. esp. Martyn, "Pauline Meta-Ethics"; Martyn, "The Human Moral Dilemma"; Martyn, "The Gospel Invades Philosophy," in *Paul, Philosophy, and the Theopolitical Vision* (ed. D. Harink; Eugene: Cascade, 2010), 13–33.

3

Sin and the Sovereignty of God in Romans
Bruce W. Longenecker

IT WOULD BE FOLLY to imagine that Paul's discourse regarding sin in Romans could be adjudicated in its complexity within a short essay such as this. Many aspects of Romans pertain to the issue in one way or another, and it is not possible to do justice to them all here. The constraints placed on this essay permit only the chance to overview the main routes that Paul's discourse takes in Romans in relation to this issue. But even this exercise of following those routes yields important results about Paul's theological commitments within this magnificent letter. In the process, we can capture something of Paul's sense of the depth and complexity of what has gone wrong in God's world, as well as capturing something of his vision about what God is doing in Christ to rectify what has gone wrong. For even if we do not stop to explore all the relevant nooks and crannies of Paul's letter to Jesus-groups in Rome, we can nonetheless recognize the extent to which Paul's theological presentation in that letter lies within the broad parameters of his discourse on sin and the sovereignty of God.

Sketching the Situation

In studies of Paul's theological discourse, it is not uncommon these days to find a distinction between Sin with a capital "S" and "sin" or "sins" with a lower-case "s." For the study of Romans, this stylistic differentiation (which

I will adopt in this essay) points to an important conceptual distinction, disentangling two dimensions of Paul's discourse in relation to the Greek word ἁμαρτία (sin/Sin): (1) a cosmological dimension of Sin as a discernible and independent entity of some kind, seemingly with intentionality and on the loose in God's world, and (2) an anthropological dimension of human sinfulness, in which sins are attributable to "the human heart" in some fashion. In the discourse of Romans, these two conceptual foci revolve around each other in a state of being almost interlocked in a relationship of mutual gravitational force, never being far from each other, even if one of these foci might take center stage at one point in Paul's presentation and the other at another point. These two foci make up what might be called "the hamartiological matrix" of Romans.[1]

A quick glance at the first major section of the letter, Romans 1–4, illustrates the point. Human sins seem to predominate in those chapters, being evident in Paul's list of transgressive behaviors in 1:18–32; or in his comments regarding those "who have sinned" in 2:12 (twice); or in his claim that "all have sinned" in 3:23; or when he speaks of "sins previously committed" in 3:25; or when he recalls scriptural passages that speak of forgiveness for sins in 4:7-8; or when he claims that Jesus Christ was handed over for "our transgressions" in 4:25.[2] These transgressions have provoked what Paul calls "the wrath of God" that is revealed from heaven against "all ungodliness and wickedness of those who by their wickedness suppress the truth" (Rom 1:18).

But if these passages highlight human sinfulness, Paul's comment in Rom 3:9 highlights not the sins of individuals but something far more ominous and threatening (not least when considered in relation to divine sovereignty, as discussed below). In that verse, Paul claims that he has "already charged that all people, both Judeans and Greeks, are under Sin." By this, he does not mean that all are under "the weight of their personal sins." That is, he is not imagining someone like Pilgrim in John Bunyan's *Pilgrim's*

---

1. On Sin as a cosmic power in Romans, see (among others) Beverly Gaventa, "The Cosmic Power of Sin in Paul's Letter to the Romans: Toward a Widescreen Edition," *Int* 58 (2004) 229–40; on human sinfulness in Paul in general, see (among others) Simon Gathercole, "'Sins' in Paul," *NTS* 64 (2018) 143–61. On the relationship between Sin and sin, see Sarah Harding, *Paul's Eschatological Anthropology: The Dynamics of Human Transformation* (Minneapolis: Fortress, 2016), esp. chs. 2–4.

2. Compare also Rom 11:27, where Paul declares that the sins of unbelieving Jews (that is, their resistance to Jesus-devotion) will be "taken away" (ἀφέλωμαι) at an astounding point in the future, because of God's covenant faithfulness to them.

Progress, nor the Robert de Niro character (Captain Rodrigo Mendoza) in the film *The Mission* (dir. Roland Joffé, 1986); both of those characters carry all their sins (or representations of them) in sacks on their back, struggling under their weight until those sins are gloriously removed once repentance has been effectively enacted. Instead, Paul seems to be referencing a cosmic power that has intentionality over and above human beings, "the power of Sin." This itself is somewhat surprising because, despite his claim, he has not, in fact, "already charged" that all people are under this cosmic power prior to 3:9—at least, not in explicitly articulated form.³ Evidently, then, while Paul's audience might have thought they were, in fact, hearing only about human sinfulness, Paul wanted them to understand that they were also hearing about a suprahuman force that lurks within God's world.

The phrase "two-level drama" comes to mind—two dramas are converging in the concrete action of individuals. But notice that, in the first section of Romans, Paul never says that human wickedness is simply and solely a perverse consequence of being enslaved to the cosmic power of Sin. If his account of human depravity in Rom 1–3 ultimately testifies to the overwhelming influence of the cosmic power of Sin, there is much in Romans that prevents us from laying all the blame solely at the feet of that cosmic power. Paul said that those who commit "all ungodliness and wickedness" (1:18) are "without excuse" (ἀναπολογήτους, 1:20); he did not say they are excused—not even that they are excused because of their unfortunate enslavement to the inexcusable cosmic power of Sin. If it makes good sense to say that God's wrath is stirred up by the cosmic power of Sin, it is also true that Paul's discourse does not follow that route; instead, the wrath of God is directed against (as one case in point) the one with a "hard and impenitent heart" (2:5).⁴

---

3. Perhaps the closest we can come to this previously stated charge is the depiction of God "handing them [sinners] over" (1:24, 26, 28) to various forms of life that testify to their being held in custody by a third party. See Beverly Gaventa, *Our Mother Saint Paul* (Louisville: Westminster John Knox, 2007), 113–23. This interpretation may not be ultimately satisfying, however. If there are forces running contrary to God in 1:24, 26, and 28, they are understood to be human attitudes and behaviors. The fact that the verb "to hand over" is often used in confrontational contexts (as Gaventa helpfully argues) cannot in itself help us define whether the confrontational "opponent" is a human or suprahuman phenomenon. If cosmic powers are in the frame of 1:24, 26, 28, that is only as a second layer of interpretation, whose foothold in 3:9 does not overturn the fact that God "gave them over" to "impurity," "degrading passions," and "a debased mind."

4. Compare also 2:9 ("there will be anguish and distress for everyone who does evil") with its curious link to 3:8; cf. 3:5–8, where God's wrath is discussed in relation to human

More of Paul's two-level drama or hamartiological matrix comes into view in Rom 5–8.[5] As a relatively self-contained section, Rom 5–8 inverts the emphasis, with the cosmological power of Sin now taking center stage. Together with the power of Death, the cosmic power of Sin acts as an enslaving and controlling overlord (5:21; 6:12, 14)—to the extent that even the well-intentioned character of Rom 7 who speaks in the first-person singular cannot counter the mastery of the cosmic power of Sin, despite a combination of good intentions and the commandment/law of God, which itself is "holy, righteous, and good" (7:12). Even that person declares, "I am sold as a slave to the lordship of the power of Sin" (7:14), which correlates to the desperate cry, "who will deliver me?" (7:24).[6] With grace and righteousness being far more potent and efficacious than the power of Sin (5:20), the matter should be all sewn up—the power of Sin is demolished in Christ, humanity is released from its ensnaring grip, and all that's left is the announcement to the world concerning God's victory over threatening forces of chaos. But even in this section of Romans, things are not clear-cut. It isn't only the power of Sin that is in play. Occurrences of ἁμαρτία in 5:12–21 are not always clear as to whether they are referencing the cosmic power or the human transgression, or perhaps a combination of both simultaneously.[7] Nonetheless, the three occurrences of the verb ἁμαρτάνειν in 5:12–16 disambiguate human sinfulness (cf. also "transgressions" in 5:20) from the related power of Sin, just as the cosmic power of Sin seems to be disambiguated from related human sinfulness in 5:21.

Evidently, then, while Paul's focus shifts from one form of ἁμαρτία to the other, he keeps them both in play in various mixtures throughout the whole of Rom 1–8. Of the two forms of ἁμαρτία, human sinfulness is easy to comprehend; less clear is the murky figure of the cosmic power of Sin. Of course, we might wonder whether Paul really imagined cosmic powers

"falsehood" and the status of "sinner" (ἁμαρτωλός).

5. I see these chapters as a fairly self-contained unit, precisely because of the rhetorical thread that runs through them at key structural points in each main text unit of those chapters—the phrase (or variations of the phrase) "through Jesus Christ our Lord" (Rom 5:1, 11, 21; 6:23; 7:25; 8:39).

6. On the identity of the speaker of Rom 7 and the interpretation of the twists and turns at Rom 7:24–25, see Bruce W. Longenecker, *Rhetoric at the Boundaries: The Art and Theology of New Testament Chain-Link Transitions* (Waco, TX: Baylor University Press, 2005), 88–93.

7. The ambiguity may be apparent in 5:12ab and 5:20, for instance, although the four articular forms of ἁμαρτία in those verses may tilt the balance in favor of seeing them as referencing the power of Sin, first introduced in Rom 3:9.

to be alive and well in God's creation, as independent suprahuman forces with their own intentionality. Perhaps this way of presenting things was simply a sensational rhetorical device that allowed Paul to conceptualize a fundamental feature of the human situation—externalizing that feature as an independent entity in order to examine it in hypostatized fashion.[8] For my part, I incline toward the view that these powers were objective entities in Paul's mental universe—the sort of thing that came easily to Jewish and non-Jewish minds of the Greco-Roman world. We might imagine them to be projections onto the heavenly screen of human psycho-socio phenomena, but Paul seems to have imagined them as objective realities that transcended the human realm and acted with intentionality upon that realm. This, at least, is how the author of Ephesians articulated the matter when he noted that "our struggle" is ultimately "against the rulers, against the authorities, against the 'cosmos-grabbers' (τοὺς κοσμοκράτορας) of this present darkness, against the spiritual forces of evil in the heavenly places" (Eph 6:12). Here the Pauline tendency has been carefully articulated in such fashion as to suggest that the cosmic powers are not simply externalizing projections of human frailties; they are, instead, cosmic realities that lie beyond an anthropomorphic grounding.[9]

Probing the Origins

Does Paul's discourse in Romans clarify how the power of Sin takes its place as an enslaving master? Two verses present themselves as most relevant to this question. The first is Rom 5:21: "the cosmic power of Sin exercised dominion in death" (ἐβασίλευσεν ἡ ἁμαρτία ἐν τῷ θανάτῳ). Here Paul seems to assume that the all-encompassing lordship of the power of Sin originates only after Adam committed his transgressive act, which resulted in death.[10]

---

8. The attempt to interpret the power of Sin as the build-up of human sinfulness within the social ethos of human culture has been put forward by Matthew Croasmun, *The Emergence of Sin: The Cosmic Tyrant in Romans* (Oxford: Oxford University Press, 2017). I am sympathetic to the attempt, but I think it ultimately does not offer the complete explanation of the situation.

9. I develop this further in Bruce W. Longenecker, "What did Paul think is wrong in God's world?" in *The New Cambridge Companion to Paul* (ed. B. W. Longenecker; Cambridge: Cambridge University Press, forthcoming).

10. The power of Sin has its masterful lordship only in relation to Death (itself conceived as a cosmic power, although with a corresponding anthropological component in 5:12–21, as in 1 Cor 15). In Rom 5, since Death/death itself comes into the world as a

There is no attempt to attribute the "disobedience of the one man" (5:19) to Sin's enslaving lordship; instead, that form of disobedience appears to be attributable to what we might call "the frailties embedded within the human heart"—narratively represented by Adam's sin even prior to the enslaving grip of a cosmic force. Evidently Paul would have us imagine that Adam's single sin, committed even before the power of Sin gained regal mastery, gave the foothold for the overwhelming power of Sin to ascend to mastery subsequently. In this scenario, the cosmic power of Sin is not the only problem to be resolved when the sovereign creator takes decisive action to rectify the created order; the human heart plays a key role in the story of relational dysfunction precisely because it takes center stage in Paul's narration of how things went wrong in the first place.

Nonetheless, even if things seem relatively straightforward in 5:21, Paul's assertion there raises questions that he does not address. Did a single transgression *give birth to* a cosmic power that hadn't existed before? Or was the power of Sin simply lurking in the cosmological wings even prior to the single transgression, just waiting for the opportunity to swoop into God's good creation once that foothold had been created? Or was the cosmic power actually influencing (rather than enslaving) the one man toward sinfulness somehow, even prior to that single transgression, and even though the responsibility for that sinful act lies ultimately with the choice of the frail human heart since "the one man" was not yet enslaved to that cosmic power?

At this point, Paul's comments in Rom 16:20 present themselves as the second verse that might offer resources for considering the relationship of cause and effect. In that verse, Paul gives voice to God's pronouncement, "I will shortly crush Satan under your feet." This declaration takes its orientation from Gen 3:15, which recounts God's declaration that the "seed of the woman" will "crush the head of the serpent" for its role in leading humanity into sin. Evidently Paul had pondered on that scriptural passage, which must have given him pause for considering that something greater

---

consequence of sin (which in 5:12b seems to suggest human sinfulness, and in particular, Adam's), the cosmic power of Sin cannot be said to have enslaved the one man, Adam, and cannot have caused him to produce the sinful transgression. The point is made by Beverly Gaventa, "Freedom in Apocalyptic Perspective: A Reflection on Paul's Letter to the Romans," in *Quests for Freedom: Biblical, Historical, Contemporary* (ed. M. Welker; Neukirchen-Vluyn: Neukirchener, 2015), 195–208. "The somewhat cryptic conclusion of 3:9 that all are under sin here becomes explicit and expansive: Adam's free disobedience renders all captive to the rule of Sin"; rebellion against God "eventuates in enslavement to the powers of Sin and Death" (202).

than Adam's sinful act needs to be referenced in order to fully explain the repertoire of the transgressive will within God's good creation.[11]

Trying to articulate the cosmological relationship between the power of Sin and human sinfulness sometimes feels like the proverbial chicken-and-egg scenario. In fact, it is hard to know whether we should be prioritizing a single utterance (i.e., Rom 5:21 or 16:20) in order to try to sort out a Pauline view of the origins of the lordship of the cosmic power of Sin, or whether Paul's theologizing on this matter simply revolves around a double polarity, at times with a bit more of one pole than the other, and at other times a bit more of the other, without trying to harmonize the various statements made in their rhetorical contexts.[12] It seems to me that the second of these options is the better of the two.

The Moral Character of Human Sinfulness

Paul's preference not to allow human sinfulness to fall out of the hamartiological matrix of Romans seems to inform several passages in Romans that need brief mention. At two points in his discussion Paul freeze-frames what the "hard and impenitent" human heart looks like, at least when relational dysfunction toward God (i.e., idolatry) overspills to relational dysfunction among human beings. Those verses crystalize the essence of relational dysfunction among humans, identifying it to be "covetousness" (1:29 [πλεονεξία]; 7:8 [ἐπιθυμία]). Unpacked more fully within the context of those verses, covetousness seems to be the moral attribute that both produces and emerges from a world of (what has been called) "social Darwinism," in which the fittest survive and dominate others through the acquisition of status and the accumulation of power over others.[13] In that world of abusive relationality, people (whether individuals or people-groups) inevitably seek their advantage over the well-being of others.[14]

---

11. On Satan in the undisputed letters of Paul, see Derek R. Brown, *The God of This Age: Satan in the Churches and Letters of the Apostle Paul* (WUNT 2/409; Tübingen: Mohr Siebeck, 2015).

12. The issue becomes far more complex if we try to insert Paul's discourse of Rom 7 into the mix, especially if, as many believe, there is an "Adamic" dimension to the voice of the "I" in that passage.

13. I should point out that I am not referencing *biological* Darwinism in this critique of *social* Darwinism.

14. The economic dimension of Paul's understanding of covetousness is explored in Bruce W. Longenecker, "Paul, Poverty, and the Powers: The Eschatological Body of Christ

If we reintroduce the power of Sin into this discussion, we can see that the moral posture of the world dominated by Sin involves hawkishly being set to pounce on any others who might show a moment of weakness, and doing so in order to appropriate whatever resources they might have, thereby bolstering one's own status. The best game-plan of the cosmic power of Sin involves harnessing the good things of God's created order (and even the good people, as in Rom 7) and drafting them into the agonistic program of social Darwinism (as in the drama of Rom 7). Paul's analysis of the human heart (as a pawn in the post-Edenic strategies of the power of Sin) would seem to have plenty of resonance throughout the course of human history, even today.

Taking Stock

Four things have emerged thus far in this study of the hamartiological matrix that Paul presents in Romans. First, Paul's discourse does not give us enough data to reconstruct a stable and precise view regarding either (a) the cosmological origins of the power of Sin or (b) its rise to cosmic dominance. Second, Paul depicts the power of Sin as having mastery over post-Edenic humanity, which imposes the "structural" context and condition in which the post-Edenic sinfulness of humanity proliferates; by definition, the one important exception to this situation is the pre-fallen Adam, whose disobedience cannot be attributed to the mastery of the cosmic power of Sin. Third, removing the cosmic power of Sin (and its accomplice, Death) from its position of dominion is both necessary and not itself sufficient if the story of God's cosmic sovereignty in Christ is truly to find its ultimate resolution without remainder. Fourth, dealing with human sinfulness that overspills from the human heart is both necessary and not in itself sufficient if the story of God's cosmic sovereignty in Christ is truly to find its ultimate resolution without remainder.[15]

---

in the Present Evil Age," in *One God, One People, One Future: Essays in Honor of N. T. Wright* (eds. J. A. Dunne and E. Lewellen; London: SPCK, 2018), 363–87. On Romans 1:29–31, see also Sylvia Keesmaat and Brian Walsh, *Romans Disarmed: Resisting Empire, Demanding Justice* (Grand Rapids: Baker Academic, 2019).

15. Regarding the necessity of dealing with human sinfulness, Walter Wink says it well (unsurprisingly) when he notes (*Engaging the Powers: Discernment and Resistance in a World of Domination* [Minneapolis: Fortress, 1992], 76): "anyone who has looked deeply within knows that not all evil has been introjected into us by the means of production or the government or patriarchy or the structures of society. Some evil would

Paul was convinced that in Christ God is both shattering the enslaving grip of the overlording cosmic power of Sin (and Death) and dealing with the sins committed by humanity as a consequence of their slavery within Sin's grip. If we choose to listen only to Paul's words pertaining to the problem of human sinfulness, we would be reducing the symphony of full orchestral resonance to a tame musical score for a string quartet.[16] At the same time, however, if we choose to listen only to Paul's words pertaining to the foreboding cosmic powers, we are in danger of losing sight of the micro-narratives of the human heart as a place where sinfulness is generated in small but not insignificant powerhouses (at least, if my inferences regarding Adam's pre-fallen freedom from the mastery of the power of Sin have merit, on the basis of what Paul says in 5:21).

If these two aspects are "joined at the hip" of Paul's theological discourse and cannot be severed without losing their essential interconnectivity, we might ask whether one of these conceptual foci predominates in Paul's theological discourse. Even if both are essential to Paul's presentation in Romans, does one form of discourse get us further to the heart of his theological discourse?

There are at least two dimensions to this. First, these conceptual foci offered Paul different kinds of theological resources that he seemed content to use in various measures, depending on the rhetorical requirements of his discourse in any given instance. If that's right, damage can be done to the complexities of Paul's discourse if we insist on forcing all of his discourse into one rigid theological package or another.[17] Paul was a flexible thinker, and our categories of interpretation need to reflect that aspect of his

---

remain in our souls regardless of the social system. Otherwise, how can we account for the creation of these alienating structures in the first place? No arrangement of social cooperation, in which power controls power and anarchy is tamed, will produce human beings free from the lust for power." See more broadly his comments throughout 74–77.

16. Ultimately, the narrative of God's sovereignty cannot be successfully resolved without the dethronement of the powers. After all, human sinfulness itself is not depicted as threatening to dethrone the sovereignty of the creator God—only the powers of Sin and Death have set themselves up in that position (together, perhaps, with the Satan figure, who enters the frame only at Rom 16:20, albeit in a highly suggestive fashion).

17. Here I depart somewhat from the view of Philip G. Ziegler when he writes (*Militant Grace: The Apocalyptic Turn and the Future of Christian Theology* [Grand Rapids: Baker Academic, 2018], 28): "redemption from [the cosmic power of] Sin represents a comprehensive account of salvation able to encompass other soteriological motifs such as atonement, guilt, and forgiveness." In my view, two somewhat different forms of discourse disambiguate in Paul which, while related, incline toward their own forms of discourse depending on whether "sins" or "Sin" is taking prominence at any given point.

discourse if we intend to respect that discourse and maximize its theological potential.

With that said, however, it also seems, secondly, that some of Paul's most intriguing and distinctive forms of theological discourse emerge in his letters at points where he foregrounds God's sovereignty in relation to the cosmic powers. When exploring that territory, Paul found novel theological resources that permitted fresh forms of articulation of the gospel, allowing him to address complex issues in theologically compelling and invigorating ways. His discourse in Rom 5–8, with its foothold in 3:9, is illustrative of this most innovative dynamic in Paul's theologizing.

Conceptual Analogies to Paul's Hamartiological Matrix

Clarifying the hamartiological matrix in Romans might be helped by offering analogies to tease out the two-level drama in relation to the sovereignty of God in Christ. This exercise comes with the important proviso that analogies are never in themselves wholly adequate. They may enlighten certain aspects of their referent, but they do so without encapsulating all the complexities of that to which they refer. Moreover, individual components of an analogy, when extrapolated beyond its place within the limitations of the analogy itself, can backfire by producing new significations that lie beyond the original conceptual point of reference. Even with these deficiencies, however, analogies are often helpful in stimulating ways of conceptualizing the matter at hand, even if they need to be employed with caution.

Since the drama of cosmic sovereignty is ultimately at stake in Paul's hamartiological matrix, analogies from the history of human warfare might provide resources for conceptualizing what God has done in Christ in relation to the two-level drama of sins and Sin. The first analogy is that of the proxy war. Dealing with human sinfulness is, in a sense, like engaging in a proxy war where minor oppositional forces are engaged, but the real threat remains disturbingly at large. In the Cold War mentality of the US in the 1960s, for instance, political regime in North Vietnam was not the real enemy that the US was battling; that regime was merely a proxy for the ultimate threat of communism that was thought to be emanating from China and the USSR.

A second analogy from human warfare derives from the Cold War mentality of the US in the 1980s—not least in Ronald Reagan's Strategic Defense Initiative, SDI or "Star Wars" program in relation to more conventional forms of warfare. The worry for conventional warfare was that Russian forces would simply cross the Bering Strait, invading Alaska and working down the western coast of Canada to invade the northwestern states. Hopefully that border transgression could be repelled by a combination of conventional forces (naval, air, and armed forces). But there was a more ominous worry—one that came from overhead. What if Soviet nuclear bombs began to shower down on US citizens from above? Initiatives to shoot them down in the air were deemed necessary, resulting in Reagan's SDI program. Here, while military readiness required troops on the ground to combat the boots on the ground in one-to-one combat (or close to it), the much scarier and devastating prospect was the rain from the sky of nuclear bombs that threatened to invert the structures of all life within the USA.

These two analogies (the proxy war and the combination of conventional and SDI initiatives) might seem to get us some way toward capturing aspects of Paul's multidimensional understanding of sin and the cosmic power of Sin. But let me propose one other analogy that frames the relationship between human sinfulness and the cosmic power of Sin in what is perhaps a more productive fashion—this time from the 1970s. In 1974, the teenager Patty Hearst was kidnapped and held captive for more than a year and a half in an effort to extract money from her rich father. Two months after her abduction, Hearst was found carrying out a bank robbery in league with her abductors, standing alongside them in their cause. If she was willingly complicit (and interpretations of her motivations vary), hers would be a classic case of the strange situation in which kidnapped people sometimes sympathetically adopt the interests and commitments of their kidnappers (a curious phenomenon popularly referred to as "Stockholm syndrome," although it has never been officially recognized as a psychological "syndrome"). In this situation, Patty Hearst needed both (1) to be rescued from her captors (much like the person of Rom 7 cries out, "Who will rescue me?" [Rom 7:25]) and (2) to be reformed in her volitional commitments (demonstrating what it means to live "according to the flesh" [Rom 8:5]). She was, in a sense, held captive "under the power of" her kidnappers, but she had also become involved in complicit "sins" of her own.

God's Sovereignty in Christ

In Romans (as elsewhere in his letters), Paul's theological canvas is huge, involving the rectification of the cosmos through the power of the sovereign God, who is faithful to creation in Christ. At its widest extent, Paul's theological canvas highlights cosmic powers that have inserted themselves deep into the structures of this world and have set themselves up as the overlording masters of God's otherwise good creation, "enclasping" all of post-Edenic humanity within their overpowering grip. The canvas is cosmic in proportion, with the major players being God and the forces that run contrary to God's will, transcending while also manipulating the realm of human transgressive initiatives. If Jesus Christ died simply to deal with the sins of sinners, and if his death and resurrection did nothing more than create a worldwide group of people who sought forgiveness for their sins, then the death and resurrection of the Son of God would have done little to dethrone the forces that threaten to remove God from the place of cosmic sovereignty. Paul does not ascribe to an anemic theology of that kind. His deity is reclaiming creation from the grip of illegitimate "cosmos-grabbers."

It is important to note, however, that this triumph of Abraham's God transpires not because God has more brute power than any cosmic opposition. It is true, of course, that in God's storehouse of power, Paul imagined resources to be inexhaustible. But in Paul's scheme God does not overthrow oppositional cosmic powers simply because God's weapons are more deadly and powerful versions of the weapons used by God's enemies. This is where the otherwise helpful analogies drawn from instances of human warfare (above) thoroughly corrupt Paul's theological calculus. God does not emerge victorious in Christ simply by outgunning all opposition with a bigger arsenal. To see things in that way is to judge things by the criteria sponsored by the cosmic powers of Sin and Death. It is one of the strategies of Sin to depict God as a super enlarged projection of the human condition under Sin. But Paul's God eschews such forms of idolatry, which have plagued the course of human history. Instead, the power of Paul's God is of a qualitatively different kind than the power of Sin—much like DC electrical power (now of a bygone age) operates completely differently to AC electrical power. The surprising triumph of God has nothing to do with God simply being the most fit to survive the cut-throat contest for power, or simply the most successful participant in this game of power-accumulation. Ironically, the surprising triumph of the sovereign God over God's cosmic competitors lies in the *renunciation* of that power complex and the *denunciation* of its rules of engagement.[18]

It is true, of course, that Paul presents the triumph of God as involving Satan being "crushed" (Rom 16:20, as noted above), and this might sound like a slightly more sophisticated version of God having a bigger club than Satan. But within the larger context of Paul's theological discourse, this crushing is not the *modus operandi*, but the end result. Paul's talk of the crushing of Satan is equivalent to Jesus's talk of "plundering the house of the Strong Man" (Mark 3:27 and parallels), with that plundering ultimately taking place in the self-giving of Jesus and God's resurrection of the same self-giving one (cf. Rom 5:6–8). In the theological discourse of both Jesus and Paul, the *modus operandi* is self-giving, and the result of that strategy is the conquering of any other strategy and all other power bases.[19] The end result is the universal acclamation of Paul's God by all people and powers (borrowing here from Phil 2:11 and Col 1:15–20, with a foothold in Rom 15:7–13).[20]

---

18. Wink, *Engaging the Powers*, 87: "The rulership [of God] thus constituted is not a domination hierarchy but an enabling or actualizing hierarchy. It is not pyramidal but organic, not imposed but restorative. It is presided over by naked, defenseless truth—the Crucified—not by a divine dictator. Christ makes all things subject to himself, not by coercion, but by healing diseased reality and restoring its balance and integrity."

19. Perhaps this is why the imagery of God crushing Satan is prefaced by Paul with the depiction of God as "the God of peace." Much the same happens in Rom 12:19–21, where the "vengeance of God" against evildoers is filtered immediately through a prism of Christian caring for enemies in need and, in so doing, "you will heap burning coals on their head." This is a fairly graphic way of speaking of the removing of the wall of hostility (as in Eph 2), the complete dismantling of the category "enemy" altogether by a modus operandi of caring other-regard. And this then spills into the next statement along the same lines—this time, more easy to understand: "do not be overcome by evil, but overcome evil with good." Things are being "overcome" in all this (graphically depicted as "heaping burning coals" on the heads of enemies), but the method of overcoming evil is through the enactment of goodness. Should it be any different for the God who, in vengeance against evil, destroys it through a power evidenced in self-giving? The author of Colossians "perfects" this line of thought when depicting the self-giving Christ as embodying "the fullness of God" and the one through whom God reconciles all things to himself, "whether on earth or in heaven, by making peace through the blood of his cross" (Col 1:19–20). Once again, we are back to "the God of peace" of Rom 16:20, whose peace comes through reconciling all things through the power of the self-giving Christ. No wonder Paul can speak in Phil 2:10 of the bending of every knee "in heaven and on earth and under the earth" at the name of Jesus.

20. The language of the "destruction" of cosmic enemies in 1 Cor 15:24–26 shifts immediately to the language of their "subjection" in 15:27–28.

The divine battle against the social Darwinism of the power of Sin is ultimately determined in relation to Jesus's act of faithful self-giving and God's act of resurrection—a creation *ex nihilo* that is characteristic of the only true sovereign of creation. The cosmic powers of Sin and Death struck at the one who obediently entered the only death that does not reinforce the reputation of Sin and Death as overlords of dysfunction.[21] For Paul, Jesus Christ entrusted himself faithfully to God, who handed him over to death (4:25; 8:32), with Jesus's obedient vulnerability to and unto death being met by God's faithfulness as the one who draws out life. The resurrection of Jesus Christ, then, ultimately announces the sovereignty of God over creation, dis-establishing all competing claims of lordship. Paul called Jesus's act of vulnerability unto death "the obedience of the one man" (5:19; and perhaps, if the subjective genitive reading of πίστις Ἰησοῦ Χριστοῦ is correct, "the faithfulness of Jesus Christ," 3:22; cf. 3:25–26). In this act of obedience lies the conviction that God is faithful and trustworthy (Rom 15:8; cf. 3:3–7). In this act of obedience, then, lies the eschewal of the Satanic lie that God is unfaithful and untrustworthy.[22] That Satanic lie has served as the foundation for the matrix of relational horror that is social Darwinism. In God's resurrection of the self-giving one, that Satanic lie itself is crushed. God's resurrection of Jesus is God's self-declaration of faithful integrity toward God's creation.[23] As such, it is also an embodiment of divine power (1:4)—a power that engorges the proclamation of the gospel itself (1:16–17). The "good news" that Paul proclaimed, then, is ultimately the announcement that sovereign power subversively undermines the damaging power structures that are deeply embedded in and ultimately destructive of God's good cosmos.

Moreover, in Paul's good news, the single act of redemptive vulnerability unto life has become the incubator for other displays of divinely-inspired power in the lives of Jesus-followers who die with their Lord and are raised to newness of life with him (e.g., Rom 6). When characterizing that form of new-life power, Paul sometimes uses the word "love," which he anchors to the notion of self-giving for the benefit of others—precisely

21. Or in the words of Romans 8:3, Jesus Christ was "in the likeness of sinful flesh."

22. On the relevance of this theme in Revelation and beyond, see especially Sigve Tonstad, *Saving God's Reputation: The Theological Function of Pistis Iesou in the Cosmic Narratives of Revelation* (London: T. & T. Clark, 2006).

23. Paul wants to affirm this while also affirming God's faithfulness to Israel; so esp. Rom 11, 15:8. The combined sense is captured in the phrase "the righteousness of God" (3:21–26).

the opposite of the covetous moral world produced by the cosmic power of Sin.[24] This is why the law that said "you shall not covet" finds its fulfillment in self-giving lives of Jesus-followers (13:8–10; cf. 8:4), who themselves utter Jesus's own denunciation of covetousness in his cry of faithful obedience, "Abba, father" (8:15; cf. Mark 14:36). This is where the power of the sovereign God is most sharply evidenced, exemplified in communities of concern for the other (14:1—15:6). Those communities advertise the short-circuiting of the mania of power-accumulation that characterizes the world of social Darwinism overseen by the cosmic power of Sin; as such, they are qualified for true worship of the sovereign God (just as 15:1–6 flows into 15:7–13). In this way, the motley communities that Paul established in urban centers of the Roman world were to be reflections of the diversity of humanity on bended knee—Jew and gentile and all other polarities united in faith-works ("the obedience that faith produces," 1:5; cf. 16:26) through the Spirit, raising their voices in joyous praise to God. If we may borrow the words of Ephesians momentarily, we might say that in communities of this kind "the wisdom of God in its rich variety might now be made known to the rulers and authorities in the heavenly places" (Eph 3:10).[25]

In contrast to the sovereign God who produces life and the conditions for its flourishing, the cosmic power of Sin seems able to produce only one thing: the conditions for the flourishing of death ("death came through sin," 5:12). This is the arena of Sin's dominion (5:21). In moral terms, the cosmic power of Sin holds dominion over all that leads to death in the realm of social Darwinism. But Sin does not have dominion over nothingness. This sounds like a strange statement. But it follows on from Paul's conviction that only the sovereign creator can work with nothingness: "God . . . gives life to the dead and calls into existence the things that do not exist" (Rom 4:17). This is true, whether that nothingness is the dead bodies of Sarah and Abraham (4:18–21) or the nothingness of the dead body of Jesus (4:24–25). That is why, in dying with Christ, his followers are

---

24. Elsewhere I have argued that the phrase "God's love has been poured into our hearts" in Rom 5:5 includes three levels of polyvalent significance: God's love for us, our love for God, and "divine" self-giving love in general. See Bruce W. Longenecker, "The Love of God (Romans 5:5): Expansive Syntax and Theological Polyvalence," in *Interpretation and the Claim of the Text* (eds. J. Whitlark et al.; Waco, TX: Baylor University Press, 2014), 145–58 and 246–48.

25. For a fuller study of the importance of worship in relation to a gathered and properly functioning community, see Bruce W. Longenecker, "Faith, Works, and Worship," in *The Apostle Paul and the Christian Life*, (eds. S. McKnight and J. Modica; Grand Rapids: Baker Academic, 2016), 47–70.

set free from enslavement to the cosmic power of Sin (Rom 6)—death is the one place where the cosmic power of Sin cannot access them. This is the irony of God's triumph: the cosmic power of Sin is overthrown in "the obedience of the one man" who went into the nothingness of death and draws his followers with him into death, where they are beyond the reach of the cosmic power of Sin. Every other instance of human death testifies to the lordship of Sin and Death, but this instance of human death becomes the power generator of newness of life beyond the power of Sin—the vortex of transformation for Jesus-followers and the matrix in which the sovereignty of God is reclaiming the world in resurrection power.

In essence, Paul saw the authentic incarnation of the self-giving God within the authentic, self-giving humanity embodied in the person of Jesus—the obedient "one man" (5:12–21) who "was declared to be Son of God with power according to the Spirit of holiness by resurrection from the dead, Jesus Christ our Lord" (Rom 1:4). Clinging to the conviction that God "did not withhold God's own Son, but gave him up" to death (8:32), Paul proclaimed the good news that Jesus-followers are freed from the power of Sin and raised to new configurations of self-giving life and love through the power of the Spirit of Christ.

4

Models for Relating Sin as a Power to Human Activity in Romans 5:12-21

A. ANDREW DAS

PAUL DOES NOT PRESENT a monolithic view of sin in his letter to the Romans. Early in the letter, sin refers to human thoughts and actions contrary to God's will. The wickedness of humanity in Rom 1:18-32 will be addressed, according to 2:5-11, by God's impartial judgment according to deeds. Then in 2:12-16 Paul addresses a potential objection to God's impartiality: the Jews' unique access to God's will in the Law of Moses. Apart from a brief, presaging nod to all humanity's being "under" (ὑπό) sin in Rom 3:9, Paul quickly reverts to individual human actions in 3:11-18 and concludes the line of thought in 3:23 with "all have sinned and fall short of the glory of God."[1]

Later in the letter, Paul presents a different understanding of sin. In Rom 5-7 he talks about sin and death as powers in the cosmos that exercise their dominion and rule over helpless human beings (e.g., 6:9, 12, 14). Sin and Death are enslaving powers from which the individual must be freed (e.g., sin in 6:6, 18). Paul also describes powers on the opposite side of Sin

---

1. Note the chain link construction as he turns to a new, saving reality in 3:21; with Bruce W. Longenecker, *Rhetoric at the Boundaries: The Art and Theology of New Testament Chain-Link Transitions* (Waco, TX: Baylor University Press, 2005), 88-102, although Longenecker does not discuss this particular instance. These sins committed by individuals (3:25) need to be forgiven (4:7-8). Paul will use the verb "to sin" as equivalent to "transgress" in 5:14, 16.

and Death. In Rom 6:19 the baptized are able to present their members as slaves not to impurity but rather to righteousness with a capital "R." Perhaps the most prominent cosmic power on the other side of the divide is Grace.

In Rom 5:20–21 Paul lists three programmatic powers: the Law, Sin, and Grace. He then systematically explores the various relationships between these three cosmic forces. In Rom 6:1 he asks about the relationship between *Sin* and *Grace*. May Christians continue sinning in order that grace may abound? In Rom 6:15 Paul turns to a second combination: he asks whether a Christian may sin since he or she is under *Grace* and not the *Law*? Paul turns to the final combination in Rom 7:7 where he asks whether the *Law* is *Sin*.[2] The Law too can be an enslaving power! Back in 6:15 Paul speaks of being "under" Grace rather than "under" the Law. The language suggests that people must be liberated from the Law (see 6:9, 14). Even as one must die to Sin (6:2), so one must die to the Law (7:4). Death frees one from both Sin (6:7, 18) and the Law (7:2–3, 6), and this freedom allows the Christian to serve in the newness of life (6:4) and the Spirit (7:6).[3] Only by sharing in Christ's death can the Christian be freed from the enslaving powers of the old age.[4] Thus Paul distinguishes in Rom 7:14–25 the thoughts and desires of an "I" (ἐγώ) from the actions of Sin as a controlling power that is external to the "I."[5]

2. Paul J. Achtemeier, *Romans* (Interpretation; Louisville: John Knox, 1985), 102.

3. Anders Nygren, *Commentary on Romans* (Philadelphia: Fortress, 1949), 268.

4. Heikki Räisänen, *Paul and the Law* (2nd ed.; WUNT 29; Tübingen: J. C. B. Mohr [Paul Siebeck], 1986), 58. Paul's analogy is a woman bound by the Law to her husband until his death frees her from the legal obligation. Similarly, a death must take place in order to free one from the power of the Law. This death took place when the Christian was buried and raised with Christ in baptism (6:3–13). Dying permits the believer *to live*! On the sequential flow of logic in this text, see Joyce A. Little, "Paul's Use of Analogy: A Structural Analysis of Romans 7:1–6," *CBQ* 46 (1984) 82–90.

5. With Susan Eastman, "Double Participation and the Responsible Self in Romans 5–8," in *Apocalyptic Paul: Cosmos and Anthropos in Romans 5–8* (ed. Beverly Roberts Gaventa; Waco, TX: Baylor University Press, 2013), 93–110, here 101: "The self operates in tandem with a lethal partner, sin, and the partner is stronger. This is a participatory, noncompetitive account of the human self as constituted in relationship to sin, yet not completely conflated with it: the self is still a responsible agent, still the subject of verbs." The self is in a relationship to sin, and sin creates a "wedge" between what the self wants and the resulting actions. The self must be liberated from this awful relationship with sin to enjoy a new relationship with Christ and the Spirit. Or, with J. Louis Martyn ("Afterword: The Human Moral Drama," in *Apocalyptic Paul: Cosmos and Anthropos in Romans 5–8* [ed. Beverly Roberts Gaventa; Waco, TX: Baylor University Press, 2013], 157–66, here 163): "Held captive by the enslaving power of Sin, human beings commit sin. The result is the dark and sinister version of dual agency. Sin is *both* an active agent,

Paul therefore presents two very different understandings of sin within the same letter. This leads to the question whether there is a model that can account for the relationship between sin and disobedience as self-conscious transgression and sin as a personified and enslaving power. Such a model would surely bear implications for Paul's thought, especially for how he understands God's saving action in Christ and the Spirit.

Personification of a Pattern of Life?

In explaining Paul's seemingly divergent understandings of sin in Romans, 5:20-21 occupies a pivotal position in the letter as Paul outlines the three key powers—Sin, the Law, and Grace. These verses are at the conclusion of a larger paragraph, 5:12-21. Whereas human beings and God had been the consistent subject of the verbs up to this point in the letter, Rom 5:12-21 offers a vivid contrast. Now sin and death are the subjects of verbs.[6] How are these personified entities to be understood?

Stephen Westerholm offered a corrective to seizing too quickly on personified powers. He notes that the other letters of Paul—1 Thessalonians, 1 Corinthians, and Philippians—do not refer to a slavery under the powers of evil. Even in Rom 5-8, there are other powers at work beyond the three programmatic ones of Sin, the Law, and Grace. Righteousness is another ruling power. Uncleanness, impurity (or lawlessness), and obedience are still more ruling powers to which one may be enslaved in Romans 6:16-23.[7] For Westerholm, the foundation was laid for these discussions in

---

an enslaving power, *and*—secondarily—a complicit act of the Adamic agent, for which he is subject to God's judgment (Rom. 3:19)." God has to invade the realm of Sin to create a new form of dual agency—the human united with the Son. Divine agency trumps human agency but in a manner that allows the human "self" to flourish and even to reign (Martyn, "Afterword," 166n20).

6. With Eastman, "Double Participation," 99.

7. Stephen Westerholm, "Paul's Anthropological 'Pessimism' in its Jewish Context," in *Divine and Human Agency in Paul and His Cultural Environment* (eds. J. M. G. Barclay and S. J. Gathercole; LNTS 335; London: T. & T. Clark, 2006), 71-98, here 79. Westerholm is restating views he initially articulated in *Perspectives Old and New on Paul: The "Lutheran" Paul and His Critics* (Grand Rapids: Eerdmans, 2004), 393-95. Paul presents a tension. On the one hand, the many were made "sinners" (5:19) and died *because* of Adam (5:15) as "the effects of his sin went far beyond that of setting a bad example for his descendants" (*Perspectives*, 394). "That sin entered and rules the world means more than that people sin, though it does not refer to the dominance of humans by demonic powers" (395). Westerholm concludes that human nature and its condition were corrupted

the earlier chapters of Romans where Paul stressed human responsibility for sin and God's handing people over to their own sinful actions (e.g., Rom 1:20-21, 32). Even in Rom 5 sin came into the world through one man, Adam (5:12).[8] Demonic forces are absent in Paul's reasoning.[9] "Each reference that might tempt one to think of 'Sin' as a demonic force is surrounded by others that militate against the notion" in drawing attention to human responsibility for sin.[10] Paul is therefore simply personifying "patterns of life" and not supernatural forces. As Westerholm put it: "[T]hough Paul undoubtedly believed in demonic forces and thought unredeemed humanity is in some sense subject to their power, he does not typically attribute human sinfulness to, or portray redemption as deliverance from, the power of demons."[11]

Westerholm is not alone in his assessment. Douglas Moo could similarly qualify Paul's language in Rom 5-8: "[I]t is not clear that Paul

---

by Adam and that the creation has been marred (cf. Rom 8:19-23). It is not clear that Paul envisions a corrupted human nature being passed down from Adam in Rom 5 at least, but Westerholm's comments in *Perspectives* appear more nuanced than in his later essay. Perhaps a better way to articulate Westerholm's overall perspective would be to adopt the position of Theodor Zahn, that ἐφ' ᾧ means "on the basis of which," with the antecedent of the neuter pronoun being the preceding clauses in which Paul explains how sin entered into the world and death permeated all humanity; Theodor Zahn, *Der Brief des Paulus an die Römer* (Kommentar zum Neuen Testament 6; Leipzig: Deichert, 1910), 261-67; so also Thomas R. Schreiner, *Romans* (BECNT; Grand Rapids: Baker, 1998), 274; Richard N. Longenecker, *The Epistle to the Romans* (NIGTC; Grand Rapids: Eerdmans, 2016), 589-90. One might speak, then, with Schreiner, of an original death that has been conveyed to all people as descendants of Adam. The notion of a corrupted nature becomes clearer with the marring of all creation in Rom 8:19-23. Thus, under which circumstances, all sin (Rom 5:12b). Joseph A. Fitzmyer concedes: "Of the relative-pronoun understandings of *eph' hō*, this one makes the best sense, and it has extrabiblical parallels" (*Romans* [AYBC 33; New York: Doubleday, 1993], 415). On the other hand, as S. Lewis Johnson, Jr., has stressed, there is no mediacy of a corrupt human nature stated in Rom 5:12-21: people simply die in relation to the one sin of the one man; "Romans 5:12—An Exercise in Exegesis and Theology," in *New Dimensions in New Testament Study* (eds. R. N. Longenecker and M. C. Tenney; Grand Rapids: Zondervan, 1974), 311. Furthermore: "Just as we are not justified by inherent righteousness, so we are not condemned by inherent corruption" (311). It is Adam's first sin that is the culprit; no intervening factors are mentioned in Rom 5:19.

8. Westerholm, "Paul's Anthropological 'Pessimism,'" 81n30: "In neither passage [Romans 1-3 or 5-7] is human sinfulness attributed to the influences of superhuman forces; still less are human innocent victims of such forces."

9. Westerholm, "Paul's Anthropological 'Pessimism,'" 98.

10. Westerholm, "Paul's Anthropological 'Pessimism,'" 79.

11. Westerholm, "Paul's Anthropological 'Pessimism,'" 79.

personalizes sin, viewing it as a 'demon' that exists prior to, and independent of, personal acts of rebellion against God."[12] Westerholm and Moo thus reduce Paul's personifications to human activity. At least in this regard, Westerholm and Moo represent an interpretive trajectory that may be traced to Rudolf Bultmann, who recognized the personifications in Rom 5–8 and that "man has lost to [these powers] the capacity to be subject of his own actions."[13] For Bultmann, this was "figurative, rhetorical language" that served to express "a certain understanding of existence" according to which the individual "is constantly confronted with the decision of choosing his lord."[14] Ultimately, the personified powers boil down to human decision and action.

Many scholars have interpreted Rom 5:12 similarly. Paul writes in the first part of the verse, "Just as sin came into the world through one man, and death came through sin"; in the second part of the verse, "death spread to all because all sinned." Whereas the first part of the verse describes a situation in Adam, in the second part death spread to all people because of their own actions in sinning.[15]

Jewish literature in Paul's day likewise attributes sin and death to Adam. The Life of Adam and Eve describes seventy plagues that God inflicted on the sinful Adam and Eve, including death (LAE 7.1; 8.2).

12. Douglas J. Moo, *The Epistle to the Romans* (NICNT; Grand Rapids: Eerdmans, 1996), 319n25 (original emphasis).

13. Rudolf Bultmann, *Theology of the New Testament* (New York: Charles Scribner's Sons, 1951/1955), 1:245.

14. Bultmann, *Theology*, 1:259. See the helpful summary of Bultmann's position on S/ sin in Matthew Croasmun, *The Emergence of Sin: The Cosmic Tyrant in Romans* (Oxford: Oxford University Press, 2017), 4–11.

15. James Denney, "St. Paul's Epistle to the Romans," *The Expositor's Greek New Testament* (ed. W. Robertson Nicoll; London: Hodder and Stoughton, 1904), 2:555–725, here 627–28; C. K. Barrett, *The Epistle to the Romans* (rev. ed.; BNTC; Peabody, MA: Hendrickson, 1991), 104: thus Paul very naturally asks, "What if there are men who do not sin? Will they not live for ever?"; John Zeisler, *Paul's Letter to the Romans* (TPINTC; Philadelphia: Trinity, 1989), 147: "Everyone is his or her own Adam . . . and cannot put the blame on the historical Adam"; Ernst Käsemann, *Commentary on Romans* (Grand Rapids: Eerdmans, 1980), 148–49; John R. Levison, *Portraits of Adam in Early Judaism: From Sirach to 2 Baruch* (JSPSup 1; Sheffield: JSOT Press, 1988), 124: "In the end individual responsibility wins out" in the tension between individual responsibility and hereditary sinfulness, although Ezra still hopes for God's undeserved mercy; Peter Schäfer, "Adam in der jüdischen Überlieferung," in *Vom Alten zum Neuen Adam: Urzeitmythos und Heilsgeschichte* (ed. W. Strolz; Veröffentlichungen der Stiftung Oratio Dominica; Freiburg: Herder, 1986), 69–93, here 73.

Pseudo-Philo traces death to the transgression of the first couple (LAB 13.8). Other Jewish writings offer striking parallels to Paul's connection between individual sins and Adam.[16] In 2 Bar. 23:4, "Adam sinned and death was decreed against those who were to be born"; but then in 54:19 the writer qualifies the earlier comment: "Adam is . . . not the cause, except for himself, but each of us has become our own Adam." Adam was thus the first but not the last. God's sentence of death justly fell upon his descendants. In 4 Ezra 3:7 God "laid one commandment" upon Adam, "but he transgressed it, and immediately [God] appointed death for him and his descendants." As in 2 Baruch and Rom 5:12, the ascription of death to Adam is qualified in 4 Ezra 7:118-20: "For though it was you [Adam] who sinned, the fall was not yours alone, but ours also who are your descendants. . . . [W]e have done deeds that bring death."[17] Human sin may be similarly traced to Eve. In Sir 25:24, "From a woman sin had its beginning, and because of her we all die" (NRSV); and yet in Sir 15:14-17, "It was he who created humankind in the beginning, and he left them in the power of their own free choice. If you choose, you can keep the commandments, and to act faithfully is a matter of your own choice. . . . Before each person is life and death, and whichever one chooses will be given." One could therefore interpret Rom 5:12a in a manner that dilutes the Adamic statements in view of the qualification immediately following that describes sin and death as ultimately the responsibility of individual human beings.[18]

---

16. Martinus de Boer has, over the years, emphasized the parallels in 2 Baruch and 4 Ezra; see *The Defeat of Death: Apocalyptic Eschatology in 1 Corinthians 15 and Romans 5* (JSNTSup 22; Sheffield: Sheffield Academic Press, 1988), 73-78, 80-83, 165-66; most recently, "Paul's Mythologizing Program in Romans 5-8," in *Apocalyptic Paul: Cosmos and Anthropos in Romans 5-8* (ed. Beverly Roberts Gaventa; Waco, TX: Baylor University Press, 2013), 1-20, esp. 11-13, here 12.

17. Martin Meiser, "Die paulinischen Adamaussagen im Kontext frühjüdischer und frühchristlicher Literatur," in *Jüdische Schriften in ihrem antik-jüdischen und urchristlichen Kontext* (eds. H. Lichtenberger and G. S. Oegema; JSHRZ 1; Gütersloh: Gütersloher Verlagshaus, 2002), 396. Jewish literature expresses this tension elsewhere as well.

18. Martinus C. de Boer ("Paul's Mythologizing Program in Romans 5-8") points out that many have understood Rom 5:12a *in terms of* Rom 5:12b, thereby subordinating the effects of Adam's one sin to the sins of individual human beings. De Boer appeals to potentially pre-70 CE traditions in 4 Ezra and 2 Baruch as parallels to Paul, but these two passages appear to *confirm* a subordination of Adam's action to the subsequent sinful actions of human beings. While de Boer *asserts* the two affirmations—Adam's determination and individual human culpability must remain in tension—the texts in 4 Ezra and 2 Baruch do appear to trace human sin ultimately to individual human actions along the pattern of Adam (12). What the two Jewish texts lack that Paul has is Rom 5:15-19,

A first model for the relationship between sin as individual action and sin as ruling power, then, is to suggest that one should not read too much into sin as a power. Paul is simply describing "patterns of life" ultimately driven by individual human actions. Or to look elsewhere to Rom 1:21–28: God is handing people who have taken the path of sin over to enslaving powers to worsen the situation.[19] Paul's comments on Adam's responsibility for sin in the first part of Rom 5:12 may therefore be subordinated to the sinful actions of his subsequent descendants. Paul explains that "death spread to all *because* [ἐφ᾽ ᾧ] all sinned." Individuals' own sins are thus the cause (ἐφ᾽ ᾧ) for death having spread to all people.[20] One could imagine death *not* having spread to all had they not themselves sinned.[21]

This reading of Rom 5:12, however, has not proven persuasive to many readers of Romans. Joseph Fitzmyer argued at length that ἐφ᾽ ᾧ is never causal throughout Paul's letters but rather should be translated "with the result that," or "so that." Thus the causal basis is not in what follows but in what *precedes*. It is precisely because death spread to all people through *Adam* that all people subsequently sinned. This reverses the logic of this part of the sentence and prioritizes Adam's sin.

Certainly in some places Paul uses ἐφ᾽ ᾧ in the manner Fitzmyer suggested. Of the other three Pauline instances of ἐφ᾽ ᾧ, Fitzmyer's best example is Phil 4:10. Gordon Fee concurred that "with reference to which" makes the best sense of the verse, which he translated: "Indeed, you have been concerned, but [*with reference to which* concern] you have had no

---

where Adam's disobedience is determinative; see below. Otherwise, Rom 5:12 might be read with 5:12b predominating—strictly on the basis of the parallels de Boer adduces. De Boer, however, stresses the presence of cosmological powers in Paul's reasoning that are lacking in the two Jewish texts (18). The presence of these powers means that "sinning is not the result of a bad choice made by an autonomous individual; it is the result and the mark of a cosmological force that has come into the world and reigned over human beings since the time of Adam" (14).

19. A possibility that J. Louis Martyn did not fully explore: that all human beings reenact in their first sin the disobedience of the Adamic agent ("Epilogue: An Essay in Pauline Meta-Ethics," in *Divine and Human Agency in Paul and His Cultural Environment* (eds. J. M. G. Barclay and S. J. Gathercole; LNTS 335 [London: T. & T. Clark, 2006], 173–83, here 179)—although Martyn would surely stress that such an approach does not adequately account for the apocalyptic realities in the cosmos.

20. E.g., Meiser, "Die paulinischen Adamaussagen," 392: this is consistent with 1:18—3:20 that holds individuals accountable for actively choosing sin.

21. Thus Paul explains in 5:14 that death indeed ruled, even in the period from Adam to Moses prior to the Law.

opportunity to show it."²² The use ἐφ' ᾧ in Phil 3:12 is not as clear. On the other hand, in 2 Cor 5:4 Fitzmyer's reading appears strained and the common causal meaning of ἐφ' ᾧ more persuasive. Murray J. Harris has noted that the ἐφ' ᾧ is parallel to a causal participle in 2 Cor 5:2: "we sigh *because* we *long* to put on our heavenly dwelling" and "we sigh *because* we *wish* to put on our heavenly dwelling." Paul is groaning in 2 Cor 5:4 *because* he wants to enjoy a spiritual corporeality.²³ Here the causal interpretation appears more likely. The ἐφ' ᾧ construction is therefore of itself ambiguous.

Romans commentators have turned for guidance to the verses that immediately follow, especially Rom 5:15-19. In v. 15 Paul is clearer: "by the transgression of the one, many died." Adam's transgression led to death for his descendants. Verse 16 even contrasts the one trespass, which brought condemnation, with the many trespasses. In v. 17 it is because of the one man's trespass that death exercised dominion through that one. In v. 18 "through the transgression of the one there resulted condemnation for all men." As S. Lewis Johnston stressed years ago, one must take seriously the one-versus-many pattern in these verses, as Paul repeatedly ascribes humanity's plight to one man's sin and not the subsequent sins of his descendants.²⁴

These comments resist a simple reduction of the problem of sin to humanity's sinful actions. Note that Paul does not talk about Adam's subsequent sinful activity or even Eve's sins. It is that first sin of Adam that remains central to Paul's thought. What Adam did in that one moment resulted in genuine consequences for his descendants. Adam's one sin bears consequences for all humanity. People are condemned and are dying because of Adam's sin and not merely because they are imitating what Adam had done. Were people solely responsible for their own sin and death, Adam would have nothing to do with it.²⁵ If Adam's sin bears such consequences

---

22. Gordon D. Fee, *Paul's Letter to the Philippians* (NICNT; Grand Rapids: Eerdmans, 1995), 426n28; C. F. D. Moule, *An Idiom Book of the New Testament Greek* (2nd ed.; Cambridge: Cambridge University Press, 1959), 132; Fitzmyer, *Romans*, 415.

23. Murray J. Harris, *Prepositions and Theology in the Greek New Testament: An Essential Reference Resource for Exegesis* (Grand Rapids: Zondervan, 2012), 141; Margaret E. Thrall, *The Second Epistle to the Corinthians* (ICC; Edinburgh: T. & T. Clark, 1994), 1:381n1336; Murray J. Harris, *The Second Epistle to the Corinthians* (NIGTC; Grand Rapids: Eerdmans, 2005), 387: the causal ἐφ' ᾧ is well recognized by several Greek grammars; cf. Fitzymer, *Romans*, 415.

24. Johnson, "Romans 5:12," 301-2, 305-7, 311.

25. Rightly Schreiner, *Romans*, 289. Likewise, as John M. G. Barclay has stressed against Troels Engberg-Pederson regarding the *converse* of humanity in relation to

for humanity, then Paul's presentation of sin cannot be reduced to mere personification of a pattern of life.

Solidarity with the Suffering Servant?

What other models are there to explain the relationship between the one sin of Adam and the individual sins of his descendants? An approach that has gained some traction is to attribute the priority of Adam's sin to Paul's Isaianic logic. Richard Hays in his 1989 classic *Echoes of Scripture in the Letter of Paul* lamented the puzzling suppression of any echoes of Isa 53 in Romans even though Paul quotes and alludes to Isa 40–55 throughout the letter.[26] As he put it: "[Paul] hints and whispers all around Isaiah 53 but never mentions the prophetic typology that would supremely integrate his interpretation of Christ and Israel.... Paul's transumptive silence cries out for the reader to complete the trope. Those who have ears to hear will hear and understand that the people of God, reckoned as sheep to be slaughtered, are suffering with Christ."[27]

Since Hays, many scholars have had ears to hear the Suffering Servant of Isa 53 in Romans. In the pre-*Echoes of Scripture* year of 1959 Morna Hooker expressed doubt about any Isaianic influence in Rom 4:25.[28] By 1998 she had changed her mind on the basis of two shared words (παραδίδωμι and δικαίωσις) and an interchange thought pattern. She concluded that

---

Sin—that is, humanity in relation to God's agency in grace—Paul *distinguishes* divine initiative in grace and the human response, and the human agent is capable of righteous action only insofar as God's anterior grace motivates and energizes it (Phil 2:12-14; 1 Cor 15:10; Gal 2:19-21; Rom 15:15-19; 2 Cor 9:8-10. See John M. G. Barclay, "'By the Grace of God I Am What I Am': Grace and Agency in Philo and Paul," in *Divine and Human Agency in Paul and His Cultural Environment* (eds. J. M. G. Barclay and S. J. Gathercole; LNTS 335; London: T. & T. Clark, 2006), 140–57, here 151–55; cf. Troels Engberg-Pedersen, "Self-Sufficiency and Power: Divine and Human Agency in Epictetus and Paul," in *Divine and Human Agency in Paul and His Cultural Environment* (eds. J. M. G. Barclay and S. J. Gathercole; LNTS 335; London: T. & T. Clark, 2006), 117–39; Troels Engberg-Pedersen, *Paul and the Stoics* (Edinburgh: T. & T. Clark, 2000).

26. Richard B. Hays, *Echoes of Scripture in the Letters of Paul* (New Haven: Yale University Press, 1989), 62.

27. Hays, *Echoes*, 63.

28. Morna D. Hooker, *Jesus and the Servant: The Influence of the Servant Concept of Deutero-Isaiah in the New Testament* (London: SPCK, 1959), 121–22, esp. 122: "Even the combination of these various terms [παραδίδωμι, δικαίωσις] can carry little weight, since it is Paul, not his predecessors, who seems to emphasize the connection between Christ 'being delivered up' and the forgiveness of sins."

Rom 4:25 clearly echoes Isa 53, and thus it is possible that a christological reading of Isaiah originated with Paul.[29]

With respect to Rom 8:32, later in the letter, J. Ross Wagner argued for a weak echo of Isa 53 on the basis of a shared word (παραδίδωμι). Ultimately, he relied on what he deemed, in contrast to Hooker's caution, to be a definite "allusion" to Isa 53 back in Rom 4:25, as well as the likelihood of an allusion to Isa 50:8 in Rom 8:33 (where God is ὁ δικαιῶν).[30] Wagner then turned to a group of interpreters who have proposed "a possible locus for echoes of Isaiah 53" in Rom 5:15-19.[31] "The idea of one person's obedience making 'many righteous' appears to echo the Hebrew text of Isa 53:11, 'the righteous one, my servant, shall make many to be accounted righteous.'"[32] Shui-Lun Shum found the conceptual parallel between Isa 53 and Rom 5:19 compelling: "Since there is no OT passage other than Isa. 53:11 which expresses so distinctive an idea that a righteous or innocent person's sufferings, righteous deeds, and death can effect justification of others, there is no reason to deny an allusive relationship between the two passages. . . . [Paul is drawing on] the prophet's concept of a *one-many-solidarity relationship*."[33]

On the other hand, against any certainty in tracing these concepts back to Isa 53, in a study of Second Temple Jewish messianic conceptions Antti Laato comments, "We have seen that there is no incontrovertible evidence that Isaiah 53 was understood to refer to the Messiah before the time of Jesus. . . . [T]here is no text in the Gospels where Jesus applies Isaiah 53 to himself. This seems to indicate that we cannot regard Isaiah 53 the text

---

29. Morna D. Hooker, "Did the Use of Isaiah 53 to Interpret His Mission Begin with Jesus?" in *Jesus and the Suffering Servant: Isaiah 53 and Christians Origins* (eds. W. H. Bellinger, Jr., and W. R. Farmer; Harrisburg, PA: Trinity, 1998), 88-103, here 101-3.

30. J. Ross Wagner, *Heralds of the Good News: Isaiah and Paul in Concert in the Letter to the Romans* (NovTSup 101; Boston: Brill, 2003), 334n106.

31. Wagner, *Heralds*, 334n106; following NA27 and NA28 margins; Richard B. Hays, "On the Rebound: A Response to Critiques of *Echoes of Scripture in the Letters of Paul*," in *Paul and the Scriptures of Israel* (eds. C. A. Evans and J. A. Sanders; JSNTSup 83; SSEJC 1; Sheffield: Sheffield Academic, 1993), 70-96, here 88: "echoes Isa. 53.11 artfully."

32. Robert Jewett, *Romans: A Commentary* (Hermeneia; Minneapolis: Fortress, 2007), 387.

33. Shiu-Lun Shum, *Paul's Use of Isaiah in Romans: A Comparative Study of Paul's Letter to the Romans and the Sibylline and Qumran Sectarian Texts* (WUNT 2/156; Tübingen: Mohr Siebeck, 2002), 198-200, here 199 (original emphasis); followed by Jewett, *Romans*, 387.

which generated the idea of the suffering Messiah."[34] Wagner himself conceded that nowhere does Paul quote from the heart of Isa 53:6, 11–12. At best, he is echoing those verses. In fact, Wagner suggested that Paul does not even read these verses of Isaiah christologically since the apostle's focus is primarily on the inclusion of the gentiles into Israel's redemptive heritage.[35] Then Wagner posed *another* explanation for the lack of a Pauline quotation of Isa 53:6, 11–12: Paul has elsewhere, in Rom 10:17, drawn on Isa 52:7 and Isa 53:1 in reference to the message of Christ that Paul himself and others are taking to the nations. In Rom 15:20, again, Paul draws on Isa 52:15 in reference to his own proclamation of the gospel. Paul is thus speaking of *himself* as one of the Isaianic preachers of the gospel. Although Wagner thought that lingering behind these connections is a "virtually unavoidable implication" that the Servant of Isaiah is Christ, alas, Paul himself does not make that identification, and the focus of his use of Isaiah's servant text is in support of his own gospel ministry.[36] If either of Wagner's explanations is correct, an echo of Isa 53 to explain the logic of Christ's saving action would be out of place. The apostle would not be reading Isa 53 christologically.

Not all commentators on Romans have had ears to hear the Isa 53 echo in Rom 5:15–19. Joseph Fitzmyer suggested rather tentatively that Paul could be alluding to Isa 53:11–12.[37] He immediately qualified the possibility by citing Käsemann's comment that "there is not the least reason to introduce the motif of the Suffering Servant into the text. The important thing is only the antithesis to Adam's disobedience and therefore again the antithetical correspondence of primal time and end-time."[38] An echo of Isa 53 in Rom 5:15–19 is certainly a possibility in light of Paul's use of Isa 40–55 elsewhere, but nothing more definite may be claimed.[39]

---

34. Antti Laato, *A Star Is Rising: The Historical Development of the Old Testament Royal Ideology and the Rise of the Jewish Messianic Expectations* (USFISFCJ 5; Atlanta: Scholars Press, 1997), 343–44: "The only possibility is the Targum but its date is uncertain. However, in the case of the Targum there is no evidence for the view that Isaiah 53 was understood as referring to a Messiah who suffers and dies vicariously on behalf of the people."

35. Wagner, *Heralds*, 334–35.

36. Wagner, *Heralds*, 335.

37. Fitzmyer, *Romans*, 421–22.

38. Käsemann, *Commentary*, 157.

39. See the concern for greater methodological control over such suggestions in A. Andrew Das, *Paul and the Stories of Israel: Grand Thematic Narratives in Galatians* (Minneapolis: Fortress, 2016).

Representative Headship

A third, more likely explanation is not exclusive of a possible Isaianic allusion but focuses, with Käsemann, on what Paul actually says in the text. Paul is contrasting Adam and Christ. Corporate categories are employed in relation to *these* two figures and not explicitly to the Suffering Servant. In speaking of corporate categories in Paul, Henry Wheeler Robinson drew attention to a body of Hebrew Bible texts that he explained on the basis of a theory of corporate personality.[40] Wheeler Robinson's notion of corporate *personality* has been criticized at length.[41] Biblical scholars have preferred the notion of corporate *responsibility* or *guilt*. Putting aside controversial theories such as Wheeler Robinson's, nevertheless, Paul views humanity in relation to Adam as parallel to humanity in relation to Christ. Paul's "in Christ" and "into Christ" expressions in the very next chapter of Romans suggest the possibility that he likewise views humanity as "in Adam" in Rom 5:12-21. Indeed, in 1 Cor 15:22 Paul says as much: "For as all die in Adam, so all will be made alive in Christ." Adam appears to function as the representative head of humanity, and so his one action bore implications for all humans to follow.

Russell Phillip Shedd stressed that all people are "in Adam" at any given point in history.[42] This realistic view of all human beings as in Adam presses Paul's language too far. If all human beings are somehow actually present in Adam long before they were born, why then is only Adam's *one* sin affecting all humanity and not *all* of Adam's sins, or at least all of Adam's sins before his first child was born? Also, how is it that human beings can exist in Adam before they are actually born and come into being? Finally, if all people are in Adam, should not the origin of sin also be traced to *all*

---

40. H. Wheeler Robinson, *Corporate Personality in Ancient Israel* (rev. ed.; Philadelphia: Fortress, 1981).

41. J. W. Rogerson, "The Hebrew Conception of Corporate Personality: A Re-Examination," *JTS* 21 (1970) 1-16; Stanley E. Porter, "Two Myths: Corporate Personality and Language/Mentality Determinism, *SJT* 43 (1990) 289-307. For instance, although Achan's theft at Ai appears imputed to the entirety of Israel, the biblical text may only be referring to the contagion of cultic impurity; Cyril S. Rodd, "Introduction," in H. Wheeler Robinson, *Corporate Personality in Ancient Israel* (rev. ed.; Philadelphia: Fortress, 1981), 7-14, here 11.

42. Russell Phillip Shedd, *Man in Community: A Study of St. Paul's Application of Old Testament and Early Jewish Conceptions of Human Solidarity* (Grand Rapids; Eerdmans, 1964), 103; at 108, even the sin of all in Rom 5:12 is nothing more than the sin of the one earlier in the verse.

people and not just *Adam* and *his* one sin? Realism has therefore suffered its share of problems as a theory.⁴³

A purely forensic notion of Adam's sin being imputed is not entirely satisfactory either, since Paul explains that all people are "made" sinners (Rom 5:19). As Thomas Schreiner pointed out in his *Romans* commentary, the Greek verb καθίστημι means "appoint" in the NT and not "make," and yet the verb never involves a judgment or appointment that does not account for the actual state of the individuals involved.⁴⁴ Despite these caveats, it does appear that Adam's one sin is somehow imputed to his descendants, even as Christ's one righteous act is as well. Adam and Christ function as representative heads of humanity, and thus their one action affects all who are "in" them. Commentators have thus often stressed the sense of "corporate solidarity" in Adam and in Christ.⁴⁵ All who are born are already in a state of inherited death. Paul simply does not provide enough insight into his thought processes to elaborate further on the precise mechanism.

Matthew Croasmun has provided a modern analogy for Paul's S/sin tension: emergentism in philosophy of science.⁴⁶ Croasmun does not overly concern himself with the exegetical tussles in individual passages, such as Rom 5:12–21. After reviewing the historic Bultmann-Käsemann debate over S/sin, supplementing that discussion with liberationist approaches,

43. Johnson, "Romans 5:12," 309–10.

44. "One cannot separate the representative and constitutive roles of Adam and of Christ in these verses. Those who are in Adam and those who are in Christ actually become sinners and righteous, respectively" (Schreiner, *Romans*, 288); e.g., Matt 24:45, 47; 25:21, 23 (seven times in the Gospels, four times in Acts, and three in Hebrews; Titus 1:4), although the translation "make" may be fitting on occasion (e.g., 2 Pet 1:8). Even when the verb means "appoint," however, it "never designates a judgment or consideration which does not conform to the actual state of the individuals involved" (Don Garlington, *Faith, Obedience and Perseverance: Aspects of Paul's Letter to the Romans* [WUNT 2/79; Tübingen: J. C. B. Mohr/Paul Siebeck, 1994], 104, following Moo, *Romans*, 345: "Paul is insisting that people were really 'made' sinners through Adam's act of disobedience just as they are really 'made righteous' through Christ's obedience").

45. Thus Anthony C. Thiselton, *The First Epistle to the Corinthians: A Commentary on the Greek Text* (NIGTC; Grand Rapids: Eerdmans, 2000), 1226: "Here Paul shows that corporate and structural dimension of 'being human' that characterizes the reign of sin and death all the more guarantees that all who are in Christ will share in solidarity with him the reality of the resurrection of the dead" (cf. 1282); Roy E. Ciampa and Brian S. Rosner, *The First Letter to the Corinthians* (PNTC; Grand Rapids: Eerdmans, 2010), 762. Thiselton elaborates that people "participate" in the order of death "represented" in Adam as well as in Jesus's resurrection (1227), which contrasts with Adam's reign and brings about a reversal (1228).

46. Croasmun, *Emergence of Sin*.

and without worrying about how modern commentators are interpreting these texts, he finds Sin as a power irreducible to sin as a human activity (cf., e.g., Westerholm and Moo). Sin is an emergent entity that derives from individual human sinful activity but cannot be reduced to the properties of individual human sin. Certainly Paul recognizes that "all people sin" in Rom 5:12, but contrary to Croasmun's reasoning, the apostle is addressing the effect not of societal sin as he does elsewhere in Romans (e.g., 1:18–32), but of the *one* sin of Adam, and it is that *one* sin that immediately precedes the explosion of Sin as power imagery in Rom 5–8. Paul is preparing his readers to understand these realities on the basis of a different logic than modern emergentism, as wonderfully intriguing as are the parallels to how Paul describes Sin as a power.

Conclusion

To draw the various strands together: Paul contends that all humanity suffers under the effects of someone else's sin, the one sin of Adam. Sin and death proceeding from Adam thus stand over the entire human race. It is but a short step from our corporate sharing in and experience of Adam's sin and death—that is, in what someone *else* has brought about—to sin and death as external powers. It is no accident, then, that Paul turns to three personified powers that will structure the next several chapters in 5:20–21, just after making these claims about the universal or cosmic effects of the one man's sin and the one man's act of righteousness. Rom 5:12–21 is not only the beginning point of Paul's discussion of sin, the Law, death, grace, righteousness, and other powers, but it also provides a foundation for understanding the connections between sin with a small "s" and with a capital "S." Even as Adam's sin, which afflicts humanity, is countered by Christ's righteous act, so also slavery to Sin and Death, which have thus reigned since Adam, can only be combatted by a greater power in Christ and his Spirit. Humanity experiences these realities as enslaving, external powers or forces.

5

Letters from the Battlefield: Cosmic Sin and Captive Sinners in 1 Corinthians

Alexandra R. Brown

I BEGIN WITH TWO Paul-inflected meditations on the cross as sin's remedy. They reveal, among other things, the depth and complexity of Paul's reading of sin in distinct idioms but in ways that lead us fruitfully into 1 Corinthians.

In the collected letters from the battlefield of William Laban Brown, a Union soldier and a Baptist from Tennessee, we find at least three citations on different occasions of the hymn "There is a Fountain Filled with Blood."[1] In one, after citing its opening lines, he writes, "this is my favorite hymn." Surrounded by war, its blood and pain and horror, this soldier took refuge of some kind in these words:

> There is a fountain, filled with blood drawn from Emanuel's veins
> And sinners plunged beneath that flood lose all their guilty stains.
> Dear dying lamb thy precious blood shall never lose its power
> Till all the ransomed church of God be saved to sin no more.
> E'er since by faith I saw the stream thy flowing wounds supply

---

1. William Laban Brown, my great-grandfather, survived the war, but not his journey home from a prison camp in Alabama. He died on the Mississippi River in the explosion of the steamship "Sultana," a ship designed to carry 376 but for mercenary reasons overloaded with more than two thousand liberated soldiers, 1500 of whom died with him, their mortal lives washed away with their sins. Another 300 died later of burns sustained in the explosion.

> Redeeming love has been my theme and shall be till I die.
> The dying thief rejoiced to see that fountain in his day;
> And there may I, though vile as he, wash all my sins away.
> When this poor lisping, stammering tongue lies silent in the grave
> Then in a nobler, sweeter song, I'll sing thy power to save.
>
> —Hymn by William Cowper (1731–1800)

Nearly two centuries later, having lived through two world wars, Karl Barth wrote in *Church Dogmatics IV* of the death of Jesus:

> In his doing this for us, in his taking to himself—to fulfill all righteousness—our accusation and condemnation and punishment, in his suffering in our place and for us, there came our reconciliation with God.
>
> —Karl Barth (1886–1968)
> *Church Dogmatics* IV/1 223

The articulations of sin and its remedy in these two testimonies—both witnesses, we might say, shaped by the experience of corporate and pervasive evil—remind us that we have in "sin and its remedy," not merely a question of definition tucked neatly away in dogmatics, nor a matter of purely personal piety, but rather a subject of urgent corporate and collective significance in our times as in theirs.[2] For us in late, late modernity the question is complicated further, for who in our times can speak meaningfully of "sin," decayed as the word is and marginalized in this secular age? Can this noun be sensibly understood at all in *our* bloodstained generation? And if the resources of Christianity, not least the letters of Paul, can be interpreted toward the healing of the world, how will the *remedy* of that menace Paul called *"hamartia"* (ἁμαρτία) be known as a power of reconciliation and compassion rather than yet another instrument of sectarian hubris? Perhaps most pressing is the question of how can we speak of "sin" today in ways that do not simply entrench fear and the loathing of self or other?

---

2. It is especially relevant to William Laban Brown's battlefield recollection of Cowper's words that Cowper was an avid abolitionist, a close associate of John Newton (who wrote "Amazing Grace" and many other hymns after his own conversion from slave trading and published with Cowper a book of hymns). Cowper's poem "The Negro's Complaint" (1788) was quoted by Martin Luther King Jr. during the Civil Rights Movement.

The Cross Event and Its Message as "Remedy" for Sin/sins

Cowper and Barth, a British poet and a Swiss theologian separated by two centuries, reflect reconciliation in Christ in strikingly different idioms and vocabularies. Cowper's "guilty stains" reflect an age not yet ashamed of the word "sin." In formal prayer as an Anglican he would still have "bewailed (his) manifold sins," would still have found "the remembrance of them grievous" and the "burden of them intolerable" (*The Book of Common Prayer*).[3] Sins *plural* played a major role in the narrative of salvation known to Cowper and in the piety known to his time. Sins plural doubtless played a major role in the piety of that soldier William Laban Brown. In his letters, he bewails the sins committed by soldiers on both sides against each other, and especially against the innocent victims of battle.[4] But these sins are hardly isolated acts of freely choosing human beings. They are acts of war; acts dictated by powers and principalities beyond the sinner. Cowper's poem somehow intimates this dual agency of sin (to paraphrase Rom 7, Paul's "I and yet not I") and answers it with a higher agency of redemption realized in baptism into Christ's death—"sinners plunged (passive) beneath that flood lose all their guilty stains." The formulation is poetic; a generous reading allows the poem to point to the mysterious dual agencies (mine and yet not mine) of *both* sin and redemption in an economy whose full mystery escapes this "lisping, stammering tongue."[5]

Barth, composing here not poetry, but systematic theology, avoids not only plural sins, but in this formula (and throughout his corpus) the word *Sünde* altogether; what Christ bore on our behalf in his suffering death "for us" was "our accusation, our condemnation, our punishment."[6] Indeed,

---

3. Confession of Sin, Holy Eucharist, Rite 1, *The Book of Common Prayer*.

4. See letter #11 of William Laban Brown, regarding the brutality of human beings at war. Of his own Union company, he wrote: "We had a company of mounted infantry with us and they robbed a house of everything and there was a little girl, the only child the man had and her sister had died and left her a fine quilt and a pin and her likeness to remember her and she begged them to leave her them and they would not and if I had a knowed [sic] it I would a died right there or she should a had them." From the transcribed letters of William Laban Brown, digitized at http://www.sounddoc.com/wlbrown/wlbrown1.html.

5. We learn in reading Cowper's biography that he suffered a severe lisp, so this is more than a poetic image. On mystery as the mode of divine presence, see Cowper's hymn "God Moves in a Mysterious Way."

6. In fact, only three headings in the entire *Dogmatics* speak expressly of

in Barth's systematics, sin appears *within*, not *prior to*, his treatment of reconciliation. In a logical shift that may derive from Paul in 1 Corinthians (see below), Barth sees the revealing of sin *as sin* for the first time in the Cross Event. That is, Christ's act of standing in our place reveals for the first time what sin actually is. In this way, Barth argues epistemologically and christologically from solution to plight, not the other way around. Barth's grammar reflects the pattern: reconciliation *has taken place* in the *indicative past*—"by his taking to himself our condemnation *came* our reconciliation with God." No human action is prerequisite to the act of reconciliation; Barth's indicative past seems in tension with Cowper's poetic "there *may I* wash my sins (plural) away," and Barth's singular collectives, "our accusation, our condemnation, our punishment," downplay Cowper's individual sins. And yet Barth was pastor to a working-class congregation, championed worker's rights, joined the Confessing Church, and in the Barmen Declaration took on the toxic, demonic policies of National Socialism. No more than Cowper's faith denied *divine rescue from cosmic power* in sin's remedy did Barth's deny *human agency as sinner* operating under the power of sin and death or, conversely, under the power of Christ.[7]

Cowper and Barth, both cross-centered, reflect the complex texture of Paul's reading of ἁμαρτία and its verbal form, ἁμαρτάνω—along with a few other related terms like ἁμάρτημα (6:18), αδικέω (6:7–8), πονηρία

---

sin—paragraphs 60, 65, and 70 in *Church Dogmatics*, Part IV, Reconciliation. Observation by Clifford Green, "Karl Barth's Life and Theology," in *Karl Barth: Theologian of Freedom* (ed. C. Green; Minneapolis, Fortress, 1991), 11–45, at 35.

7. See Beverly Gaventa's thoroughgoing treatment of sin in Romans as a cosmic power, a fundamental theme of her work compellingly articulated in her chapter "When in Romans, Watch the Horizon," in *When in Romans: An Invitation to Linger with the Gospel according to Paul* (Grand Rapids: Baker Academic, 2016), 23–46, 42–43. In his treatment of sin in Paul as "emergent" from complex systems of human transgressions, Matthew Croasmun understands the alternate "powers," Body of Sin and Body of Christ, as descriptive of social "world bodies" that each "exercise dominion through the control of the moral reasoning of members of its body." In this way, Croasmun accounts both for sins as discreet acts of human beings and for the complex cumulative powers arising from (emerging from) human agents and, in a circular continuum, applying downward causation now experienced as bodies of power that hold human beings in patterns of behavior that Paul identifies with Sin or Christ. The overlap of the "ages" in 1 Cor 10:11 manifests the coexistence of these two bodies of power: "The existence of these two world bodies is the material manifestation of the overlap of the ages in which Paul understands himself and his churches to be living (1 Cor 10:11)" (Croasmun, *The Emergence of Sin: The Cosmic Tyrant in Romans* [Oxford: Oxford University Press, 2017], 177).

(5:8)—across the corpus but in ways especially relevant to 1 Corinthians.[8] Both reflect consciousness of cosmic war, of "primordial catastrophe" ("in Adam all die") and its lasting effects, and so make sense of the language of *deliverance* that the cross strangely generates—"for as in Adam all die, so also in Christ shall all be made alive" (15:22). Both assume, too, a *perceiving human actor*. One *sees, if* one sees,[9] the cross now piercing through the darkness—one's own darkness and the web of shared darkness—exposing Sin and Death as false powers and creating a new world as the form of this world passes away (7:31). It is fair to say that while Cowper and Barth assume very different "ways in" to sin's remedy, for both, human beings participate bodily and communally, acting and being acted upon, in the progressive yet not final conditions of "being saved or perishing" (1:18).[10] Together they illustrate the hermeneutical limitations of binaries like *sins v. Sin, human agency v. divine agency, personal v. personification* for assessing Paul's theology of sin.

I begin with the cross because Paul begins with it in 1 Corinthians. Everything he has to say in this letter about sin, corporate or individual, sin as a cosmic power or a human act, sin singular or sins plural, begins in his particular theological construal of the cross. His beginning with the crucifixion, moreover, is aimed at an epistemological shift founded in his vision of Christ, a way of knowing in the "mind of Christ" as he puts it in

8. Jeffrey Siker surveys the varied vocabulary associated conceptually with "sin" in the New Testament in his newly released *Sin in the New Testament* (Oxford: Oxford University Press, 2019).

9. The language of perception—seeing, knowing, judging—is especially pervasive in 1 Corinthians. What Paul seem to intend to engender here is an epistemology of the cross, i.e., a way of knowing through the lens of the crucifixion of the Messiah.

10. In his perceptive review of an early presentation of this paper, theologian John Coakley noted a key distinction between Barth and Cowper in their respective allowances for *functional entry points* to their conceptual frameworks for salvation. Recalling a quip by Dutch scholar Sperna Weiland to the effect that "Barth's theology constitutes a great and beautiful building which has *no door*," Coakley notes that in contrast "Cowper is *all* doors." That is to say, whereas Barth's resistance to religion (and for that matter, natural theology) limits human agency as a "way in" through experience, Cowper's theology virtually relies on the *felt experience* of sin and repentance. Coakley, in personal correspondence, cites E. M. Conradie: "Sperna Weiland portrays Barth's *Church Dogmatics* accordingly as 'a gigantic building without a door.' He adds, 'One can walk around in it, one can marvel at the architecture and ask oneself the question why the word *Nein!* is written on the wall just where one would expect a door'" (E. M. Conradie, *Saving the Earth: The Legacy of Reformed Views on 'Recreation,'* [Muenster: LIT Verlag, 2013], 269). The citation opens up a world of interesting comparisons and contrasts between Barth and Schleiermacher.

2:6, without which all discourse about sin is but "a noisy gong, a clanging cymbal" (13:1).

We notice immediately in 1 Cor 1–2 the proliferation of terms of perception as Paul strives to put into language the way into salvation he means. The reality of the deliverance he proclaims is not in question; nor is the new creation itself dependent upon the perceiving organ of human consciousness. (Barth's complaints against natural theology seem, to me, justified especially by 1 Cor 1–2.) Nevertheless, he *proclaims to human actors* in *human contingencies* the message of Christ and him crucified; he writes letters *addressed to human beings* calling them to see the cross, and in seeing to be transformed from agents of Sin into agents of righteousness.[11] Indeed, as we hear echoing in Barth, he announces that this transformation has already been accomplished in the very Event he proclaims—"for Christ *is made* our righteousness [δικαιοσύνη], our sanctification [ἁγιασμός], and our redemption [ἀπολύτρωσις]" (1:30), with the result that "*you* [plural] were washed [ἀπελούσασθε], you were sanctified [ἡγιάσθητε], you were justified [ἐδικαιώθητε]" (6:11). In language that sometimes suggests cosmic power and sometimes the effects of that power on and in human perception and action, Paul elaborates the "eucatastrophe" of the cross (to borrow J. R. R. Tolkien's incisive term), the remedy whose cosmic horizon radically resituates the human agent *vis-à-vis* God, other human beings, and indeed the creation itself. Since this Event was, in Paul's perspective, undertaken "for us" and, more to the point, somehow "for our sins" (15:3), human beings as *agents* of Sin, witting and unwitting, remain clearly in view for him, not least because the first-person plural pronoun "us" defines the reader as a part of the complex fabric of *human community*. Thus, Paul expends considerable energy in 1 Corinthians on matters of mundane human behavior, often calling his audience to right perception, occasionally using the vocabulary of ἁμαρτία (and related terms) with respect to human agents of sin through specific actions, and in every instance setting those human actions within the larger anthropological, communal, and cosmic contexts reflected in his theology of the cross.[12]

---

11. Elsewhere I elaborate on this perceptual motif in 1 Corinthians by way of speech-act theory: the word of the cross, I argue, is a performative utterance through which Paul draws his audience into the perlocutionary act of being taken up into the new world it articulates. See Alexandra R. Brown, *The Cross and Human Transformation: Paul's Apocalyptic Word in 1 Corinthians* (Philadelphia: Fortress, 1996).

12. Susan Eastman writes persuasively in conversation with neuroscience of the defining webs of relationships that define human identity. See Susan Grove Eastman, *Paul*

Sin, Sins and Agency in 1 Corinthians

In his work on Substitutionary Atonement,[13] Simon Gathercole seeks to reclaim a place for sins as "acts and dispositions of human beings" in Pauline theology and practice. The reclamation, an appeal for Substitutionary Atonement, is in part about restoring to the theology of the cross Paul's stated claim, as in 1 Cor 15:3, that the Christ died *for our sins,* "in our place *and* instead of us," and in part it is about the pastoral implications of that claim, the release from anxiety that Calvin, for example, attributed to the doctrine of substitution whereby the Son of God transferred to himself the "vengeance" for wrongdoing (collective and individual) that otherwise would fall on human beings.[14]

Gathercole is in dialogue, in particular, with the seeming opposite of Substitutionary Atonement, namely, current "apocalyptic" readings of Paul's theology.[15] This "apocalyptic" reading Gathercole associates with J.

---

and the Person: Reframing Paul's Anthropology (Grand Rapids: Eerdmans, 2017), 110–12 and throughout.

13. Simon Gathercole, *Defending Substitution: An Essay on Atonement in Paul* (Grand Rapids: Baker Academic, 2015).

14. Gathercole (*Substitution*, 17) cites John Calvin, *Institutes* 2.16.5. On Calvin's anxiety, see William J. Bouwsma, "John Calvin's Anxiety," *Proceedings of the American Philosophical Society*, 128 (1984) 252–56. Susan Eastman finds Calvin helpful in her argument for a participatory model of apocalyptic theology. She cites *Institutes* 4.17.2, which reads in part, "We cannot be condemned for our sins, from whose guilt he has absolved us, since he willed to take them to himself as if they were his own . . . taking the weight of our iniquity upon himself, he has clothed us with his righteousness" (Susan Grove Eastman, "Apocalypse and Incarnation: The Participatory Logic of Paul's Gospel," in *Apocalyptic and the Future of Theology* (eds. J. B. Davis and D. Harink [Eugene: Cascade, 2012] 169n10). In *Institutes* 3, Calvin's address on "progress in sanctification" holds the indicative mood of justification together with the imperative mood of sanctification through repentance: "I interpret repentance as regeneration, whose sole end is to restore in us the image of God that had been disfigured and all but obliterated through Adam's transgression. . . . Accordingly, we are restored by this regeneration through the benefit of Christ into the righteousness of God; from which we had fallen through Adam. . . . And indeed, this restoration does not take place in a moment or in a day or one year; but through continual and sometimes even slow advances, God wipes out in his elect the corruptions of the flesh, cleanses them of guilt, consecrates them to himself as temples renewing all their minds to true purity that they may practice repentance throughout their lives and know that this warfare will only end at death" (*Institutes* 3.3.8; *Institutes of the Christian Religion* [ed. J. T. McNeil; Philadelphia: Westminster, 1960]; cited in essay online by Les Galinski, http://www.imagochrististudio.org/wp-content/uploads/2017/09/John-Calvins-Doctrine-of-Sanctification.pdf, 11).

15. Principal scholars advocating the "apocalyptic model of deliverance" are J. Louis

Louis Martyn: "Martyn argues that for Paul, the plight of humanity does not consist of sins (a self-caused plight) but of enslavement."[16] That is, "[t]he human situation is fundamentally one of being subject to hostile cosmic forces and of Christ's invasion of the cosmos to rescue humanity from those forces."[17] A corollary of this position is that the plight of the creation and of the human beings within it is addressed in Paul's theology not by the granting of "forgiveness (of sins) from on high" (a response to human repentance) but by an invasive act of "liberation on the ground."[18]

I am sympathetic to Gathercole's objection that this "cosmological" apocalyptic version of sin in Paul tends to neglect the range of ἁμαρτία uses, singular *and* plural, that we find in his letters. For Gathercole, echoing Calvin, this muting of the language of human agency robs the believer of the assurance that her or his sins *in particular* are taken up by Christ who substitutes himself "on our behalf and in our place." Gathercole holds, however, that the apocalyptic approach he outlines is not *incompatible* with the atonement model he calls for. His point is all the more pressing in 1 Corinthians where (unlike Galatians and Romans) the concrete instances of human sinning (i.e., sinful actions or attitudes attributed to human beings) indicated by plural *sins* or human sinning at least equal the instances of Sin as singular dominating power. Here, I want to suggest what *compatibility* between these two models might actually look like in 1 Corinthians. In short, I will argue that Paul's language of sins plural as "acts and dispositions of human beings" makes sense only *within* the apocalyptic model of Sin singular as a cosmic entity whose enslaving power is ended in fact by

---

Martyn, Beverly Gaventa, Martin de Boer, and Susan Eastman. Characteristic expressions can be found in J. L. Martyn, *Theological Issues in the Letters of Paul* (Edinburgh: T. & T. Clark, 1997), and Beverly Gaventa, ed., *Apocalyptic Paul: Cosmos and Anthropos in Romans 5-8* (Waco, TX: Baylor University Press, 2013). Each author has extensive additional bibliography, some of which is also cited by Gathercole.

16. Gathercole, *Defending Substitution*, 43, citing J. Louis Martyn, *Galatians* (AYBC 33A; New York: Doubleday, 1997), 97.

17. Gathercole, *Defending Substitution*, 43.

18. Susan Eastman, in "Apocalypse and Incarnation: The Participatory Logic of Paul's Gospel," 170-71, cites J. L. Martyn's *Galatians*: "God would not have to carry out an invasion in order merely to forgive erring human beings. The root trouble lies deeper than human guilt, and it is more sinister. The whole of humanity—indeed the whole of creation (3:22)—is, in fact, trapped, enslaved under the power of the present evil age" (J. L. Martyn, *Galatians* [AYBC 33A; New York: Doubleday, 1997], 105). Eastman takes the matter a step further, from *invasion* to the fuller implications of *incarnation*—"Christ's death with us and for us is 'an inside job'. . . . [D]ivine power condescends to operate in and through human weakness" ("Apocalypse and Incarnation," 171).

the suffering death of Christ "for us" and in practice where the defeat of Sin is realized in human perception.

This path is supported by the structure and content of the letter as a whole and by the way in which a "history of sin," so to speak, unfolds from the exposition on the cross in chapter 1 to the announcement of sin's end in chapter 15. Most of the work on sin's *history*, admittedly, has focused on Romans and for good reason: there, especially in chapters 5–8, sin takes on a narrative life, and depending on how you read the narrative, sins and their cosmic master Sin can be understood as co-dependents, with Sin as the stronger, tyrannical partner. Here the careful exegetical work of Susan Eastman on Pauline anthropology is especially persuasive.[19]

While sin's "history" is more elusive in 1 Corinthians than in Romans, in this letter's penultimate chapter, 1 Corinthians 15, Paul shifts our focus to the *cosmic* horizon[20] as if to gather up the pieces of a faintly emerging narrative frame—built in part from the Israel/Christ typologies that punctuate chapters 5 and 10[21]—into the culminating Adam/Christ type that encompasses all time and space.[22]

> For since through a human being came death, so also through a human being comes about the resurrection of the dead. For just as all die in Adam, even so shall all be brought to life in Christ." (15:22)

From this universal and cosmic perspective, Sin and Death are revealed to have been powerful but doomed actors on the human stage (indeed active in "our sins") since the beginning.[23] Death will be vanquished and with it the sting of sin, both swallowed up in the victory of resurrection from the dead.

19. See Eastman, *Paul and the Person*, 124.

20. Gaventa, "When in Romans, Watch the Horizon," 23.

21. The paschal lamb in ch. 5 and the type of Israel in the wilderness in ch. 10 are figures that open out, as it were, into the Adam/Christ typology in ch. 15, that final type perfecting and completing the Israel/Christ typologies.

22. For my own more developed treatment of the typologies in 1 Corinthians, see Alexandra R. Brown, "Kairos Gathered: Time, Tempo, and Typology in 1 Corinthians," *Interpretation* 72 (2018) 43–55.

23. Pannenberg calls our attention to the power of the concept of original Sin to transform our moral consciousness: "The universality of Sin forbids the moralism that will not accept solidarity with those who become the instruments of the destructive power of evil" (Wolfhart Pannenberg, *Systematic Theology* [vol. 2; trans. G. Bromiley; Grand Rapids: Eerdmans, 1994], 238).

> When the perishable puts on the imperishable and the mortal puts on immortality, then shall come to pass the saying that is written: "Death is swallowed up in victory." "Oh Death, where is thy victory? Oh Death, where is thy sting?" The sting of death is Sin [ἡ ἁμαρτία; singular] and the power of Sin [ἡ δὲ δύναμις τῆς ἁμαρτίας] is the Law. (15:54–56)

Here, as in Rom 7, singular Sin, through its alliance with Death, is an entity whose power derives from the Law (that is, the Law taken into the "hands" of Sin so as to thwart human effort) and whose fate is sealed with the end of Death:

> For he must reign until he puts all his enemies under his feet. The last enemy to be destroyed is Death. (15:25–26)

In the Corinthian correspondence we see Paul's preparation for the more pervasive and coherent history of Sin he provides in Romans—the exchange narrated in the Adam-Christ typology wherein Adam's (enslavement to) Sin and Death is powerfully addressed by Christ's entering that Death, being made Sin who knew no Sin (2 Cor 5:21), thereby vanquishing both for the sake of human (and all) life. Following this participatory typology, we glimpse already in 1 and 2 Corinthians what becomes clearer in Rom 7, a treatment of sin as both cosmic power and a poison that corrupts a still weak human agency. There the remedy for sins/Sin that Paul rejects is the hijacked Law without Christ—that is, the Law in the "hands of Sin."[24] The remedy he proclaims is the liberation of human agents from malevolent power through the Christ who so deeply identified with the human plight as to become the bearer of Sin and Death in the "eucatastrophe" (Tolkien) of the crucifixion. The same narrative arc is present in 1 Corinthians, though again, it is not so structurally coherent as in Romans: chapter 1 narrates the cross as the saving (and counterintuitive) divine entry/invasion/incarnation into the human condition; chapter 15 announces the universal consequences of that divine entry—the swallowing up of Sin and Death at the Resurrection. Between the opening and closing discourses on the cross and the resurrection Paul addresses the concrete concerns and practices of the community now living at the turning of the ages (1 Cor 7:31; 10:11), that is between the events of the cross and the resurrection. In broad terms, Paul's treatment of particular ethical and ecclesiastical questions in

---

24. Paul W. Meyer, "The Worm at the Core of the Apple," in *The Word in this World* (eds. P. W. Meyer and J. T. Carroll; Louisville: Westminster John Knox, 2004), 57–77.

the body of the letter must be read within this overarching narrative frame. To be sure, Sin singular plays a leading role in both the narrative arc of 1 Corinthians and in individual instances of community strife (sins plural) Paul addresses there. A review of the particular uses of ἁμαρτία vocabulary in the letter provides evidence for evaluating the compatibility of substitutionary atonement for "sins" with apocalyptic readings of Sin as a cosmic power in Pauline theology.

Sinning as "Human Act" in 1 Corinthians

1 Corinthians 7:28, 36

Not every use of ἁμαρτία vocabulary is theologically weighty. Not every ἁμαρτία is, well, a sin! We are counseled wisely by Erin Roberts who surveys ancient literature to discover a wide variety of ἁμαρτία connotations in classical sources. Thus, ἁμαρτία is *sometimes* used in the sense of infraction against the gods, that is, with the theological inflection we typically see in translations of Christian texts, but is often rendered rather as "mistake," "error," or "things we get wrong."[25] While I want to acknowledge Paul's right (indeed his propensity) to create new meanings for vocabulary now taken up into a new reality, it is worth pondering whether Christian theology has, as Roberts suggests, obfuscated *nuances* in Paul's thought by assigning the English "sin" or "sins" to every instance of ἁμαρτία. In fact, at times, "sin" in the theological sense seems truly to *distort* the plain reading. So, for example, in 1 Cor 7, Paul writes that, his preference for celibacy notwithstanding, persons who marry under various named circumstances do not "sin" (ἁμαρτάνω, 7:28[x2]; 7:36). Might it make more sense of the situation he outlines to say that one who marries "can't go wrong?"[26] In a unit that seems to encourage a "divestment" from the worldly institution of marriage, reference to sin is here, at any rate, relatively free of theological importance.[27]

---

25. Erin Roberts, "Reconsidering Hamartia as 'Sin' in 1 Corinthians," *MTSR* 26 (2014) 340–64.

26. As an aside, it is tantalizing that Paul's uses of ἁμαρτία are associated here, and I believe *only* here, with uses of ἀφίημι, now meaning "divorce," rather than "forgiveness," all in the context of divestment from worldly affairs—does Paul, in addition to divesting (see Barclay below) from institutional structures of marriage, also divest from the traditional patterns of sin/forgiveness as "economic" justifications in the Christ event?

27. John M. G. Barclay, "Apocalyptic Allegiance and Divestment in the World: A

1 Corinthians 6:18

In contrast, two other more *theologically* weighted instances of ἁμαρτία/ ἁμάρτημα "frame" the advice on marriage in chapter 7. In 6:18, a particular sort of sin, πορνεία, is in view and ἁμαρτία is an act committed within that field of influence against one's own body, a wrong-doing compounded and made explicitly theological by the fact that the body houses the Holy Spirit:

> Shun immorality [πορνεία]. Every other sin [ἁμάρτημα] which a person does is outside the body; but the immoral person [ὁ δὲ πορνεύων] sins [ἁμαρτάνει] against his own body.

Since the human body is, for Paul, spiritually united with the Lord (6:13), the body is a temple for the Holy Spirit and in that sense, the ἁμάρτημα pollutes not only the human being, but the Spirit of Christ within him. While there is not space for exegesis of this text and its complicated reception history, we note that in this instance—whether or not Paul is correcting a libertine Corinthian slogan such as "every sin is done outside the body" (making the body morally irrelevant *or* the sin irrelevant for the church body or Body of Christ)[28]—he takes up the terminology of personal sin explicitly as *sin against the Holy Spirit*.

1 Corinthians 8:12

In chapter 8, individual sin is not first against the self or one's own body but is against the "weak" (ἀσθενοῦσαν), the other who is "destroyed" by the one who flaunts his superior knowledge that "an idol has no real existence." This know-it-all scandalizes the weak by eating food offered to idols in the presence of those whose conscience is weak.

> And so, by your knowledge this weak man is destroyed, the brother for whom Christ died. Thus, sinning [ἁμαρτάνοντες] against your

---

Reading of 1 Corinthians 7:25–35," in *Paul and the Apocalyptic Imagination* (eds. B. C. Blackwell et al.; Minneapolis: Fortress, 2016), 257–74.

28 In this context, Paul seems to advise that sexual activity, perhaps uniquely, carries profound implications for the spiritual integrity of both the person and the church. Anthony Thiselton gives characteristically helpful attention to modern attempts to parse this difficult verse. He concludes, with wide support from the literature, that Paul's point here is to assert (against an alternative Corinthian view) that the sexual act engages the whole person as *soma*, and is not, therefore, a peripheral and spiritually negligible act. See Anthony C. Thiselton, *The First Epistle to the Corinthians* (NIGTC; Grand Rapids: Eerdmans, 2000), 472–74.

brethren and wounding their conscience when it is weak, you sin [ἁμαρτάνετε] against Christ. (8:11–12)

This act, like the act of union with the πόρνη in chapter 6 but *unlike* the *adiaphora* of marriage in chapter 7, is a sin, ultimately, against Christ. In both chapters 6 and 8, one's participation *in Christ* in the body—in one's own body and one's neighbor's body—means that when one does wrong in these instances, the wrong-doing is understood by Paul theologically; it is a "sin" against God. Anthropologically, it harms the whole network of human relations.[29]

1 Corinthians 15:3 and 15:17: The climax and center of Gathercole's argument

Paul's citation of the traditional formula in 15:3 has stimulated much discussion about the degree to which he accepted the theological implications of the tradition he cites. As Gathercole notes, Paul claims straightforwardly that the formula is of *primary* importance.

> For I delivered to you as of *first importance* what I also received, that Christ died for our sins [ὑπὲρ τῶν ἁμαρτιῶν [plural] ἡμῶν] according to the Scriptures.

Debate centers on the relation of the formula here[30] to Isa 53. Gathercole argues for the direct influence of Isa 53:4ff in the formula *and* for deliberate adoption of Isaiah's substitutionary death motif by Paul.[31] Objections from apocalyptically-minded interpreters generally reflect concerns that the remedy implied in the substitution tradition is "forgiveness of sins"—a formula surprisingly rare in the undisputed Paulines—rather than liberation from enslavement to the cosmic actor Sin.[32] While I find no exception

---

29. Corporate models for both sin and divine power persist through Paul's writings. Persons exist in webs of relation influenced by Sin or by Grace.

30. And in Rom 4:25, and the expression "gave himself for our sins" in Gal 1:4.

31. Gathercole, *Defending Substitution*, 68–71.

32. Gathercole challenges Stendahl's famous argument that Paul is concerned not with forgiveness but with justification. Gathercole finds insufficient the argument that Paul is citing Hebrew Scripture when he uses the formula in Rom 4:7 (cf. Ps 32:1–2) and Rom 11:27 (cf. Isa 59:20). Even if one consigns these uses (and other such citations) to a nuance in Scripture not actually shared by Paul, one must still account for Paul's meaning (if it is not the equivalent of "forgiveness of sins") in a place like 2 Cor 5:19: "God was in Christ reconciling the world to himself, not counting people's trespasses [παραπτώματα]

in 1 Corinthians to the rule that Paul does not speak of forgiveness as the remedy to sin, cosmic or otherwise, I am not certain that the substitution metaphor requires "forgiveness of sins" so much as, say, *putting oneself in the place of another in order to undo the enemy.*[33] This seems to be very close to the way Paul puts the matter in 2 Cor 5:21: "for our sake, he made him to be sin who knew no sin, so that in him we might become the righteousness of God." Perhaps something like this is what Gathercole means when he says apocalyptic and substitutionary remedies are not incompatible.

A similar substitution through participation in Christ's resurrection is the point of 1 Cor 15:17: "If Christ has not been raised, your faith is futile and you are still *in your sins* [ἐν ταῖς ἁμαρτίαις ὑμῶν]." While *sins* in the plural is, again, unusual usage in Paul, especially personalized as "in *your* sins," the expression here echoes the creedal statement in 15:3 (above) that Christ died *"for our sins."* Perhaps Paul uses the expression intentionally to connect to the traditional formula as if to confirm that his resurrection teaching is no idiosyncratic add-on of Paul's but is central to the kerygma handed down from the beginning. Clearly, this conditional declaration belongs to Paul's own rhetorical pattern—a set of syllogisms to refute some who question or deny the resurrection. The net effect of the rhetorical move is to set *bondage* to personal sins (a function of the prepositional phrase) against the new reality of in-breaking resurrection life and to state the matter in such a way as to reflect traditional (i.e., not newfangled) kerygma.[34] Both substitution (resurrection in the place of sins) and liberation (resurrection as seal of divine liberation from Sin/s) are operative here.

---

against them." This, Gathercole argues, "is clear evidence that Paul is interested in the forgiveness of sins" (*Defending Substitution*, 50n68, where he also cites Krister Stendahl, *Paul Among Jews and Gentiles* [Philadelphia: Fortress, 1976]).

33. See Cilliers Breytenbach on the probability that early Christian use of Isa 53 as "dying for someone" comes through the LXX and reflects the Greek notion of "delivering someone over to a hostile power" ("The Septuagint Version of Isaiah 53 and the Early Christian Formula 'He was Delivered for our Trespasses,'" *NovT* 51 [2009] 339-51).

34. As Richard Hays notes, "Paul goes back to this bedrock confession in order to make the point that 'resurrection of the dead' is not merely some idiosyncratic speculation that can be set aside by those who claim more sophisticated knowledge" (*First Corinthians*, [Interpretation; Louisville: John Knox, 1997], 255).

A Final Step toward Coherence: The Holy Spirit as Co-Agent in the Defeat of Sin as sins in Daily Life

Immediately after the cross discourse in chapter 1, Paul brings in the Spirit as the authenticating witness to the mystery (2:1) of the cross he proclaims in "fear and trembling" (a stock expression in apocalyptic literature, by the way). The Spirit is the guide to the mystery (μυστήριον) of the cross and brings the Word of the cross to bear on the consciousness of the hearer so that she may know "what God has prepared for those who love God" (2:9). This knowledge, says Paul, is *apocalypsed* (ἀπεκάλυψεν) through the Spirit (2:10). We have seen in places where Paul uses sin terminology of human action (i.e., in chapter 6 and chapter 8) the over-reach of freedom based on claims to *false* knowledge, that is, to knowledge not grounded in the cross-revealed love of God. In Paul's economy, that is to say that the offending knowledge does not reflect the message of the cross that is communicated by the Spirit. In 3:16, the integrity of the Spirit to the body as its "temple" (individual and collective) is such that to compromise the body (say, as in chapters 6 and 8) in allowing one's physical desires to overrun the spiritual integrity of the body (individual or collective) is to risk cutting the self off from the Spirit as the source of life. In 5:5, it is precisely to save the spirit (that part to which the Spirit of God communicates—2:6–16) that the incestuous man is to be removed from the Church. Moreover, in the context of 1 Corinthians, it is not merely human agency that moves this person toward salvation. The cross bears the power that invades the perverted structures of being under which this man is now enslaved. And its communication through the Spirit will be, it is implied, his deliverance.

In Paul's final calling out of human sin, neglect of this Spirit-apocalypsed knowledge is once again in view:

> If the dead are not raised, "Let us eat and drink, for tomorrow we die." Do not be deceived [μὴ πλανᾶσθε]. . . . Come to your right mind (sober up) and sin no more [μὴ ἁμαρτάνετε]. For some have no knowledge of God. I say this to your shame. (15:32–34)

Rather than derailing the apocalyptic reading of the cross by its imperative to "sin no more," this parenetic utterance calls the hearers out of toxic indifference to the web of true life (from enmeshment in counterfeit goods and relationships) and back into the network of Spirit-knowledge that formed them as the body of Christ. If the "some" who "have no knowledge" are outsiders to the community, then the "shame" is in the Corinthians' drawing outsiders into their misguided (πλανᾶσθε) ignorance. Again, a deceiving agency not merely human seems to lurk in the background.

Conclusion

Attending to the overarching Adam-Christ typology (and the history of Sin it encompasses) that frames Paul's final words to the Corinthians helps to sum up themes of anthropology and pneumatology that interpret his understanding of S/sin. In the cross as the turning point between the ages, the one defined by Adam and the one defined by Christ (10:11), Paul perceives the advent of new creation.[35] This Event both exposes Sin as the power exploiting the Adamic ψυχή, drawing human beings into webs of ignorance, indifference and violence, *and* liberates human beings as sinners captive to Sin into life out of that death by incorporation in the living πνεῦμα of Christ (15:45). Finally, Paul sets the narrative of Sin/sins within an immanent and universal Christology of victory over death (15:26) and articulates a pneumatology of co-inherence—Spirit communicating to spirit (2:6–16). By this mystery of divine communication, human agency is transformed and taken up into divine agency in such a way as to reveal Sin singular in its cosmic dimension and sins plural in their human dimensions as temporal but *temporary* impediments to divine co-inherence when "God will be all in all" (1 Cor 15:28). The one who "sins" acts in captivity to that hostile power Sin whose reign is coming to an end. The interpretive framework for the relation of human sins to cosmic Sin remains what I am calling the "apocalyptic" one without diminishing the lived reality of sins plural as "acts and dispositions of human beings."

---

35. Near the end of his work on the emergence of sin, Croasmun (*Emergence*, 186–87) faces the question of the "disanalogy" between the emergent Body of Sin and the Body of Christ as "cosmic, collective bodies." The distinction he draws from the work of Philip Clayton (via Hartshorne) rests theologically on the doctrine of God's *antecedent* nature as "Ground or Source of all things." Human beings come to know God through emergent properties of the physical world taken as a whole (the creation) and in this sense the Body of Christ emerges, i.e., is an instance of causative emergence. But whereas the Body of Sin, that "counterfeit deity," has *only consequent and not antecedent* nature, the Body of Christ is the realization of the antecedent (not merely consequent) Creator so that in the Body of Christ, the created integrity of the human subject is delivered from the Body of Sin. Croasmun cites Elsa Tamez to helpful effect: "The sovereignty of God coincides with the realization of the human being. The sovereignty of the idol coincides with dehumanization" (Elsa Tamez, *The Amnesty of Grace: Justification by Faith from a Latin American Perspective* [Nashville: Abingdon, 1993], 145; cited in Croasmun, *Emergence*, 187).

Afterword

Modern readers of the Pauline letters sometimes find the language of cosmic Sin in the singular off-putting, primitive, mythological, and unhelpful. In it they see a binary universe that neglects the complexity of systemic sins in favor of a mythical being to whom the blame is magically attributed. They sense a contradiction to human responsibility, to Christian ethics, and to the work of sanctification that Paul himself affirms. The language of substitutionary atonement helps, but only so much, since it too assumes mythologically construed entities and circumstances as the deity steps in to bear the penalty for sins and thus to clear the sinner. In a world rife with systemic evil there is need for a hermeneutic of Sin/sins that speaks authentically and prophetically from the Christian tradition to the human condition, recognizing the ways in which human beings participate in sin while at the same time they are dominated and controlled by it. Recent work cited here by Gaventa, Eastman, and most recently Croasmun demonstrate against more superficial readings highly nuanced and realistic treatments of Paul's Sin/sins language with respect to anthropology, biology, neuroscience, and human behavioral sciences. For each of these authors, Paul's discourse on Sin/sins reveals in his time and ours a complex understanding of human nature, individual and collective. They demonstrate in different registers ways in which sins as human acts arise from (and contribute to) worlds of experience that complicate simpler notions of free will and discreet moral acts. Born into webs of relationships that dominate, corrupt, or nurture the "I," no person is independent of larger social entities that make claims upon him/her/them. Approached by way of newly discovered understandings of personhood as irreducibly relational (Eastman) or of the way complex human social realities "emerge" from simpler bases in human activity and then exercise power over the entities from which they emerge (Croasmun's "downward causation"), Paul's cosmic Sin can be understood as inseparable from yet irreducible to discreet acts of human sinning.

First Corinthians fits the pattern outlined more fully in recent exegesis of Romans. Where Paul faces the fractionalization of community through acts of hubris, callous self-elevation, neglect of the poor, and the like, he names these behaviors "sins." In this letter, more perhaps than in Romans, the emergent power of Sin is defined epistemologically—an arrogant group-think emerging from the actions of some reflects amnesia of the cross-generated new creation. When Paul commands the Corinthians to "sin no more" he does not appeal as a moralist to the individual sinner but points to a force field of ignorance, a christological amnesia controlling the collective mind. "Do not be deceived, sober up, and sin no more!" (15:34). Sinning is not exactly caused by amnesia (drunkenness of perception), as if a power totally alien to the human experience intervenes, but amnesia operates from the ground up, now larger than the act of any personal agent, as the death-dealing slave master (Sin) that perpetuates Sin-dominance.[36]

In the end, both Cowper's palpable *sins washed away* and Barth's cosmic power of condemnation (herein named "Sin") find place in Paul's Corinthian theology. Indeed, the relationship of sins to Sin is, in this letter, manifested uniquely in the ways in which dissension, division, and blind disregard for the weak and vulnerable are the fruits of epistemological blindness and arrogance. In 1 Corinthians, then, the "remedy" Paul offers to the disintegration of human being and community is the wake-up call of the cross kerygma through which the divine election of the Creator (over the counterfeit emergence of dehumanizing powers) is announced:

> But God elected what is foolish in the world to shame the wise; God elected what is weak in the world to shame the strong; God elected what is low and despised in the world, even things that have no being, to bring to nothing things that have being so that no human being may boast in the presence of God. He is the source of your life in Christ Jesus, whom God made our wisdom, our righteousness and sanctification and redemption; therefore, as it is written, "Let him who boasts, boast in the Lord." (1 Cor 1:27–31)

---

36. In the Corinthian correspondence, Paul explicitly and repeatedly juxtaposes "part" to "all," division to unity, in ways that suggest this dynamic.

6

Divine Generosity in the Midst of Conflict: Sin and Its Remedy in 2 Corinthians

DOMINIKA KUREK-CHOMYCZ

THE VOCABULARY OF ABUNDANCE and overflowing pervades the canonical letter of Second Corinthians. Images and terminology from the world of commerce, employed to describe God's—but also Paul's own, and those of his communities—actions and behavior, recur in this letter. Yet, as Frances Young and David Ford observe, while "[m]ost economies are characterized by their ways of coping with scarcity, ... Paul's vision is of more than enough of the central resource."[1] In chapter 8, Paul recalls the paradox of extreme poverty overflowing in a wealth of generosity on the part of Macedonians (8:2), mirroring the generous act of Jesus Christ, who, being rich (πλούσιος ὤν), became poor, in order that by his poverty others might become rich. God as portrayed in 2 Corinthians is a generous God, who does not count trespasses (5:19), who bestows God's Spirit as a deposit (1:22; 5:5), and who causes both Christ's sufferings and consolation to abound for Paul (1:5).

The notion of sin is of particular theological significance, yet it remains somewhat elusive in this letter, especially when compared with the prominence of personified Sin in Romans. Remedy for sin, as I shall suggest, however, is rooted in divine generosity, which is the divine characteristic constitutive of who God is. Christ's generous act of being made "sin"

---

1. Frances Young and David F. Ford, *Meaning and Truth in 2 Corinthians* (Biblical Foundations in Theology; London: SPCK, 1987), 172.

by God enables our wondrous transformation, so that humans, too, can partake in God's generosity. Generosity continues to produce further good, becoming a nonviolent "weapon" (cf. 2 Cor 6:7) to address situations of conflict and to enable reconciliation.

This essay is divided into two parts. In the first part, I discuss the vocabulary of sin and related terms in 2 Corinthians, with a short excursus on the issues of translation. The second part consists of three sections. I first focus more specifically on 2 Cor 5:21 and its context, then look at how forgiveness is envisaged in 2 Corinthians, and how this relates to theological themes of 2 Cor 5:14–21. In the third section I explore the significance of the ἵνα clause in 5:21, and of δικαιοσύνη θεοῦ in 2 Corinthians more generally, as well as how it relates to human δικαιοσύνη in this letter. In my concluding remarks I consider how the results of my discussion illuminate the question of "sin's remedy" in 2 Corinthians, and comment on the title of the paper.

Before I begin, some preliminary remarks are in order. First of all, the unity and integrity of 2 Corinthians are assumed in what follows.[2] Secondly, I follow Reimund Bieringer in his understanding of this letter as a particularly good example of Paul's "theology in the making," in that it gives us an insight into how the development of specific theological themes is related to particular circumstances of the apostle's relationship with the Corinthians, its challenges and highlights.[3] And finally, I do not find convincing the idea that some of the Pauline statements in the letter are part of a "pre-Pauline" tradition, as was fashionable in the past, and thus consider it unwarranted to play down any specific sayings as allegedly "un-Pauline."

---

2. See especially Reimund Bieringer, "Plädoyer für die Einheitlichkeit des 2. Korintherbriefes: Literarkritische und inhaltliche Argumente," in *Studies on 2 Corinthians* (eds. R. Bieringer and J. Lambrecht; BETL 112; Leuven: Leuven University Press/Peeters, 1994), 131–79, and more recently, Reimund Bieringer, "Love as That Which Binds Everything Together? The Unity of 2 Corinthians Revisited in Light of ἀγαπ-Terminology," in *Second Corinthians in the Perspective of Late Second Temple Judaism* (eds. R. Bieringer et al.; CRINT 14; Leiden: Brill, 2014), 11–24. Recent contributions to the debate in support of the unity of 2 Corinthians include Ivar Vegge, *2 Corinthians—A Letter about Reconciliation: A Psychagogical, Epistolographical and Rhetorical Analysis* (WUNT 2/239; Tübingen: Mohr Siebeck, 2008); Thomas Schmeller, "No Bridge over Troubled Water? The Gap between 2 Corinthians 1–9 and 10–13 Revisited," *JSNT* 36 (2013) 73–84.

3. Reimund Bieringer, "Looking Over Paul's Shoulder: 2 Corinthians Evidence for Paul's Theology in the Making" (paper presented at Annual Meeting of the SBL, Boston, MA, November 23, 2008). For a published version in Dutch, see idem, "Verzoening met God in 2 Korintiërs 5,18-21: Een voorbeeld van paulinische theologie in wording," *Collationes* 39 (2009) 21–30."

Sin, Wrongdoing, and Issues of Translation in 2 Corinthians

The substantive ἁμαρτία occurs in 2 Corinthians only three times. Two of the three occurrences, however, are in a theologically significant passage, in 5:21. Paul speaks here of the one "who did not know sin" (τὸν μὴ γνόντα ἁμαρτίαν) whom God "made sin" (ἁμαρτίαν ἐποίησεν), while contrasting "sin" with δικαιοσύνη θεοῦ.[4] The third occurrence, in 11:7, is in a very different context, and it may even be debated whether rendering ἁμαρτία as "sin" there is justified. I shall return to this question in a moment.

To continue with the use of ἁμαρτία and its cognates in 2 Corinthians, the simple verb ἁμαρτάνω and the nouns ἁμαρτωλός and ἁμάρτημα are entirely absent from this letter. The compound προαμαρτάνω, however, does occur twice, in 2 Cor 12:21 and 13:2, in reference to certain Corinthians who "previously sinned." Based on the second part of 12:21, it seems that these "previous" sins pertain primarily to the sexual sphere: Paul fears that he may have to, as the NRSV renders it, "mourn over many who previously sinned and have not repented of the impurity, sexual immorality, and licentiousness [ἐπὶ τῇ ἀκαθαρσίᾳ καὶ πορνείᾳ καὶ ἀσελγείᾳ] that they have practiced." Paul's concern with sexual purity echoes 1 Cor 6:12–20.[5] In this passage the understanding of the Corinthians' bodies as part of the body of Christ, and the metaphor of the body as "a temple of the Holy Spirit" (τὸ σῶμα ὑμῶν ναὸς τοῦ ἐν ὑμῖν ἁγίου πνεύματός ἐστιν, 6:19), ground the prohibition of πορνεία, and of sexual union with a πόρνη more specifically. Similar concerns, as we will see shortly, also appear earlier in 2 Corinthians, even if the vocabulary to express what Paul considers "sinful" behavior differs. Paul's "fears," however, were not limited to the Corinthians' sexual

---

4. Translating the Greek substantive δικαιοσύνη, especially in the Pauline letters, is notoriously difficult. While English translations tend to use primarily "righteousness" (when speaking of God's quality) and "justification" (in reference to God's action towards humans), with some notable (mainly Catholic) exceptions, among scholars there is a growing recognition that in a number of cases "justice" would be more appropriate (and easier to grasp by contemporary readers) than "righteousness." See Ronald Damholt, "*Rightwiseness* and Justice, a Tale of Translation," *ATR* 97 (2015) 413–32, for the history of rendering δικαιοσύνη into English in biblical translations. Although I am sympathetic to the arguments of those who support the use of "justice" to render δικαιοσύνη in certain contexts, in my essay I try to retain the Greek original whenever possible, given that I am mainly interested in the specific connotations of this term in 2 Corinthians, and in particular its theological significance in relation to the topic of this paper.

5. On 1 Cor 6:18, see, in this volume, chapter 5, Alexandra Brown, "Letters from the Battlefield: Cosmic Sin and Captive Sinners in 1 Corinthians."

behavior. In the verse preceding 2 Cor 12:21 he provides a "catalog of vices" which he fears (φοβοῦμαι) he might find in the Corinthian community when he arrives: ἔρις, ζῆλος, θυμοί, ἐριθίαι, καταλαλιαί, ψιθυρισμοί, φυσιώσεις, ἀκαταστασίαι ("quarreling, jealousy, anger, selfishness, slander, gossip, conceit, and disorder," 12:20 [NRSV]). The list resembles similar lists in 1 Corinthians, Galatians, and Romans,[6] as well as in other ancient writings. Yet even though commentators refer to it as "comprehensive,"[7] the catalog does not include "greediness" (πλεονεξία). According to Stanislas Lyonnet, greediness is the "sin" that Paul would seem to single out elsewhere as particularly serious,[8] given that πλεονεξία or the adjective πλεονέκτης appears in both lists in 1 Corinthians, as well as in Rom 1:29 (albeit not in Galatians). It is perhaps not surprising that Paul does not list it as a Corinthian "vice" in a letter in which he devotes so much attention to the need to contribute to the collection, but in which he also defends himself against accusations of having taken advantage of the Corinthians (note the different forms of πλεονεκτέω in 2 Cor 7:2; 12:17-18; cf. also the use of πλεονεξία in 9:5).

That the word ἁμαρτία does not occur frequently in 2 Corinthians is not uncharacteristic of Paul; indeed, Romans is untypical with its forty-eight occurrences of the noun, as opposed to only four in 1 Corinthians, three in Galatians, and none in Philippians, to name just the main letters. Yet it would be misleading to conclude that Paul is unconcerned in this letter with the reality of what the readers are likely to associate with sin. In English, too, the term is somewhat nebulous, and trying to determine what sin consists in, or what its nature is, according to Paul, without prejudging the outcome, does not make our task easier. Still, considering the broader semantic domain of wrongdoing beyond ἁμαρτία and its cognates, but frequently associated with them, we note one occurrence of the noun παράπτωμα, in 5:19, thus in the same passage as that of which 5:21 is the culmination. Furthermore, the verb ἀδικέω occurs three times (once in 7:2, and twice in 7:12) and the cognate noun ἀδικία once (12:13). There is also the noun ἀνομία in 2 Cor 6:14,[9] where it, similarly to ἁμαρτία in

---

6. Cf. 1 Cor 5:11; 1 Cor 6:9-10; Gal 5:19-21; Rom 1:29-31; 13:13.

7. Margaret E. Thrall, *A Critical and Exegetical Commentary on the Second Epistle to the Corinthians* (2 vols; ICC; London: T. & T. Clark, 2000), 2:862.

8. Stanislas Lyonnet, "The Notion of Sin," in *Sin, Redemption, and Sacrifice: A Biblical and Patristic Study* (eds. S. Lyonnet and L. Sabourin; AnBib 48; Rome: Biblical Institute Press, 1970), 1-57, here 50.

9. 2 Cor 6:14—7:1 has often been considered non-Pauline or even anti-Pauline, but

5:21, is contrasted with δικαιοσύνη. In the same passage Paul speaks of the "defilement of flesh" (μολυσμὸς σαρκός), of which we should be cleansed (7:1). In this way he introduces the notion of pollution, with which modern readers may feel uncomfortable, yet which can be best interpreted both in light of ancient and contemporary conceptions of the body as porous, unbounded, and malleable.[10] The need to keep the body "pure" is, similarly to 1 Corinthians, related to its status as the "temple of the living God" (ναὸς θεοῦ ζῶντος) in 2 Cor 6:16.[11]

To complete the overview, one could also include the distinction that Paul makes in 5:10 between good (ἀγαθόν) and bad (φαῦλον) that we do "through the body" (διὰ τοῦ σώματος), and for which we shall receive a recompense when we appear before the judgment seat of Christ. And finally, in 13:7, the contrast is between what is κακόν (bad/evil) and what is καλόν (lit. beautiful, but here in the ethical sense, thus "good"). The precise content of "wrongdoing" in most of the above passages eludes us, but the two spheres Paul seems to be primarily concerned with are human sexuality and interpersonal relationships, in both cases with a focus on how wrongdoing affects not just individuals involved, but the entire community.

What is the relevance of the passages speaking of human wrongdoings in 2 Corinthians for our understanding of how Paul conceptualizes sin in a theological sense? The problem with deciding which verses are relevant to

---

arguments in favor of an interpolation tell us more about their authors' presuppositions and how they envisage Paul, than about Paul's theology. For a survey of different exegetical positions, and their hermeneutical implications, see Emmanuel Nathan, "Fragmented Theology in 2 Corinthians: The Unsolved Puzzle of 6:14—7:1," in *Theologizing in the Corinthian Conflict: Studies in Exegesis and Theology of 2 Corinthians* (eds. R. Bieringer et al.; BTS 16; Leuven: Peeters, 2013), 211–28. Cf. also George J. Brooke, "2 Corinthians 6:14—7:1 Again: A Change in Perspective," in *The Dead Sea Scrolls and Pauline Literature* (ed. J.-S. Rey; Leiden: Brill, 2013), 1–16.

10. Dale B. Martin, *The Corinthian Body* (New Haven, CT: Yale University Press, 1995), is now a classic on Greco-Roman ideologies of the body and Paul's discourse in 1 Corinthians. For lucid overviews of contemporary views on the body and the self with reference to Paul's anthropology, see Susan Grove Eastman, *Paul and the Person: Reframing Paul's Anthropology* (Grand Rapids: Eerdmans, 2017); and chapter 3 of Matthew Croasmun, *The Emergence of Sin* (Oxford: Oxford University Press, 2017).

11. See also George H. van Kooten, *Paul's Anthropology in Context: The Image of God, Assimilation to God, and Tripartite Man in Ancient Judaism, Ancient Philosophy and Early Christianity* (WUNT 232; Tübingen, Mohr Siebeck, 2008), 203, who argues that in 2 Cor 6:14–16 there is a connection between being "God's temple" and being "God's image," achieved through "a contrast between the individual believer as the temple of God, on the one hand, and εἴδωλα, on the other."

our theme highlights important issues of translation. Because of the connotation that the term "sin" has in contemporary English, we tend to make a much sharper distinction between "sin" and words such as "wrongdoing" or "shortcoming." For this reason I am sympathetic to the concerns expressed by Erin Roberts, who cautions us against a consistent rendering of the word ἁμαρτία as "sin" in the New Testament and other ancient Jewish and Christian literature.[12] Yet in the context of 2 Corinthians, there are reasons to render all three occurrences of the substantive in this way. Other English words may be used for other terms listed above, yet in view of the connection between Paul's theologizing and the specific Corinthian circumstances, there is no doubt that there exists a tight link between individual acts and dispositions of the Corinthians, and how Paul understands sin and God's ways of dealing with sin.

As to when the translation "sin" should be retained in the case of Paul's letters, and in 2 Corinthians more specifically, 11:7 is especially problematic in this regard ("Η ἁμαρτίαν ἐποίησα ἐμαυτὸν ταπεινῶν ἵνα ὑμεῖς ὑψωθῆτε, ὅτι δωρεὰν τὸ τοῦ θεοῦ εὐαγγέλιον εὐηγγελισάμην ὑμῖν;). English translations disagree on its rendering:

> "Have I committed *an offence* in abasing myself that ye might be exalted, because I have preached to you the gospel of God freely?" (KJV)

> "Did I commit *a sin* by humbling myself so that you might be exalted, because I proclaimed God's good news to you free of charge?" (NRSV)

> "Did I make *a mistake* when I humbled myself so that you might be exalted, because I preached the gospel of God to you without charge?" (NABRE)

Is "an offence," "a sin," or "a mistake" appropriate in this context? The NABRE translation is certainly possible insofar as ἁμαρτία is used in Greek literature in this sense. The ὅτι clause provides the content of Paul's ἁμαρτία here, namely preaching the gospel without charge. Rendering ἁμαρτία as "sin" has resulted in the commentators' speculating whether the Corinthians may have deemed manual labor as "sin" in that it violated the Lord's command, or whether there was another aspect that made the Corinthians (or the opponents) think of "sin" in this context. In commenting on

---

12. Erin Roberts, "Reconsidering Hamartia as 'Sin' in 1 Corinthians," *MTSR* 26 (2014) 340–64.

whether Paul's critics may have suggested that his behavior was sinful, or whether this was "ironical exaggeration," Margaret Thrall suggests that the former must not be discarded too easily: "Whilst 'sin' may still be somewhat too strong a term, in Graeco-Roman society the refusal of a proffered benefaction would nevertheless be seen as an insult to the benefactor(s) and as likely to engender hostility."[13]

The decision not to use the word "sin" in 11:7 could be the easiest way to avoid similar scholarly speculation. And yet, having earlier said in 5:21 that God made sin (ἁμαρτίαν ἐποίησεν) the one who did not know sin, it is likely that Paul's ironic use of the term in 11:7 (ἁμαρτίαν ἐποίησα) is deliberate.[14] This is confirmed, to my mind, when later in 12:13 Paul uses ἀδικία in a similarly ironic way, and in a similar context: τί γάρ ἐστιν ὃ ἡσσώθητε ὑπὲρ τὰς λοιπὰς ἐκκλησίας, εἰ μὴ ὅτι αὐτὸς ἐγὼ οὐ κατενάρκησα ὑμῶν; χαρίσασθέ μοι τὴν ἀδικίαν ταύτην ("In what way were you less privileged than the rest of the churches, except that on my part I did not burden you? Forgive me this wrongdoing!"). We note that χαρίσασθέ μοι τὴν ἀδικίαν ταύτην echoes the language that Paul has earlier (in chapter 2) used in reference to a wrongdoer. While full of irony, Paul's vocabulary is scarcely accidental here. This is why in spite of its dangerous potential, there are good reasons to retain consistency in rendering both ἁμαρτία and ἀδικία in 2 Corinthians (and, as we shall see momentarily, also the verb χαρίζομαι).

Sin, Sins, and Generosity, Divine and Human

Second Corinthians 5:21 and Its Context

Based on the review of the vocabulary above, we saw that chapter 5 is likely to be central to Paul's understanding of sin in this letter. Second Corinthians 5:21 ends the apostle's discourse on God's reconciling activity, culminating in what could also be considered a concluding statement to vv. 14–20: τὸν μὴ γνόντα ἁμαρτίαν ὑπὲρ ἡμῶν ἁμαρτίαν ἐποίησεν, ἵνα ἡμεῖς γενώμεθα δικαιοσύνη θεοῦ ἐν αὐτῷ. The verse begins with asyndeton, which may underscore its significance, but also makes its relationship with what precedes more difficult to determine. It has puzzled interpreters throughout

---

13. Thrall, *Second Corinthians*, 2:683.

14. I refer here only to the verbal parallel; I realize of course that the syntax of the two clauses differs, in that in 2 Cor 5:21 there is a double accusative, so the verse does not speak of God "committing sin."

the centuries, and it continues to do so, especially in view of its soteriological and christological implications.

Three main lines of interpreting the main clause in v. 21 (ὑπὲρ ἡμῶν ἁμαρτίαν ἐποίησεν) are attested since antiquity[15]: (1) ἁμαρτία as sin offering; (2) ἁμαρτία as "sinful flesh," in analogy to Rom 8:3; (3) ἁμαρτία as referring to Jesus becoming subject to what sinners are subject to, and in particular suffering (and dying) as sinners do.

The sin-offering interpretation, even though it is still defended by some contemporary interpreters,[16] ultimately fails to convince. The main reasons quoted by commentators include the following: the meaning of the word ἁμαρτία would need to change radically within just a few words; it is not clear what the contrast between sin offering and δικαιοσύνη θεοῦ would mean; and finally, ἁμαρτία does not mean sin offering anywhere else in the Pauline letters or the New Testament more generally.[17] Similarly, the reference to "sinful flesh" seems unlikely; in Rom 8:3 Paul speaks of the "likeness of sinful flesh," or literally "flesh of sin" (ἐν ὁμοιώματι σαρκὸς ἁμαρτίας). What is more, even though incarnation may be included in Jesus being "made sin," it is at death that he suffered "as a sinner."

The third option itself encompasses a wide range of more specific interpretations. But broadly, in this view the focus is usually on the death of Jesus. Verse 21 would thus be read as parallel to v. 15 with its ἵνα clause, except that in v. 21 the emphasis is on the fact that Jesus suffered and died *as a sinner*.[18] Here ἁμαρτία is usually understood as a metonymy ("sin" to

---

15. For the history of interpretation of 2 Cor 5:21 from the patristic period to the first part of the twentieth century, see Léopold Sabourin, "Christ Made 'Sin' (2 Cor 5:21) Sacrifice and Redemption in the History of a Formula," in *Sin, Redemption, and Sacrifice: A Biblical and Patristic Study* (eds. S. Lyonnet and L. Sabourin; AnBib 48; Rome: Biblical Institute Press, 1970), 185–296; for an overview of the different interpretations of 2 Cor 5:21, and their main proponents, see Reimund Bieringer, "Sünde und Gerechtigkeit in 2 Korinther 5,21," in *Studies on 2 Corinthians* (eds. R. Bieringer and J. Lambrecht; BETL 112; Leuven: Leuven University Press/Peeters, 1994), 461–514.

16. These include Ralph P. Martin, *2 Corinthians* (2nd ed.; WBC 40; Grand Rapids: Zondervan, 2014), 140; Thomas Stegman, *The Character of Jesus: The Linchpin to Paul's Argument in 2 Corinthians* (AnBib 158; Rome: Pontifical Biblical Institute, 2005), 186–87; Linda L. Belleville, *2 Corinthians* (IVPNTC; Downers Grove, IL: IVP Academic, 1996), 158–59.

17. See Thrall, *Second Corinthians*, 1:440–41; Murray J. Harris, *The Second Epistle to the Corinthians: A Commentary on the Greek Text* (NIGTC; Grand Rapids; Eerdmans, 2005), 453; Raymond F. Collins, *Second Corinthians* (Paideia; Grand Rapids: Baker Academic, 2013), 126.

18. This, in turn, evokes another shocking verse, Gal 3:13, which Luther understood

denote a "sinner"). One could ask, however, whether v. 21 does not go even further: just as according to Rom 8:3 God "condemned sin in the flesh," may we envisage that in the suffering inflicted on the innocent victim, sin (Sin?) is being put to death on the cross, in a performance of sorts?[19]

That someone who did not "know" sin might be "made" sin implies that sin is conceptualized here as a personal being, although its status is unclear. But we should also note that ultimately v. 21 is not so much about sin as such, as about its remedy: this is already suggested by the prepositional phrase ὑπὲρ ἡμῶν, which I take to mean "for our benefit," and which is then explicated in the final ἵνα clause: ἵνα ἡμεῖς γενώμεθα δικαιοσύνη θεοῦ ἐν αὐτῷ. To its meaning we shall also return in the last section.

Presently we consider the immediate context of v. 21, namely vv. 14–20. There are parallels between vv. 14–15 and v. 21, with which the latter forms an *inclusio*: these include a soteriological use of ὑπέρ, "for us" in v. 21, and "for all" in vv. 14 and 15 (although we may ask whether it is used in the same sense in all these cases); the fact that Paul avoids referring directly to Jesus/Christ; and finally the ἵνα clauses. As suggested above, v. 15 is especially relevant. But it not only makes the reference to the death of Jesus in v. 21 more plausible. In addition, that one died "for all" (ὑπὲρ πάντων), "in order that the living may no longer live for themselves but for the one who died and rose for them," provides possible content for the δικαιοσύνη θεοῦ, which we are to become. Still, there are also differences between vv. 15 and 21: the subject is different, and the beneficiaries (those "for whom" the "one" dies, and is "made sin") are "all" in v. 15 and "we" in v. 21. The latter verse is thus more theocentric and brings the reality of God's reconciliatory act closer to Paul's own (and presumably the Corinthians') experience.[20]

There are also other important connections between v. 21 and vv. 16–20, further illuminating v. 21. Ἐν Χριστῷ in v. 17 is echoed in ἐν αὐτῷ

---

to mean the same as 2 Cor 5:21. See also Morna Hooker, "On Becoming the Righteousness of God: Another Look at 2 Cor 5:21," *NovT* 50 (2008) 358-75, on how Gal 3:13 can illuminate our understanding of 2 Cor 5:21.

19. Cf. the performance envisioned by Susan Eastman, *Paul and the Person*, 126–50, in her imaginative retelling of Phil 2:6–11 as that of a divine actor playing on human stage.

20. There is no agreement as to the referent of specific first person plural forms in 2 Cor 5:16–21 among interpreters. I take the "we" of vv. 18–20 as referring primarily to Paul and possibly other apostles and their coworkers. The switch to second-person plural towards the end of v. 20 signals that the "we" of v. 21 also includes the recipients.

in v. 21, implying that our participation "in Christ," being "in Christ," is the sphere in which new creation becomes a reality, and thus presumably being God's δικαιοσύνη is part of the reality of new creation. In v. 16 Paul speaks of his changed mode of knowing Jesus (εἰ καὶ ἐγνώκαμεν κατὰ σάρκα Χριστόν, ἀλλὰ νῦν οὐκέτι γινώσκομεν), using then the same verb (γινώσκω) in an experiential sense in v. 21. Furthermore, God as subject connects v. 21 with v. 19, as in v. 21 the subject remains implicit. Finally, there is the link between τὰ παραπτώματα in the participial clause in v. 19b and ἁμαρτία in v. 21 (cf. Rom 5:12–18). Τὰ παραπτώματα which God does not count are in this context presumably individual sinful acts committed by humans, which are the consequence of their immersion in the realm of sin, but also simultaneously contribute to the expansion of the power of sin.

More generally, there is no explicit cultic imagery in vv. 14–21, no reference to the divine wrath, and while δικαιοσύνη could evoke court imagery, the latter is not explicit.[21] The two prevailing images for how God deals with the world affected by sin are (1) the aforementioned banking metaphor of not counting trespasses, and (2) reconciliation, a metaphor originating in a political, and in particular, military-diplomatic sphere.[22] In the context of 2 Corinthians, however, the imagery of reconciliation is possibly to be read against the backdrop of friendship, influenced by, on the one hand, Paul's own Damascus experience, and on the other, by his own troubled relationship with the Corinthians.

---

21. That none of these are explicit does not mean that they have not been read into the text by commentators. Cultic metaphors are implied in the interpretation of ἁμαρτία in v. 21 as "sin offering," or as a scapegoat. Divine "wrath" is ubiquitous especially in older commentaries. Cf., e.g., C.K. Barrett, A *Commentary on the Second Epistle to the Corinthians* (BNTC; London: Black, 1973), 180: "he came to stand in that relation with God which normally is the result of sin, estranged from God and the object of his wrath." Forensic imagery is present first and foremost in the penal substitution interpretation, which is typically associated with Calvin and his followers, but also other interpreters who understand v. 21b to refer to being "acquitted" envisage this as a forensic action.

22. See esp. Cilliers Breytenbach, *Versöhnung. Eine Studie zur paulinischen Soteriologie* (WMANT 60; Neukirchen/Vluyn: Neukirchener Verlag, 1989); Cilliers Breytenbach, "Salvation of the Reconciled (with a Note on the Background of Paul's Metaphor of Reconciliation)," in *Salvation in the New Testament: Perspectives on Soteriology* (ed. J. G. van der Watt; NovTSup 121; Leiden: Brill, 2005), 271–86.

Forgiving the Wrongdoer, Forgiving Human Sins

We shall return to the meaning of δικαιοσύνη θεοῦ in v. 21 shortly. But first, let us briefly consider Paul's notion of forgiveness, which presumably precedes reconciliation, and which is often related to the concept of sin. It is sometimes asserted that Paul is not interested in forgiveness. While it is true that apart from the quotation of Ps 31:1 in Rom 4:7, Paul does not use the verb ἀφίημι in the sense "to forgive," in 2 Corinthians he employs another verb, χαρίζομαι, to express this. If Paul's language about Christ becoming "sin" is opaque, his references to the specific wrongdoer, the person who seems to have harmed the community and/or Paul, are rather obscure, too. They do nonetheless offer a glimpse into his theologizing. This individual is only in chapter 7 referred to as the "wrongdoer" (cf. τοῦ ἀδικήσαντος in 7:12), where the significance of the wrongdoing as such is played down. When the offender is first mentioned in chapter 2, the focus is on the result of his wrongdoing: the fact that he (assuming that the Greek grammatical gender pertains also to this person's biological gender) has inflicted pain (Εἰ δέ τις λελύπηκεν, οὐκ ἐμὲ λελύπηκεν, 2:5). While Paul acknowledges that it was appropriate to punish the wrongdoer, he also urges the Corinthians to forgive him. The verb translated "to forgive," used repeatedly in this context (once in 2:7 and three times in 2:10), is not ἀφίημι, but χαρίζομαι, a cognate of χάρις, a gift. Incidentally, Paul also uses it in 12:13, the aforementioned verse in which he ironically asks the Corinthians to "forgive" him the wrongdoing of not burdening them (χαρίσασθέ μοι τὴν ἀδικίαν ταύτην).

While ἀφίημι implies that there is a burden that needs to be taken away, χαρίζομαι suggests a more positive notion of forgiveness: a gift that enables the offender to start a new life, and thus, in the case of a broken relationship, pave the way for reconciliation. Notably, neither ἀφίημι nor χαρίζομαι presupposes that the offender has repented.[23] The use of χαρίζομαι in this sense is rather unusual, and in the seven undisputed Pauline letters is unique to 2 Corinthians. While χαρίζομαι in the sense "to

---

23. As Thomas Schmeller, "'Anyone whom you forgive, I also forgive' (2 Cor 2:10): Interpersonal Forgiveness and Reconciliation in 2 Corinthians 2:5–11" (paper presented at Annual Meeting of the SBL, Boston, MA, November 24, 2008), notes, "It is conspicuous that there is no indication that the offender had in any way shown repentance of his deed. That he felt pain from being excluded need not imply that he felt pain concerning his deed."

grant" is attested throughout the New Testament, the meaning "to forgive," besides 2 Corinthians, is found only in Col 2:13, Col 3:13, and Eph 4:32.[24]

Interestingly, in the above listed verses in 2 Corinthians, human beings are always the subject of χαρίζομαι, whether Paul or his addressees; only in Colossians and Ephesians does God also become the subject of this verb. In 2 Corinthians, the notion of forgiveness as *giving* is likely to be implied in God's not counting human trespasses in 5:19, although here it seems to be even more radical. In this context we once more turn briefly to 1 Corinthians, where the so-called "hymn" about love in chapter 13 already anticipates some of the main theological themes in 2 Corinthians. For our purposes, especially important is what Paul says about ἀγάπη at the end of v. 5: [Ἡ ἀγάπη] οὐ λογίζεται τὸ κακόν, literally "it does not count evil." Most English translations paraphrase this text, so the notion of counting is generally absent from our English Bibles. In the LXX, only in Ps 31:2 is the negated verb λογίζομαι used with ἁμαρτία as direct object. Yet the idea that God will not remember, or will erase sins/transgressions, is present in a few passages in the Hebrew scriptures, notably in Isa 43:25 and Jer 31:34 (LXX 38:34). Interestingly, in Ps 31:1–2, both the image of taking away (and covering) sins, and that of not counting them, occur. The fact that Paul will quote these two verses in Rom 4:7–8 shows that he was not essentially opposed to the notion of forgiveness as "taking away." However, the recurrent use of χαρίζομαι in 2 Cor 2, and the introduction of the banking metaphor in 2 Cor 5 (a chapter deemed by many to be of particular theological significance), suggest that his preference was for a different way of envisaging forgiveness. Human forgiveness in the form of "giving" (χαρίζομαι) seems to be Paul's way of expressing how humans ought to imitate God's not being resentful, and thus preparing the ground for reconciliation.[25] Just as

---

24. The only references that LSJ provides for this meaning are 2 Cor 12:13; Col 2:13 (with indirect object); and 2 Cor 2:7 (an absolute use).

25. Cf. Reimund Bieringer, "Reconciliation to God in the Light of 2 Corinthians 5:14–21," in *Reconciliation in Interfaith Perspective: Jewish, Christian and Muslim Voices* (eds. R. Bieringer and D. Bolton; Leuven: Peeters, 2011), 39–58, at 56–57: "Both in 1 Cor 13:5 and in Rom 4:3.5.8 Paul uses the verb *logizomai* in the sense of unconditional or graceful counting. The counting or not counting happens purely because of grace and mercy, not because of any merit or duty. It is therefore highly unlikely that in 2 Cor 5:19b the condition for not counting trespasses is Jesus' death on the cross. The participial clause 'not counting their trespasses against them' tells us why God was able to reconcile the world to himself." Simon Gathercole, "'Sins' in Paul," *NTS* 64 (2018) 143–61, at 161, somewhat surprisingly seems to identify the "not counting" of v. 20 with the "content of the ministry of reconciliation." But surely, if this verse is about forgiveness, as he argues,

δικαιοσύνη is one of God's key characteristics, so is the fact that God does "not count trespasses"; the latter is not "earned" by Jesus's death on the cross. What is more, the two are related. This brings us to the last part of 5:21: what does it mean that we are to become δικαιοσύνη θεοῦ?

God's δικαιοσύνη as God's Generosity—and Ours!

In the traditional understanding of v. 21, influenced by the view that justification was central to Paul's theology, "becoming God's δικαιοσύνη" was taken to mean "becoming justified by and before God."[26] Taking into account the motif of reconciliation in the verses preceding v. 21, and the parallel between being "justified" (δικαιωθέντες) and "reconciled" (καταλλαγέντες) in Rom 5:9-10, it may be tempting to interpret 2 Cor 5:18-21 in light of Rom 5. However, such an understanding can hardly be deduced from 2 Corinthians alone, and due to the asyndeton in 2 Cor 5:21, ascertaining how Christ's being made sin and our becoming δικαιοσύνη θεοῦ relates to reconciliation is not straightforward.[27] What is more, in 2 Corinthians Paul does not use the verb δικαιόω, and the broader context makes it unlikely that the point about becoming δικαιοσύνη θεοῦ is the status of having been justified.

The Corinthians, based on what we know from 1 Corinthians, were already familiar with Paul's reference to Christ Jesus who "became [ἐγενήθη] wisdom for us [ἡμῖν] from God, as well as δικαιοσύνη and sanctification and redemption" (1 Cor 1:30). Even though Paul does not literally say that this δικαιοσύνη is "of God," it is implied with the reference to wisdom as

---

then forgiveness precedes reconciliation.

26. Thrall, *Second Corinthians*, 1:442. To be more precise, there are two competing "traditional" ways of understanding the text. Frank J. Matera, *II Corinthians: A Commentary* (NTL; Louisville: Westminster John Knox, 2003), 144-45, commenting on this, concludes: "On the one hand, the immediate context favors an 'imputed' righteousness. For, just as God viewed Christ as if he were a sinner, though he was sinless, so God views humanity as if it were righteous, though it is sinful, since God 'imputes' his own righteousness to humanity. On the other hand, Paul has already spoken of those who are "in Christ" as being a new creation (v. 17), suggesting that something transformative has happened to them in Christ."

27. Note that even in the case of Romans, the relationship between reconciliation and "justification" is a matter of debate. Cf. Joseph A. Fitzmyer, "Reconciliation in Pauline Theology," in *To Advance the Gospel: New Testament Studies* (2nd ed.; Grand Rapids: Eerdmans, 1998), 162-85, at 172-73, according to whom "justification takes place in view of something, viz., reconciliation, so that reconciliation does not 'sharpen and point up the doctrine of justification' in Pauline thought. It is rather the other way round."

being ἀπὸ θεοῦ (cf. also 1 Cor 1:24). The substantive δικαιοσύνη occurs in 1 Corinthians just once; in 2 Corinthians it appears seven times, but apart from 5:21, there is only one verse in which clearly God's δικαιοσύνη is implied, in 9:9. In chapters preceding 5:21, the substantive is used only in 3:9, to denote the subject or object of διακονία. Without going into exegetical detail, in view of the parallel with ἡ διακονία τῆς κατακρίσεως, an objective genitive seems preferable. Ἡ διακονία τῆς δικαιοσύνης is ministry which brings about δικαιοσύνη. Similarly, in 5:18 Paul speaks of the ministry τῆς καταλλαγῆς, of reconciliation, which I take to mean "ministry which brings about reconciliation," although here, too, the genitive may be understood in different ways. But Paul's appeal to the Corinthians (καταλλάγητε τῷ θεῷ) in v. 20 suggests that this is a more plausible reading. Verses 14–20 of chapter 5 leave no doubt that reconciliation affects humanity in a radical way, and the elliptic καινὴ κτίσις is most likely not limited to human beings. But human transformation, effected by the Spirit (cf. also ἡ διακονία τοῦ πνεύματος in 3:8) is already envisaged in 3:18. The δικαιοσύνη of 3:9 is not characterized as θεοῦ. But if we take the διακονία τῆς δικαιοσύνης to refer to the ministry which strives to bring about the becoming δικαιοσύνη θεοῦ for those whom it serves, then 3:18 is likely to be relevant. If we understand the *hapax legomenon* κατοπτριζόμενοι in 3:18 as meaning "to reflect as a mirror,"[28] then human participation in δικαιοσύνη is best taken as a reflection of God's δικαιοσύνη.

While in chapter 3 the relationship between human and divine δικαιοσύνη is possibly implied, later in chapter 9 it becomes more explicit. In his appeal to the Corinthians to give generously, after having explained in 9:8 that God is able to make every grace/gift abundant for them (δυνατεῖ δὲ ὁ θεὸς πᾶσαν χάριν περισσεῦσαι εἰς ὑμᾶς) so that they may abound in every good work (ἵνα ... περισσεύητε εἰς πᾶν ἔργον ἀγαθόν), in 9:9 Paul quotes Ps 111:9 LXX: "As it is written, 'He scatters abroad, he gives to the poor; his δικαιοσύνη endures forever" (καθὼς γέγραπται· ἐσκόρπισεν, ἔδωκεν τοῖς πένησιν, ἡ δικαιοσύνη αὐτοῦ μένει εἰς τὸν αἰῶνα). Incidentally, the psalm which Paul quotes speaks not of God, but of a *man* fearing God (ἀνὴρ ὁ φοβούμενος τὸν κύριον), and thus δικαιοσύνη αὐτοῦ in the original context does not pertain to God! Lest one should think that Paul was hesitant to ascribe δικαιοσύνη to a human being, in the subsequent verse he comments: "The one who supplies seed to the sower and bread for food will

---

28. See Laura Tack, "A Face Reflecting Glory: 2 Cor 3,18 in its Literary Context (2 Cor 3,1—4,15)," *Biblica* 96 (2015) 85–112.

supply and multiply your seed and increase the harvest of *your* δικαιοσύνη" (ὁ δὲ ἐπιχορηγῶν σπόρον τῷ σπείροντι καὶ ἄρτον εἰς βρῶσιν χορηγήσει καὶ πληθυνεῖ τὸν σπόρον ὑμῶν καὶ αὐξήσει τὰ γενήματα τῆς δικαιοσύνης ὑμῶν[29]). As Bieringer observes, "In 2 Cor 9:9–10 we meet a Paul who according to some scholars seems rather unconcerned about using the noun δικαιοσύνη in a way that could be (mis)construed as one's own righteousness based on works of the law, a concern that he had displayed earlier in his letter to the Philippians."[30] Even more importantly, in these verses δικαιοσύνη seems to refer to human generosity and benevolence, which does, I contend, shed light on 5:21b. It would probably be too farfetched to propose that in 5:21b δικαιοσύνη should be *translated* as "generosity." But in light of v. 15b (no longer living for oneself), and God's generosity present in God's "not counting" trespasses in v. 19b, the aspect of God's δικαιοσύνη that Paul draws attention to is God's lavishness in giving, which in turn humans are to reflect once reconciled to God. If this is so, this may also have implications for how we interpret the metaphor of "weapons τῆς δικαιοσύνης" in 6:7. Rather than employing military imagery to bolster his claims that "righteousness" is on his side, Paul would be using it in a more subversive way, with δικαιοσύνη serving to disarm the opponent in a way similar to how God's overflowing generosity disarms human attachment to sin (cf. also Paul's claim in 10:3 that he is not waging war κατὰ σάρκα).

There is still more to divine generosity in 2 Corinthians. Let us return to the beginning of 5:21 to consider the participial phrase τὸν μὴ γνόντα ἁμαρτίαν. What precisely does Jesus's "not knowing sin" consist in? It is usually interpreted in a general sense as pertaining to Jesus's sinlessness during his earthly existence.[31] I do not disagree with this, but I think that there is also a more positive content that may be implied here. First of all, in 2 Cor 1:19–20, Paul speaks of the "yes," ναί, which came into being (γέγονεν) in Jesus Christ. This could possibly imply that the notion of sin as *disobedience* is thus also present in this verse, albeit indirectly. Yet Jesus Christ's becoming

---

29. As a glance at the textual apparatus shows, there are a number of variants in this verse, but for the present purposes I follow the text of NA28.

30. Reimund Bieringer, "The δικαιοσύνη of God and the δικαιοσύνη of the Corinthians (2 Cor 9:9–10)" (paper presented at Annual Meeting of the SBL, San Diego, CA, November 22, 2014).

31. Although note Vincent P. Branick, "The Sinful Flesh of the Son of God (Rom 8:3): A Key Image of Pauline Theology," *CBQ* 47 (1985) 246–62, who argues that "not knowing sin" pertains to preexistent Jesus. According to Branick, Paul does not claim that during his earthly existence Jesus was "without sin," as it is usually understood.

ναί is also a theological statement about God's faithfulness to God's promises, and thus the focus is not so much on faithfulness and obedience to God, as about Jesus Christ as impersonating divine promises.[32] But an especially important christological statement appears only later in the letter, the significance of which is not always appreciated due to its being part of Paul's appeal to the Corinthians for financial contribution: γινώσκετε γὰρ τὴν χάριν τοῦ κυρίου ἡμῶν Ἰησοῦ Χριστοῦ, ὅτι δι' ὑμᾶς ἐπτώχευσεν πλούσιος ὤν, ἵνα ὑμεῖς τῇ ἐκείνου πτωχείᾳ πλουτήσητε ("For you know the gracious act of our Lord Jesus Christ, that for your sake he became poor, being rich, so that by his poverty you might become rich," 2 Cor 8:9). As John Barclay has argued, the participial clause πλούσιος ὤν is best understood as causal, rather than concessive, thus "because he was rich," rather than "although he was rich."[33] Here is yet another reminder of how generosity is constitutive of divinity. If "not knowing sin" pertains to incarnation, then divine generosity, expressed in the incarnation, is the antithesis of sin, while his being made sin is the ultimate expression of Christ's willingness to give. Only in this act can human attachment to sin be exposed so as to pave the way for reconciliation. Only in him (ἐν αὐτῷ) are human transformation and the capacity to no longer live for oneself enabled. Having died and being made sin, he did not cease to be God's δικαιοσύνη.[34] Both this and his resurrection are fundamental to Paul's argument.

What then about the various references to "wrongdoings" in 2 Corinthians, referred to in the first part of this essay? As Morna Hooker puts it, "If Christ is the source of 'righteousness and sanctification' (1 Cor 1:30), then those who, in him, become what he is, should also embody righteousness and sanctification. Perhaps this explains why Paul goes on, in 6:14—7:1, to urge

---

32. This could possibly support N. T. Wright's understanding of δικαιοσύνη θεοῦ in 2 Cor 5:21 as "God's faithfulness to the covenant" (see his *Paul and the Faithfulness of God* [London: SPCK, 2013], 881; originally argued for in N. T. Wright, "On Becoming the Righteousness of God: 2 Corinthians 5:21," in *Pauline Theology, vol. 2: 1 and 2 Corinthians* (ed. D. M. Hay [Minneapolis: Fortress, 1993], 200–208). I am not convinced, however, that the immediate context of chapter 5 justifies this.

33. John M. G. Barclay, "'Because he was rich he became poor': Translation, Exegesis and Hermeneutics in the Reading of 2 Cor 8.9," in *Theologizing in the Corinthian Conflict: Studies in the Exegesis and Theology of 2 Corinthians* (eds. R. Bieringer et al; Leuven: Peeters, 2013), 331–44.

34. I agree with Morna Hooker, "Interchange in Christ," *JTS* 22 (1971) 349–61, at 353, that "The interchange of experience is not a straightforward exchange, for we become the righteousness of God *in him*. If Christ has been made sin, he has also been made our righteousness."

Christians to live holy lives: righteousness and lawlessness cannot be partners, any more than can Christ and Beliar."[35] Embodying righteousness and sanctification includes the body. If in order to become δικαιοσύνη θεοῦ one needs to be united with Christ, this necessitates an uncompromising stance concerning all that, in Paul's view, pollutes one's body. To become δικαιοσύνη θεοῦ is to mirror, however imperfectly, God's perfect generosity, maintaining purity both of one's own body, and of the whole body of Christ.

Concluding Remarks

I began this essay by pointing to the vocabulary of abundance and overflowing in 2 Corinthians. In line with this, there is more than one way of speaking of sin and its remedy.[36] Even if the substantive ἁμαρτία occurs only three times in 2 Corinthians, there is a range of terms which Paul uses in reference to human wrongdoings. Notably, while Paul is highly critical of followers of Christ associating with "unbelievers," he shows much more openness towards the "wrongdoer," recommending forgiveness, but expressed with the verb χαρίζομαι. In forgiving, one imitates the divine attitude of "not counting trespasses."

Paul especially singles out sins pertaining to sexuality, as well as a range of antisocial behaviors, which affect the community. But he appears to consider the continuation of some of these behaviors as his personal failure (cf. "God may humble me" in 13:21). This is not to say that humans are not to be held responsible for their sins. The reference to the "judgment seat of Christ" in 1 Cor 5:10 leaves no doubt about that. Yet, this surely is not a matter of "works based righteousness," for whatever "righteousness" or "justice" they may perform is rooted in, and enabled by, God's δικαιοσύνη. The notion of sin (singular) remains somewhat nebulous in 2 Corinthians, but clearly if not for God's act in Christ, humans would continue to be entangled in the reality of sin—however one envisions that. In this sense, sin's remedy is the whole drama which begins with incarnation—whereby Jesus Christ "became poor because he was rich [in generosity]"—and culminates in his being "made sin," which not only exposes sin's utter terror, but through Christ's death *and* resurrection also enables both reconciliation between God and humans, and

---

35. Hooker, "Becoming," 373.

36. Of course, this is true not only of 2 Corinthians. Unsurprisingly, one of the sections in Gathercole's "'Sins' in Paul" is entitled: "The Abundance and Variety of Paul's 'Transgression' Language."

the reality of new creation to emerge. But the drama continues in that in order for humans to become δικαιοσύνη θεοῦ and in this way to embody divine activity in their midst, human response is required.

The above can best be illustrated in the table below, where the left column refers to actions of God/Jesus, which in light of our focus can be characterized as part of God's grand "remedial" plan, while in the right column are ἵνα clauses specifying the purpose and benefit of these actions. By formulating these as purpose clauses Paul not only makes them more dynamic, but, crucially, leaves space for a human response. In 2 Corinthians 5:20d, Paul begs the Corinthians: καταλλάγητε τῷ θεῷ. The willingness to reconcile themselves with God is the precondition for any of the purpose clauses to become reality.

Action of God/Jesus Christ	Purpose/Human Benefit
2 Corinthians 5:15—καὶ ὑπὲρ πάντων ἀπέθανεν,	ἵνα οἱ ζῶντες μηκέτι ἑαυτοῖς ζῶσιν ἀλλὰ τῷ ὑπὲρ αὐτῶν ἀποθανόντι καὶ ἐγερθέντι.
2 Corinthians 5:21—τὸν μὴ γνόντα ἁμαρτίαν ὑπὲρ ἡμῶν ἁμαρτίαν ἐποίησεν,	ἵνα ἡμεῖς γενώμεθα δικαιοσύνη θεοῦ ἐν αὐτῷ.
2 Corinthians 8:9—γινώσκετε γὰρ τὴν χάριν τοῦ κυρίου ἡμῶν Ἰησοῦ Χριστοῦ, ὅτι δι' ὑμᾶς ἐπτώχευσεν πλούσιος ὤν,	ἵνα ὑμεῖς τῇ ἐκείνου πτωχείᾳ πλουτήσητε.
2 Corinthians 9:8—δυνατεῖ δὲ ὁ θεὸς πᾶσαν χάριν περισσεῦσαι εἰς ὑμᾶς,	ἵνα ἐν παντὶ πάντοτε πᾶσαν αὐτάρκειαν ἔχοντες περισσεύητε εἰς πᾶν ἔργον ἀγαθόν

Ultimately, the "remedial" plan which takes place is rooted in divine generosity, and just as God was reconciling the world in the midst of a cosmic conflict, so are the Corinthians, who become δικαιοσύνη θεοῦ, expected to act justly and generously, and thus to embody God's lavishness, both in the midst of the local conflict and elsewhere. Acting generously includes both nonliteral giving in forgiving, as in Paul's experience with the person who has hurt him (the "wrongdoer"), and literal contributing to the Jerusalem collection. But it also involves being generous towards one's own body and the community, the body of Christ, by guarding it against pollution and living for others rather than boasting of one's own achievements. Only in this way can they, as a mirror that reflects the divine glory, continuously rid themselves of their blurs and impurities, in an ongoing process of transformation (3:18).

7

Sin, Slavery, Sacrifice, and the Spirit: The Human Problem and Divine Solution in Galatians

DAVID A. DESILVA

WHERE HAS HUMANITY GONE wrong, necessitating God's restorative interventions? Where does it still go wrong on this side of the coming of Christ? What forces are at work constraining humanity to continue to go wrong (and to have gone wrong hitherto)? If we approach these questions merely on the basis of an analysis of passages using the lexical terminology most fundamentally associated with the idea of "sin," we will not find all that much with which to work in Galatians. In Romans, "sin" is a focal topic. The word counts make this abundantly clear: forms of the noun ἁμαρτία appear in Romans forty-eight times, but only sixteen times across the remaining twelve letters associated with Paul's name; forms of the verb ἁμαρτάνειν appear seven times in Romans, and only sixteen times across the remainder of the Pauline corpus. Nevertheless, each of those few passages in Galatians that foreground the lexicography of sin cracks open larger conversations within Paul's letter and the situation he addresses that can lead us toward some helpful observations.

The Vocabulary of "Sin" and the Human Plight in Galatians

Galatians 1:4

The first relevant passage appears in the opening paragraph, within Paul's wish for "grace and peace" upon his troubled and troublesome congregations in Galatia:

> Grace to you and peace from our Father God and the Lord Jesus Christ who gave himself for the sins we committed [ὑπὲρ τῶν ἁμαρτιῶν ἡμῶν][1] in order that he might rescue us out from the present, evil age according to the will of our God and Father. (Gal 1:3-4)

This is an important verse that sets the stage for much that will follow.[2] It provides the Galatian Christians with an essential reminder of their debt to Jesus such that they ought to take great care neither to "set aside God's grace" (as Paul claims *he* is careful to avoid doing in 2:21) nor to lose Christ's benefits by falling from this grace (a clear and present danger facing them, according to Paul's strong declarations of the consequences that would follow upon the wrong choice in 5:3-4). Already from the outset we find Paul concerned both with "sins" as discrete acts in regard to which some sacrificial death is necessary and with a larger cosmic framework that is experienced in some way as oppressive and from which we therefore needed "rescue."[3] This is important to note in connection with ongoing debates in Pauline theology concerning whether Paul conceives the human problem to consist of "sins" as affronts against God that require forgiveness

---

1. I read the genitive pronoun as subjective rather than possessive: the "sins" are actions we've done, not items we possess (see, further, David A. deSilva, *The Letter to the Galatians* [NICNT; Grand Rapids: Eerdmans, 2018], 118).

2. It also resonates with another credal summary found in 1 Cor 15:3, there also in connection with Christ's reconciling work (rightly, Simon Gathercole, "'Sins' in Paul" [*NTS* 64 (2018) 143-61], 159-61).

3. Caird and Hurst gave theologians a good lead in regard to investigating "sin": "What sin means to those who commit it may be seen most clearly reflected in the language of redemption: for justification, consecration, reconciliation, and redemption imply a guilt to be cancelled, a stain to be erased, an enmity to be dispelled, and a servitude to be abolished" (G. B. Caird and L. D. Hurst, *New Testament Theology* [Oxford: Clarendon, 1994], 87).

and reconciliation or "Sin" as an enslaving power from which human beings require liberation.[4]

Paul will develop quite explicitly the notion of sins as discrete acts or patterns of behavior as he speaks of the "works of the flesh" (5:19), the actions prompted by "the flesh with its passions and desires" (5:24):

> And the works born of the flesh are clearly evident: sexual immorality, impurity, shameless debauchery, idolatry, drug-induced spells, displays of enmity, strife, fanaticism, angry outbursts, self-promoting acts, dissensions, factions, acts born of envy, drunken bouts, gluttonous parties, and other things like these. (Gal 5:19-21)

These are, moreover, acts and patterns of behavior with clear consequences: "Concerning these things I tell you in advance, just as I warned you before: Those who keep on practicing such things will not inherit the kingdom of God" (5:21; see also 6:8a). "Flesh" does not signify, of course, the "meat" of our physical person. Rather, the term encapsulates those impulses, urges, and desires that lead people away from other-centered virtues toward self-gratification and self-promotion, often at the expense of others' interests and well-being, of communal harmony, or of the accomplishing of God's desires for human life and community. It is a potent force that can manifest itself in thought, word, and deed, in the yearnings of mind and soul as well as body.[5] It is not, however, an enslaving force external to the human being. Jurgen Becker expresses well the power of the "flesh": "The compulsion to give in to desire is one's own and at the same time is felt as foreign domination."[6] What Paul calls "flesh" is, in Galatians at least, a force internal to the person, even if it is not the person in the truest sense, namely that moral faculty that can recognize and resist the impulsive desires of the flesh.

---

4. The latter position was strongly promoted by E. P. Sanders (see, e.g., his *Paul and Palestinian Judaism* [Philadelphia: Fortress, 1977], 500). See the judicious discussion of the question and the evidence in Gathercole, "'Sins' in Paul." It is not simply a matter of whether Paul speaks more frequently of "sins" in the plural or "sin" in the singular (against J. D. G. Dunn, *The Theology of Paul's Letter to the Galatians* [Cambridge: Cambridge University Press, 1993], 43), since Paul often uses the singular to denote a particular transgression and not an enslaving power (rightly, Gathercole, "Sins," 154, citing Rom 4:8; 5:13b, 20; 14:23; 2 Cor 11:27) or a "pattern of life" in contrast with obedience (Gathercole, "Sins," 154, citing Rom 6:16, 18, 20).

5. deSilva, *Galatians*, 447.

6. Jurgen Becker, *Paul: Apostle to the Gentiles* (Louisville: Westminster John Knox, 1993), 392.

At the same time, Paul gives significant attention in this letter to those forces that *do* act upon the individual person from without to constrain his or her heart and practice to move in other than God-ward directions—and thus result in multiplying sins *qua* actions contrary to God's vision for God's creatures and their common life. This brings us, in Galatians, chiefly to τὰ στοιχεῖα τοῦ κόσμου. The στοιχεῖα represent the fundamental building blocks of the world, but not in the sense of the physical elements from which the physical world is constituted,[7] though this meaning does provide a close analogy. They are the organizing and regulatory principles that create the "order" that constitutes the *kosmos* to which Paul celebrates having been crucified so as to live no longer within its constraints (6:14). This is the "world" of human systems, interaction, and activity as these have taken shape in humanity's rebellion against, rather than submission to, God. The στοιχεῖα arise from human ordering and activity, the accumulated residue of human sin's effects on the environment of the sinners that "twists conditions in which others must live."[8] They represent "the systemic nature of sin," calling us to recognize "the manner in which structures embody and perpetuate harm and wrong."[9]

The στοιχεῖα are, especially, the categories that divide, order, and create hierarchy within social reality, as well as the rationales that undergird the same. Paul will name and sweep away three of these paired categories that had hitherto ordered human community and assigned priority and relative value across those categories in Gal 3:28: Jew versus Greek, slave versus free, male versus female. They are the rules and values that each child, born into and confronted with the society that had long since taken shape on the basis of such rules and values, must inevitably internalize, accept, and live by. They are the individual parts of "the way the world works," to which each child must adapt himself or herself, by which each child must be willingly constrained as his or her mind, practices, and life trajectory are shaped thereby. These regulatory principles begin outside of us but, at some point within the long process of our socialization into the world as *kosmos*, become part of us, become internal strictures within us. This is the slavery into which every person is born, and which most never recognize as such.[10]

---

7. Contra Dunn, *Theology of Paul*, 108.

8. Mark E. Biddle, "Sin," in *Dictionary of Scripture and Ethics* (eds. J. B. Green et al.; Grand Rapids: Baker Academic, 2011), 730–33, here 732.

9. Biddle, "Sin," 733.

10. This paragraph is slightly adapted from deSilva, *Galatians*, 347; for a full

The human predicament consists, for Paul in Galatians, both of sins committed and slavery endured.[11] Thus God's remedy must consist of the restoration both of righteousness and freedom.

Galatians 2:15, 17, 18

The next three occurrences of the language of "sin" and "sinner" come from the extended version of Paul's response to Peter in Syrian Antioch:

> We, Jews by nature and not sinners [ἁμαρτωλοί] from the nations . . . (Gal 2:15)

> Now, if while seeking to be set right in Christ we were found also ourselves to be sinners [ἁμαρτωλοί], then is Christ sin's servant [ἁμαρτίας διάκονος]? Heck, no! (Gal 2:17)

This says something about what sin is *not* for Paul, at least not anymore. It is *not* to be found in the neglect of those practices that maintain the separation of Jew from gentile once Jew and gentile have been reconciled to God and to one another in Christ. We could go further: sin *is* to be found now, on this side of Christ's coming, above all in the rejection of the "way out" that God the Father (1:4) has provided from this predicament through the death and resurrection of God's Son (1:4; 2:20) and provision of God's Spirit (3:2–5, 13–14; 5:13–25). "Sin" is choosing now not to align oneself with God's provision for the *re*-alignment of human beings as individuals *and* humanity as community with God's Self and God's vision for both—refusing, that is, God's provision for "rectification," the setting right, of the human situation before God. This was, far from incidentally, Paul's understanding of his own primary sin as he reflects on his own story (Gal 1:13–16; 1 Cor 15:8–10). It was not his sins against the law (in regard to which he could boast to be "blameless," Phil 3:6) but his opposition to God's Righteous One that God had to intervene to correct by "revealing his Son to me" (Gal 1:15).

In the immediate context of 2:15 and 2:17, Paul is confronting Peter in Syrian Antioch as a man who "stood condemned" (2:11)—strong

---

discussion of the subject and defense of the interpretation given here, see deSilva, *Galatians*, 348–53.

11. "Paul is a sophisticated thinker who . . . considers people both responsible, and also denizens of a universe occupied by malevolent beings" (Gathercole, "Sins," 156–57), the latter of which exercise influence upon human beings.

language indeed, calling attention to the amplitude of Peter's transgression. This transgression, however, is specifically a transgression against the solution that God has put in place and is bringing about in the community of those "in Christ." By withdrawing from table fellowship with the gentile Christians there who had been similarly reconciled to God and cleansed from their sins by the blood of Christ, and who had been similarly received into God's family as attested by their reception of God's Holy Spirit, Peter has moved against God's own currents; he has not kept walking straight in the direction of the truth that the gospel is bringing about (2:14).[12] He has taken a serious misstep by returning to a practice that suggested that the boundaries between the Jew and the Greek still had value in God's sight and needed to be observed. Even if Peter was just "putting on an act"—the language is that of theater (συνυπεκρίθησαν, τῇ ὑποκρίσει, Gal 2:13)—for the people who came from James, his shift in practice belied what God was doing in the new community of the Jews and gentiles sanctified together in Christ and by the Spirit. Paul provides explanatory commentary on 2:17 along these very lines in the immediately following verse. In what does "sin" now consist as far as the question of Jew-gentile boundaries and the Torah that legislated these boundaries are concerned? "If I erect afresh the very things that I tore down, I establish myself to be a transgressor" (παραβάτην, 2:18).[13]

The episode in Antioch incidentally offers a good case study for the interplay between sin as discrete act and sin as the result of systemic forces and predispositions that are hostile to God's purposes and interventions. Peter's cowardice, as Paul interprets the situation, led him to transgress the truth that the gospel was calling into reality; the στοιχεῖα, in the person of the human beings (the "men from James") who had been shaped by them and continued to live in line with them, created the social environment in which significant forces were being exerted upon Peter to dispose him to fail to keep walking straight in line toward the truth that the gospel was calling into reality.

12. This is how I would render the phrase ὀρθοποδοῦσιν πρὸς τὴν ἀλήθειαν τοῦ εὐαγγελίου. The preposition quite clearly indicates a direction; the genitive seems to me best understood to indicate the "producer" or "source" of the particular truth in question.

13. Similarly, for the gentile Galatian Christians to take on the liturgical observances of the Jewish calendar (4:9–10)—which in the first-century context was one element that clearly marked the Jew and set him or her apart from the gentile—was, for Paul, to participate in building up again what *God* broke down in the sending of God's Holy Spirit upon Jew and gentile together in Christ.

Galatians 3:19, 22

The next cluster of occurrences finds Paul presenting the Torah as the *non*-remedy for the sin that had taken root in all the nations, the Jewish nation as well as the gentile nations:

> Why, then, the law? It was added for the sake of transgressions [τῶν παραβάσεων χάριν] until the Seed, to whom the promise was given, should come. (Gal 3:19)

The terse phrase τῶν παραβάσεων χάριν has been quite variously interpreted. Paul's own further development of this topic in 3:23–25 seems to me to point quite clearly to the Torah's role in keeping a particular people in some degree of check in regard to transgressions, as the pedagogue kept the behavior of his minor charges in check with his close supervision and his ready stick. It might include the view that the Torah was given to make some provision for transgressions, even as the pedagogue would teach his charges to say, "I'm sorry," when they make missteps.[14]

The more relevant component is the temporary role assigned to the law in regard to transgressions. It was not the means by which God would rectify the human predicament, but the means by which God would preserve the seedbed from which the Seed was to emerge. At the same time, the law served to confirm the human predicament. Paul presents life under law as life lived under the threat of a curse—a threat that came to be realized far too often in the collective life of "Israel according to the flesh." The law as "pedagogue" in Gal 3:23–25—an oppressive but, at least, benevolent figure—gives way to the law as "slavery" in 4:24–26, akin to slavery under the στοιχεῖα (a kinship already established in 4:1–11). Pushing aside the law as potential remedy, Paul concludes that:

> Scripture shut up everything under sin [ὑπὸ ἁμαρτίαν] in order that the promise might be given on the basis of trusting Jesus to those who trust. (Gal 3:22)[15]

---

14. See further the discussion and assessment of the various options for the meaning of this phrase in deSilva, *Galatians*, 315–17.

15. I do not regard this translation of Gal 3:22 to be problematically redundant since Paul is answering two related but distinct questions throughout the central section of Galatians: *On what basis* do we arrive at God's promised, good ends for us (ἐκ πίστεως Ἰησοῦ Χριστοῦ)? *To whom* are God's good ends promised (τοῖς πιστεύουσιν)? Both answers involve "trust." Indeed, the second element of this clause—"to those who *continue to* trust" (highlighting the imperfective aspect of the substantive τοῖς πιστεύουσιν)—may also introduce the *conditions* under which those to whom God's good ends are promised

This is the closest Paul will come to the kinds of expressions familiar from Romans that speak of sin as a power that dominates, even subjugates, the human being, but the concept is not nearly so fully developed yet in Galatians. Sin is here a prison, a holding cell, not a triumphant conqueror.

At the close of this verse, Paul draws attention to the remedy for the predicament of living "under sin." We find the content of the promise to which Paul refers here earlier in Galatians, in the only other passage in the letter in which "Scripture" appears as a grammatical subject: "Scripture, seeing in advance that *God would make the nations righteous on the basis of trusting*" (3:8). This was the "good news" that Scripture murkily announced ahead of time to Abraham when it was promised to him that "all the nations will be blessed in you" (3:9; Gen 12:3; 18:18). This "blessing" turns out to be none other than the Holy Spirit, which Paul identifies as the promised good that, received through trust, would make many righteous:

> Christ redeemed us from the law's curse by becoming a curse on our behalf . . . in order that the blessing of Abraham might come to the nations—in order that we might receive the promised Spirit through faith. (Gal 3:14)[16]

This verse underscores the importance both of Christ *and* the Spirit in God's setting things right, and especially of the Spirit, which emerges as the divine force and provision for the "making right" of the nations in 5:13–25.

Galatians 6:1

The final occurrence of a word explicitly and obviously associated with "sin" appears in Paul's closing exhortations to his congregation:

> Brothers and sisters, even if a person should be caught in some trespass [ἔν τινι παραπτώματι], set about restoring such a person,

---

will see those ends, since these conditions are in question in Galatia at the time of Paul's writing. See, further, deSilva, *Galatians*, 229–37 on the translation of διὰ/ἐκ πίστεως Ἰησοῦ Χριστοῦ (Gal 2:16).

16. Paul does not make explicit the path by which he identified the giving of the Holy Spirit with the promise of Abraham. He does understand that promise to include God's "making the Gentiles righteous" (Gal 3:8), and the role of a fresh outpouring of the Holy Spirit in empowering righteousness before God is a well-established aspect of Paul's prophetic heritage (most notably, Ezek 11:19–20; 18:31; 36:26–27). Andrew Das (*Galatians* [St. Louis, MO: Concordia, 2014], 334) suggests the collocation of the pouring out the Spirit upon the "seed" of the addressees and "blessing" upon "descendants" in Isa 44:3 might also have played a role in Paul's thinking.

you in-Spirited ones, in a spirit of gentleness—maintaining vigilance over yourself, lest you also be tempted. (Gal 6:1)

Even while Paul suggests with his language ("*even* if") that trespasses should be exceptional rather than regular occurrences in the redeemed community, he makes provision for how to respond to these eventualities. It is clear once again that Paul has not lost sight of sins as discrete acts.[17] Paul also presupposes a good deal of moral autonomy on this side of having trusted Christ. As he writes at the close of this paragraph:

> Whatever a person sows, that shall he or she also reap, because the one who keeps sowing to his or her flesh will harvest destruction from the flesh, but the one who keeps sowing to the Spirit will harvest eternal life from the Spirit. (Gal 6:7-8)

Whatever else might be said of life apart from Christ and prior to receiving the Holy Spirit, Paul addresses the Galatian Christians as people in whose power it now lay to sow to the flesh or to the Spirit.

God's Remedy: The Freedom for Righteousness

In Paul's understanding, righteousness—a life characterized by alignment with God's good desires for human beings and human community—remains God's goal for humanity. Paul uses the noun δικαιοσύνη, a word denoting an ethical quality that would have been widely recognized as such (being one of the four cardinal virtues lauded by Greco-Roman ethicists), to speak of this goal in Galatians, and not δικαίωσις, as if God's remedy for human sin consisted merely in acquittal. At the climax of Paul's initial statement of his position (2:15-21), he forcefully asserts: "I'm not pushing God's grace off to the side: for if righteousness[18] comes by means of the law, Christ died for no reason" (Gal 2:21). Paul presumes that his audience will agree that Christ's death (and, intimately bound up with this, God's gracious favor) was not gratuitous and will be led to conclude that, therefore,

---

17. Gathercole ("Sins," 154 and n59) rightly stresses the importance of the synonyms of ἁμαρτία that broaden the evidence that Paul is concerned with "sins" as acts of disobedience against God's righteous standards: e.g., παράβασις (Rom 2:23; 4:15; 5:14; Gal 3:19); παράπτωμα (Rom 4:25; 5:15 [2x], 16, 17, 18, 20; 11:11, 12; 2 Cor 5:19; Gal 6:1).

18. Most English translations render δικαιοσύνη correctly here as "righteousness"; the NRSV unjustifiably renders it here as "justification" (as it does also at Rom 5:21; 2 Cor 3:9) as if Paul had written δικαίωσις (a word with this meaning with which Paul is familiar, given his use of it in Rom 4:25; 5:18) here.

righteousness does not in fact come by means of aligning oneself with the Torah. He does not, however, oppose their quest for "righteousness" here, only their contemplation of adopting a Torah-observant lifestyle on this side of the Christ-event as the means to attain it. A similar point is made just a few paragraphs later: "Is the law poised against God's promises? Heck, no! For if a law capable of giving life had been given, then righteousness would indeed have been on the basis of law" (Gal 3:21). The implication is not only that the law was *incapable* of giving life and, thus, not the basis for embodying righteousness in God's sight, but that God's promises will indeed result in life *and* righteousness.

Paul makes this explicit still a few more paragraphs later in this argument: "For it is *we* who, by the Spirit and on the basis of trusting, await the righteousness [δικαιοσύνη] for which we hope" (Gal 5:5).[19] The "we" here stands in contrast to another group, from whom Paul hopes his converts will now decisively distance themselves, who seek righteousness by means of alignment with the stipulations of Torah. Paul nevertheless very positively and clearly affirms the goal of "righteousness" as one indeed to be sought—but by the right path. Christ died in order to make possible what the law had not made possible, namely for human beings to live righteously and, thus, to become righteous in God's sight rather than remain sinners.[20] It was a death "for our sins" (Gal 1:4), bringing acquittal for past transgressions, but it was also a death that secured for those who trust Jesus the provisions necessary for a life of righteousness—a life that would be acquitted as righteous *indeed* by the just and impartial Judge of all.[21] Further evidence that Paul expected trusting Jesus (and all this entailed) to lead to "righteousness" comes from the contrary statement in 5:19-21:

> And the works born of the flesh are clearly evident: sexual immorality, impurity, shameless debauchery, idolatry, drug-induced spells, displays of enmity, strife, fanaticism, angry outbursts,

---

19. I understand the genitive to express the object of the verbal noun "hope" (with NIV; J. D. G. Dunn, *The Epistle to the Galatians* [Peabody: Hendrickson, 1993], 270), though it may also be taken as a genitive of apposition with the same effect (as does Ernest deWitt Burton, *A Critical and Exegetical Commentary on the Epistle to the Galatians* [New York: Scribners, 1920], 279).

20. So also Burton, *Galatians*, 278; Gorman, *Inhabiting*, 72; Dunn, *Galatians*, 269-70.

21. A number of Pauline scholars have come to realize that the apostle had "a stronger theology of final vindication on the basis of an obedient life than is evident in most analyses of Pauline theology" (Simon Gathercole, "A Law unto Themselves: The Gentiles in Romans 2.14-15 Revisited" (*JSNT* 24 [2002] 27-49, 48).

self-promoting acts, dissensions, factions, acts born of envy, drunken bouts, gluttonous parties, and other things like these. Concerning these things I tell you in advance, just as I warned you before: Those who keep on practicing such things will not inherit the kingdom of God.

The ongoing presence of sinful behaviors disqualifies one from God's kingdom (compare Gal 6:7-8, where the same leaves a person to rot in the grave rather than enter into eternal life). God has intervened in the life of the believer so as to effect a radical change in orientation and practice. The sins—the self-serving actions that reflected non-alignment with God's good desires for human life and human community—that formerly characterized his or her life, necessitating the self-giving death of Jesus, no longer have any place in the believer's life, which is instead to be characterized by the virtues identified as the Spirit's "fruit" (5:22-23) or, in a word, "righteousness."

This righteousness takes shape within human beings as *Christ* takes shape in—as Christ comes to life and increasingly lives *through and among*—those human beings individually and collectively. In a moment of disarming transparency, Paul speaks of his own experience of discovering life and righteousness:

> Through the law,[22] I died to the law in order that I might live to God. I have been crucified together with Christ. It's not me living any longer, but Christ is living in me. What I'm now living in the flesh, I live by trusting the Son of God who loved me and handed himself over on my behalf. (Gal 2:19-20)

Experiencing Christ's death as a death "for me," as an expression of the love of the Son of God "for me," is a crucial element in this process of deliverance. It is this radical act of love "for me" that arrested Paul and changed the entire orientation and direction of his life, such that, in a fair return, Paul gives the remainder of his own life "in the flesh" (by which, here, he means "in the body") over to Christ and, in so doing, over to the righteousness that the Righteous One will work in and through him.[23] The new life that

---

22. How a dying *to* the law could also come about *through* the law is a topic taken up in 3:11-14, 19-25; 4:4-5). Paul speaks here from his own perspective as a Jewish Christ-follower; Paul's statements later about dying to the flesh and dying to the world (both, again, using the distinctive imagery of crucifixion; 5:24; 6:14) will speak more directly to the experience of gentile Christ-followers among his audience(s).

23. Troels Engberg-Pedersen (*Paul and the Stoics* [Louisville: Westminster John

Paul lives (2:20), the new life that the law could not initiate (3:21), is the life of the living Christ taking on flesh in, so as to live through, the redeemed person.[24] Paul describes it as a "coming alive to God" in a decisively new way. This is the "making alive" that also brings "righteousness" (3:21).[25] It is the essential act of "new creation" that God is bringing about (6:15), the perfect restoration of the divine image in the redeemed by virtue of the perfect image-bearer of God, namely the Son of God, coming to life in the person.[26] It is also the "gift of God" that Paul refuses now to set aside, as if such "righteousness" as Christ has brought to life for Paul and in Paul could have come by any other means. This is the paradigmatic experience in Paul's own life that he passionately desires for his converts as well: "my little children, with regard to whom I am again suffering labor pains until Christ takes shape in you!" (4:19).[27]

Knox, 2000], 145) captures this exchange of grace and response to grace beautifully: "Christ has the very specific role in the Christ event of *enabling* human beings to *respond* to the event *in the way they were meant to by God*. When Christ, the mediator, bent down in love and gave *himself* up 'for my sake' ([Gal] 2:20), that is, by *his* suffering (vicariously) in order to bring '*me*' help in a situation which was negative for '*me*' (cf. 1:4 and 3:13), then "I" *responded in kind* and through that response came to live for God and so 'live'" (italics original).

24. On the importance of this verse to an understanding of Pauline theology, see Scott Shauf, "Galatians 2:20 in Context," *NTS* 52 (2006) 86–101, and Michael Gorman, *Inhabiting the Cruciform God* (Grand Rapids: Eerdmans, 2009), 63–86.

25. "Making alive" clearly indicates something more than biological existence, which all the addressees enjoyed both before and after coming to trust in Jesus and receiving the Holy Spirit (see also Ronald Fung, *Galatians* [Grand Rapids: Eerdmans, 1988], 162–63; Mark Seifrid, *Christ Our Righteousness: Paul's Theology of Justification* [Downers Grove, IL: InterVarsity, 2000], 82; and Engberg-Pedersen, *Paul and the Stoics*, 170).

26. This lends credence to Biddle's suggestion that "Paul's understanding of sin involves the assertion, explicit in Rom. 3:23, that human beings universally 'miss the mark' (*hamart-*) by 'falling short' // (*hyster-*) of the 'glory of God' (a near synonym in Paul for 'image of God' [see 1 Cor. 11:7; cf. 2 Cor. 3:18; 4:4, 6])" (Biddle, "Sin," 731–32). See also R. R. Reno, "Sin, Doctrine of," in *Dictionary for Theological Interpretation of the Bible* (ed. K. Vanhoozer et al.; Grand Rapids: Baker Academic, 2005), 748–51, 750: "The universality of sin is not peripheral to human identity. Sin shapes life. To use Paul's language, sin enslaves, dictating the direction of human life.... For this reason, the very identity of the sinner is defined by sin, and that identity must be destroyed. Echoing Paul again, the old man [sic] must die and a new man must be born if one is to turn from a life defined by sin to a life of righteousness (Rom. 6:6–8)."

27. The theme of transformation into Christ-likeness as the path to life, resurrection, or glory is also explicit in Rom 8:29; Phil 3:8–11; and 2 Cor 3:18. See also discussion in J. Louis Martyn, *Galatians* (AB 33A; Garden City, NY: Doubleday, 1997), 425, 430–31; D. A. deSilva, *Transformation: The Heart of Paul's Gospel* (Bellingham, WA: Lexham, 2014),

The Holy Spirit is the agent of this transformation, the "best gift divine" secured by Jesus in his death for those who trust Jesus's mediation (3:2-5). Christ takes shape in the believer as he or she walks more and more closely in line with the Spirit, yielding less and less to the impulses of the "flesh," those self-serving and self-promoting desires and responses that lead one away from "righteousness" before God. By the Spirit we participate in Christ's death, dying both to enslaving powers and to our own "flesh with its passions and desires" (2:19; 5:24; 6:14); by the Spirit we come alive to God in a hitherto unimagined way (2:19-20; 5:22-24). Paul describes this new life as the freedom for which Christ set us free in his death (5:1)—a freedom won for us at such cost that we dare not cast it aside. This freedom is not license to sin (5:13-14); rather, this freedom is the liberation from all the drives and forces, whether internal to our psyches or socially and externally imposed, that had hitherto disposed us to sin and hindered living righteously before God.

Paul is not interested merely in our deliverance from the consequences of sin, but in our deliverance from the internal bifurcation of the person that leaves us bound to continue in sin.[28] And he is entirely optimistic about the Holy Spirit's power to achieve God's good ends in us: "Keep walking by the Spirit and there's no way you'll make what the flesh craves a reality" (5:16).[29] Paul's emphasis on faith or trust as the path to righteousness includes faith or trust that the provision secured by Jesus for all who trust him (3:2-5, 13-14; 4:6-7)—the Holy Spirit—is indeed sufficient to bring Christ's followers to the place where they will stand well-aligned with God's righteous standards. Attaining righteousness remains the result of God's grace, since it is God's own self that both empowers and directs righteous living in the Christ-follower through the Holy Spirit.[30] The Christ-follower

10-14, 44-66.

28. This is rightly stressed by Jurgen Becker, *Paul: Apostle to the Gentiles* (Louisville: Westminster John Knox, 1993), 390.

29. The second half of this verse uses the "emphatic future denial" construction. The RSV and NRSV mistakenly render this as a second command ("and do not gratify") rather than an assured result ("and there's no way you'll gratify"). Michael Bird describes Paul's thought here with characteristic clarity: "Paul's anthropological pessimism about the human inability to keep the law is matched only by his pneumatological optimism that Spirit-empowered persons will be able to fulfill the requirements of the law" (*The Saving Righteousness of God: Studies on Paul, Justification, and the New Perspective* [Milton Keynes: Paternoster, 2007], 173).

30. The image of "fruit" subtly keeps in focus the fact that it is the *Spirit* that produces the virtuous orientations and practices that constitute righteousness.

need simply "continue to fall in step" (στοιχῶμεν, 5:25) with the Spirit, living out the reality of his or her co-crucifixion with Christ to all the forces of ungodliness and his or her coming alive with Christ to the new life, the Spirit-led life.[31] The challenge, of course, is consistently *choosing* thus to "keep sowing to the Spirit" with a view to the Spirit's harvest: "eternal life" (6:7–8).[32]

Paul, as we have noted already, is also very well aware of the external aspect of our liberation. Christ died to pull us out from the matrix—indeed, the mire—of the present evil age, the *stoicheia*-shaped life with its regulations and limitations, and to create for us a spiritual and social space—the space defined as "in Christ"—wherein the Spirit can bring order to our own unruly wills and affections *and* order our common life. Indeed, the death of Jesus is not explicated in this letter in terms of atonement, reconciliation, or cleansing; it is explicated in terms of rescue and liberation *from* a life defined by one set of conditions (and preconditions) *for* a different life defined by quite other conditions. Christ's death for the believer invites the believer not only to die to "the flesh with its passions and cravings" (5:24), but also "to the world" (κόσμῳ, 6:14)—that is, to the ordering of life and human community determined and constrained by "the regulatory principles of the world" (τὰ στοιχεῖα τοῦ κόσμου, 4:3) that characterizes the life of the old humanity that is not "in Christ" and keeps people in ideological and systemic bondage to the structures of a fallen human community.

Conclusion

Paul's analysis of the human predicament is, as is appropriate to the subject matter, complex. On the one hand, he acknowledges that the most fundamental problem is that each one of us has affronted the Creator and Sustainer God by disregarding God's righteous standards for God's creatures' hearts and practice. Simply put, we have *sinned*, and the record of these sins stands as a testimony to our ingratitude and rebellion. On the other hand, Paul acknowledges that the individual human being finds himself or herself at the mercy of coercive pressures to conform not to the righteousness of

---

31. See also N. T. Wright (*Justification: God's Plan and Paul's Vision* [Downers Grove, IL: IVP Academic, 2009], 189): "The Spirit enables the Christian ... freely to become that which is pleasing to God."

32. See, on this point, J. M. G. Barclay, *Obeying the Truth: Paul's Ethics in Galatia* (Minneapolis: Fortress, 1991), 226–30.

God, but to the ordering of the world established by the collective sin and rebellion of generations of human beings (the social and systemic pressures that Paul calls slavery to the "regulatory principles of the world," τὰ στοιχεῖα τοῦ κόσμου, 4:3) and to the disordered desires and impulses of our own hearts (the "passions of the flesh" that are experienced as both internal to us and as "foreign domination").[33]

God's remedy involves reconciliation, the restoration of righteousness, and rescue from the forces that conspire against that restoration. The first element, reconciliation, is not emphasized in Galatians, though it is present *in nuce* in the kerygmatic formula concerning Christ's death "for the sins we committed" (1:4) and perhaps also in the "exchange curse" of 3:13. More prominent in Galatians is the attention Paul gives to the restoration of righteousness before God, the hope that is attained by trusting Jesus and the gift secured for his followers by Jesus—the Holy Spirit, who brings with him the possibility of freedom from the oppressive drag of the "passions of the flesh" and, thus, the possibility of walking in righteousness as the Spirit produces his fruit in believers (5:22–24), as the Spirit brings Christ to life within and to live through each believer (2:20; 4:19). As the community orders its steps by the Spirit, its members experience freedom from the world's way of ordering human life (the coercive pressures of τὰ στοιχεῖα τοῦ κόσμου) and discover the freedom of life "in Christ," where the lines drawn by τὰ στοιχεῖα no longer constrain and construct—where there is no longer "Jew nor Greek, slave nor free, not 'male and female,'" but all are one in Christ Jesus (3:28).

---

33. Becker, *Paul*, 392.

8

Dead in Your Trespasses: Sin as Infraction and Sphere of Power in Colossians and Ephesians

John K. Goodrich

It is significant that the notion of sin as a power or force is missing from Ephesians.[1]

Paul regards man's state as a contradiction of the sonship for which he is eternally ordained. He is under a spell. He is living under tyranny. His own actions, his παραπτώματα, his trespasses, are the explanation for this state, and it amounts to the same thing if we say that the actions themselves constitute the bondage, the chains which hold him.[2]

SIN TERMINOLOGY, THOUGH LIMITED in frequency, is central to the message of both Colossians and Ephesians. The concept of sin, to be sure, surfaces in these letters in places well beyond the occurrences of explicit sin language. But even if this were not so, the terms ἁμαρτία and παράπτωμα bear a theological weight in Colossians and Ephesians that is disproportionate to their few usages and to the limited attention they have received from contemporary scholarship. It should not be surprising, therefore, that close

---

1. Andrew T. Lincoln, *Ephesians* (WBC 42; Nashville: Word, 1990), 29.
2. Karl Barth, *The Epistle to the Ephesians* (ed. R. D. Nelson; trans. R. M. Wright; Grand Rapids: Baker Academic, 2017), 105.

study of sin terminology in Colossians and Ephesians repays the efforts of the careful exegete, providing fresh insight into the intriguing and diverse ways that Paul conceives of the human plight, to say nothing of the different ways he talks about its divine solution.[3] What we find in these letters is that Paul's use of sin language is polyvalent. As is shown in this essay, sin is a way of referring not only to moral-religious infractions, but also to a sphere of power that traps and controls its occupants. Both of these senses can be present in a single occurrence of a term, and both find their remedy in the person and work of Jesus Christ, who not only provides forgiveness for wrongdoing but also freedom from sin's grip.

Sin as Moral-Religious Infraction

The noun "sin" (ἁμαρτία) occurs only twice in Colossians and Ephesians, once in each letter, and in both instances the term appears in the plural. This stands in contrast to its use in Romans, where the singular form predominates and is employed almost exclusively to refer to an enslaving power. In Col 1:14, Paul announces that "in [Christ] we have redemption, the forgiveness of sins" (ἐν ᾧ ἔχομεν τὴν ἀπολύτρωσιν, τὴν ἄφεσιν τῶν ἁμαρτιῶν). Likewise, in Eph 2:1 Paul asserts that "you also were dead in your trespasses and sins" (καὶ ὑμᾶς ὄντας νεκροὺς τοῖς παραπτώμασιν καὶ ταῖς ἁμαρτίαις ὑμῶν).[4] The use of the plural noun ἁμαρτίαι, its attribution to individual people through the personal pronoun ὑμῶν (Eph 2:1), its coupling with παραπτώματα (Eph 2:1), its stated remedy as forgiveness (ἄφεσις, Col 1:14), and the use of the verbal form in Eph 4:26 for immoral behavior (μὴ ἁμαρτάνετε) together suggest that Paul conceives of ἁμαρτία in both Col 1:14 and Eph 2:1, *in the first place*, not as a power but as a moral-religious infraction.

This inference is supported by the way "trespasses" (παραπτώματα) is used interchangeably with "sins" (ἁμαρτίαι) elsewhere in Colossians and Ephesians. For example, while παραπτώματα joins ἁμαρτίαι in Eph 2:1, a similar clause in Col 2:13 attributes the spiritual death of Paul's readers to their participation "in trespasses and in the uncircumcision of [their]

---

3. Although Colossians and Ephesians are among the disputed Pauline epistles, I refer to the author as Paul out of convenience, realizing that while plausible arguments can and have be made in defense of Pauline authorship, such is often doubted in critical scholarship.

4. All translations are my own.

flesh" (καὶ ὑμᾶς νεκροὺς ὄντας [ἐν] τοῖς παραπτώμασιν καὶ τῇ ἀκροβυστίᾳ τῆς σαρκὸς ὑμῶν). The dative τοῖς παραπτώμασιν communicates in Col 2:13 what is meant by the expanded phrase τοῖς παραπτώμασιν καὶ ταῖς ἁμαρτίαις in Eph 2:1. Moreover, Paul's twin references elsewhere to "the forgiveness of *trespasses*" (χαρισάμενος ἡμῖν πάντα τὰ παραπτώματα, Col 2:13; τὴν ἄφεσιν τῶν παραπτωμάτων, Eph 1:7), rather than to the forgiveness of *sins* (Col 1:14), demonstrates that the apostle is comfortable in both epistles using παραπτώματα and ἁμαρτίαι interchangeably to refer to moral-religious infractions. Ostensibly, then, in Col 1:14 and Eph 2:1, ἁμαρτίαι is shorthand for what Paul means elsewhere by "evil deeds" (οἱ ἔργοι οἱ πονηροί, Col 1:21), "disobedience" (ἀπείθεια, Eph 5:6; cf. Col 3:6), and "(former) practices" (πράξεις, Col 3:9), including the many vices enumerated in the paraenetic sections of these respective letters (Col 3:5, 8–9; Eph 4:17—5:20).[5]

If the above preliminary sketch of sins and trespasses is correct, then the first plight of humanity worth noting is indebtedness to God. The accumulation of trespasses, the apostle remarks, is tantamount to the Colossians being issued "a certificate of debt against [them] because of regulations" (τὸ καθ' ἡμῶν χειρόγραφον τοῖς δόγμασιν).[6] A certificate of debt (χειρόγραφον), Julien Ogereau explains, "generally designated a document recording some form of credit operation, which thereby placed the debtor under a formal, legal obligation to repay whatever was due."[7] In the case of Paul's readers, this certificate "is opposed to [them]" (ὃ ἦν ὑπεναντίον ἡμῖν) because it itemizes the violations or debts that disqualify them from being in right standing before God. This includes breaking regulations (δόγματα, 2:14; δογματίζω, 2:20) that arise from "the divinely decreed ordering of cosmos and society," notably the Law of Moses (cf. Eph 2:15).[8]

The second plight of unbelievers, which arises due to their debt, is their estrangement from God. Their infractions have created hostility between humanity and its creator. As Paul diagnoses the problem in Col 1:21,

---

5. Ernest Best, "Dead in Trespasses and Sins (Eph. 2.1)," *JSNT* 13 (1981) 9–25, at 12.

6. The dative τοῖς δόγμασιν is probably best taken as causal (e.g., Eduard Lohse, Colossians [Hermeneia; Minneapolis: Fortress, 1971], 109–10).

7. Julien M. Ogereau, "Χειρόγραφον in Colossians 2:14: The Contribution of Epigraphy to the Philology of the New Testament," in *Epigraphical Evidence Illustrating Paul's Letter to the Colossians* (eds. J. J. Verheyden et al.; WUNT 411; Tübingen: Mohr Siebeck, 2018), 93–122, at 101.

8. James D. G. Dunn, *The Epistles to the Colossians and to Philemon* (NIGTC; Grand Rapids: Eerdmans, 1996), 165.

"you . . . were once alienated and hostile in mind, in evil deeds" (cf. Eph 4:18). Moreover, because of their rebellious actions and estranged status, unbelievers have "no inheritance in the kingdom of Christ and of God" (Eph 5:5). In fact, "on account of these the wrath of God is coming upon the sons of disobedience" (Eph 5:6; cf. 2:3; Col 3:6). Thus, the plight of unbelieving humanity, while beginning with sinful behavior and resulting in separation from God, also entails a punitive consequence. Rather than enjoying the blessing of eschatological inheritance in God's long-awaited kingdom, those who remain culpable for their sins will experience God's justice. The nature of future divine retribution lacks clear elucidation in Colossians and Ephesians, though the profusion of darkness and death imagery throughout these letters leaves a sufficiently negative impression (Col 1:13; 2:13; Eph 2:1; 5:8, 14).

Some means of peace and reconciliation is therefore required on behalf of sinful humanity, and this is precisely what is provided in Christ. Those who were once estranged, Christ "has now reconciled in the body of his flesh through death, to present [them] holy and blameless and irreproachable in his presence" (Col 1:22). The mechanics of Christ's conciliatory work are not explained here in detail, yet they are implied in the immediately prior verse, where reconciliation and peace are said to have been made "by the blood of his cross" (Col 1:20). Or, as Paul puts it in Ephesians, Christ has "reconcile[d] both [Jews and Gentiles] in one body to God *through the cross, killing the hostility* in him" (Eph 2:16; cf. 1:7).[9] In light of the impending wrath destined for unbelievers, it is difficult to conceive of the death of Jesus in these verses as operating in any sense other than by means of substitution. The penalty sinners deserved was satisfied through the vicarious death of Jesus. This is made more explicit in Eph 5:2, where Paul asserts that "Christ loved us and gave himself for us [παρέδωκεν ἑαυτὸν ὑπὲρ ἡμῶν], an offering and sacrifice to God for a fragrant aroma." The phrase ὑπὲρ ἡμῶν in Eph 5:2 is key, for it indicates that Christ's *death* (his "giving himself") was *for* us, *on behalf of* us—that is, in place of *our death*. As Simon Gathercole shows (in the parallel in Rom 5:8), "the death 'for' another is not merely a death 'for the benefit of' another—'for their

---

9. Although "the hostility" (ἡ ἔχθρα) is between the circumcised and uncircumcised in Eph 2:14, the hostility mentioned in 2:16 is likely between God and humanity, since the reconciliation that takes place is "to God" (τῷ θεῷ). This same vertical dimension is emphasized in the ensuing verses, as the proclamation of peace is made separately "to you who were far off" and "to those who were near" (2:17), resulting in access for each group "to the father" (πρὸς τὸν πατέρα, 2:18).

sake' in a general sense. Nor is it a death *with* them. Rather, it is ... a 'doom-averting death,' a death that averts death."[10] Fleming Rutledge agrees: "The accursed, Godforsaken death suffered by Jesus was, in some way that we cannot fully articulate, the death that should have been ours, a death under the cursing voice of the Law wielded as a weapon by the Power of Sin."[11]

Thus, the enmity and estrangement between God and humanity has been abolished through the substitutionary death of Jesus, resulting in both the forgiveness of sins (Col 1:14; 3:13; Eph 1:7; 4:32) and the mending of divine and human relationships (Col 1:20, 22; Eph 2:11–18). It is therefore by means of Christ absorbing the consequence for sins as moral-religious infractions that people can avoid the coming day of God's judgment (Col 3:6; Eph 5:6) and, in the light of which, anticipate "the day of redemption" (Eph 4:30).

Sin as Sphere of Power

The above account, however, is not the full story of sins in Colossians and Ephesians. While trespasses and sins should be understood in the first place as the cause and instrument of at least one dimension of the human predicament, they also constitute the unredeemed condition itself. Humans violate ordinances and are thereby alienated from God, yet their unredeemed state also results in continued participation *in* said trespasses, as both epistles make sufficiently clear. In Col 2:13 and Eph 2:1, Paul's multivalent use of the dative τοῖς παραπτώμασιν (καὶ ταῖς ἁμαρτίαις) conveys not only the *cause* and *instrument* that brought about the spiritual death of unbelievers; it also indicates the *sphere* in which this mortality is experienced.[12] By vir-

---

10. Simon Gathercole, *Defending Substitution: An Essay on the Atonement in Paul* (Grand Rapids: Baker Academic, 2015), 106–7 (original emphasis).

11. Fleming Rutledge, *The Crucifixion: Understanding the Death of Jesus* (Grand Rapids: Eerdmans, 2015), 531.

12. Lincoln, *Ephesians*, 93: "Trespasses and sins both bring about the condition of death and characterize the existence of those who are spiritually dead." For "in sin" as a sphere or realm of power, see Stephen E. Fowl, *Ephesians: A Commentary* (NTL; Louisville: Westminster John Knox, 2012), 68; Harold W. Hoehner, *Ephesians: An Exegetical Commentary* (Grand Rapids: Baker, 2002), 308; John Eadie, *A Commentary on the Greek Text of the Epistle of Paul to the Ephesians* (2nd ed.; New York: Robert Carter and Bros., 1861), 122. Markus Barth suggests the trespasses and sins "are at the same time the cause, the instrument, the manifestation, the realm, and the consequence of death" (*Ephesians 1–3: A New Translation with Introduction and Commentary* [AB 34; Garden City, NY: Doubleday, 1974], 213). For strictly the dative of sphere, see Benjamin L. Merkle,

tue of this locative reading, "trespasses (and sins)" constitute an inescapable prison that confines people to disobedience. Unbelievers remain, as Paul Foster amplifies the phrase, "*trapped* in [their] trespasses."[13]

This spherical notion of sin is more explicitly conveyed by way of the preposition ἐν in Col 3:7 and Eph 2:2. In the Colossians discourse, Paul begins by instructing his readers to "put to death" (νεκρώσατε) their "earthly members" (τὰ μέλη τὰ ἐπὶ τῆς γῆς, 3:5a). The term τὰ μέλη refers to those parts of the human anatomy closely associated with sinful activity.[14] This is apparent through the way the apostle immediately identifies (by way of metonymy) these bodily members with a host of ethical vices ("fornication, impurity, passion, evil desire, and greed, which is idolatry," 3:5b), "on account of which [δι' ἅ] God's wrath is coming" (3:6). With these vices still in view, Paul next asserts that his readers "also once *walked in* them, when [they] *lived in* them" (ἐν οἷς καὶ ὑμεῖς περιεπατήσατέ ποτε, ὅτε ἐζῆτε ἐν τούτοις, 3:7).

The concept of "walking" in Colossians, as in the rest of the Jewish halakhic tradition, conveys, on the one hand, the idea of human behavior, whether acceptable or unacceptable to God (e.g., Lev 18:3–4; Bar 1:18). However, the abundance of spatial language in Colossians introduces a modification to the scriptural idiom of walking, such that the expression here implies not only a *manner of conduct* but a *sphere of control*, with the

---

Ephesians (Exegetical Greek Guide to the New Testament; Nashville: B&H Academic, 2016), 53; William J. Larkin, *Ephesians: A Handbook on the Greek Text* (Baylor Handbook on the Greek New Testament; Waco, TX: Baylor University Press, 2009), 27; Daniel B. Wallace, *Greek Grammar beyond the Basics: An Exegetical Syntax of the New Testament* (Grand Rapids: Zondervan, 1997), 155. Against John Muddiman, who suggests that νεκροὺς τοῖς παραπτώμασιν is a dative of respect ("dead to trespasses"; cf. Rom 6:11) and is thus "more naturally understood to be a positive idea, i.e. delivered from them through union with the crucified Christ" (*The Epistle to the Ephesians* [BNTC; Peabody: Hendrickson, 2001], 101). However, such a reading makes for an awkward recurrence of καὶ ὄντας ἡμᾶς νεκροὺς τοῖς παραπτώμασιν in 2:5 and disregards the clear pattern of καὶ ὑμᾶς ὄντας established in Colossians (1:21; 2:13), where the readers' previous way of life is in view.

13. Paul Foster, *Colossians* (BNTC; London: T. & T. Clark, 2016), 268 (emphasis added).

14. It is noteworthy that all of the other 28 occurrences of μέλος in the Pauline corpus have an anatomical sense, whether literal or metaphorical. Thus, Dunn maintains, "the person's interaction with the wider world as through organs and limbs is what is in view.... Despite the power of their having been identified with Christ in his death, there were still things, parts of their old lives, habits of hand and mind, which tied them 'to the earth' and hindered the outworking of the 'mind set on what is above' [3:2]" (*Colossians and to Philemon*, 212).

object of the preposition serving as the constraining force. In the case of Col 3:7, the two grammatical objects of the preposition ἐν are two pronouns, οἷς and τούτοις, but the antecedents of the pronouns are the vices from 3:5—οἷς and τούτοις (3:7) refer back to ἅ (3:6), which refers back to τὰ μέλη (3:5), which is related (by metonymy) to the vices.[15] Thus, the Colossian readers are said to have once *walked and lived in the sphere of sinful vices* (cf. ἐν τοῖς ἔργοις τοῖς πονηροῖς, Col 1:21).[16]

This much is further demonstrated in the ensuing parenesis. In 3:8, Paul instructs his readers to "lay aside" (ἀπόθεσθε) not only those vices mentioned in 3:5, but in fact "all (such evil) things" (τὰ πάντα), including "anger, wrath, malice, slander, obscene speech from your mouth." And if that were not enough, after warning his readers no longer to lie to one another, he exhorts them to *"strip away* the old person with its practices" (ἀπεκδυσάμενοι τὸν παλαιὸν ἄνθρωπον σὺν ταῖς πράξεσιν αὐτοῦ). The imagery of these metaphorical demands—"laying aside" (ἀπόθεσθε, 3:8) and "stripping away" (ἀπεκδυσάμενοι, 3:9)—suggests that Paul does not conceptualize these vices as merely discrete practices (cf. πράξεσιν, 3:9) performed by perfectly autonomous beings. Instead, they constitute a part of the unredeemed condition that has attached itself to both individual and community and managed thereby to restrict the thought patterns, affections, and behaviors of the former self.

---

15. Admittedly, the phrase "on the sons of disobedience" (ἐπὶ τοὺς υἱοὺς τῆς ἀπειθείας, 3:6b) is attested in some manuscripts, which calls into question the antecedent of at least τούτοις in 3:7. However, the shorter reading of 3:6b represented in my exegesis is supported by P46 and B, and according to Dunn, is preferred by "almost all commentators" (*Colossians and to Philemon*, 210). Some suggest that the shorter reading creates a tautology with the pronouns in 3:7. Yet, as David W. Pao shows, 3:7 forms a chiasm with developing clauses: "[I]n context a progression of thought seems clear. In light of 2:6, the metaphor of walking provides a general context in reference to lifestyle and behavior, while 'living' points back to 2:20, where Paul makes a distinction between living in the world and dying to it with Christ" (*Colossians and Philemon* [ZECNT; Grand Rapids: Zondervan, 2012], 222). Cf. Rom 6:1–4. If, however, ἐπὶ τοὺς υἱοὺς τῆς ἀπειθείας is authentic, then only ἐν οἷς refers to the vices, while ἐν τούτοις refers to "the sons of disobedience" ("when you lived *among them*"); see, e.g., R. Mcl. Wilson, *Colossians and Philemon* (ICC; London: T. & T. Clark, 2005), 248. On either reading, ἐν οἷς refers to the realm of the vices.

16. For ἐν τοῖς ἔργοις τοῖς πονηροῖς (Col 1:21) as indicating sphere, see Scot McKnight, *The Letter to the Colossians* (NICNT; Grand Rapids: Eerdmans, 2018), 172: "I take 'in your evil deeds' to be the sphere they inhabit." Cf. T. K. Abbott, *A Critical and Exegetical Commentary on the Epistles to the Ephesians and to the Colossians* (ICC; Edinburgh: T. & T. Clark, 1897), 225.

Thus, in Col 3 believers are instructed to exit what Lightfoot called "this atmosphere of sin,"[17] by removing it and its attendant vices like an old piece of clothing. In its place, they must enter into the realm of the Spirit by putting on the new self through union with Christ (3:10). This happens as believers die with Christ (3:3) and are raised and seated with Christ (3:1). When believers die with Christ, so must their earthly members die, together with their vices (3:5), their old self, and their evil practices (3:9). And when believers are raised with Christ, so too must their moral reasoning be directed towards things above (3:2) as their lives begin to be patterned after the image of Christ their creator (3:10). Thus, instead of continuing to "walk *in sin*" (ἐν οἷς καὶ ὑμεῖς περιεπατήσατέ ποτε, 3:7), believers must now "walk *in him*" (ἐν αὐτῷ περιπατεῖτε, 2:6). By doing so, the Colossians will begin to don the virtues that accompany this new sphere of existence—namely, compassion, kindness, humility, gentleness, patience, grace, and above all, love (3:12–14).[18]

The use of ἐν in the portrayal of sin as a sphere of power also surfaces in Eph 2. As the apostle advances from 2:1 to 2:2, Paul asserts that trespasses and sins cannot be reduced to the disobedient actions unbelievers once committed or the habitual patterns that defined their prior behavior.[19]

---

17. J. B. Lightfoot, *Saint Paul's Epistle to the Colossians and to Philemon: A Revised Text with Introductions, Notes, and Dissertations* (London: Macmillan and Co., 1875), 279.

18. Cf. John Paul Heil, *Colossians: Encouragement to Walk in All Wisdom as Holy Ones in Christ* (Early Christianity and Its Literature; Atlanta: Society of Biblical Literature, 2010), 143: "That they [sic] once 'walked' (περιεπατήσατέ) in these immoral ways (3:7) stands in contrast to the exhortation that they are to 'go on walking' (περιπατεῖτε) in the Christ, Jesus the Lord, whom they received (2:6)."

19. Against F. F. Bruce, who suggests that the notion of walking in sins implies merely that "these were the things that characterized you" (*The Epistles to the Colossians, to Philemon, and to the Ephesians* [NICNT; Grand Rapids: Eerdmans 1984], 280). Best concurs: "Unlike τὰ παραπτώματα which relates to individual sins 'the uncircumcision of their flesh' refers to a condition, the condition of their not being Christian. For this reason the dative [τῇ ἀκροβυστίᾳ, Col 2:13] cannot be causal or instrumental but is rather one descriptive of circumstances, and this will apply also to τοῖς παραπτώμασιν. . . . [W]e can no more here [in Eph 2:1] than in Col. 2.13 take the dative 'trespasses and sins' in a purely causal manner. Sins and trespasses cause death but the life (if the paradox may be pardoned) which continues thereafter is characterised by sins and trespasses: the lifestyle of the dead is one of sins and transgressions" ("Dead in Trespasses and Sins," 12, 19–20). This would be consistent with how Paul often uses the idiom περιπατέω + ἐν. However, it is also true that the primary denotive force of the expression is not manner but locale or sphere. What is conveyed in such instances is movement along a particular pathway constituted by a particular moral norm (LXX Lev 18:3–4; John 8:12; Eph 4:1;

Sins in this passage, like in Col 3:7, comprise the *realm* "in which [unbelievers] formerly walked" (ἐν αἷς ποτε περιεπατήσατε, 2:2).[20] As in Colossians, the pervasiveness of spatial language in Ephesians transforms the idiom of walking from a metaphor describing conduct to an image implying control—in this case, people are imprisoned *in* the sphere of their sins.

The sphere of sins, however, need not be a permanent place or mode of existence. Those who are "dead *in* sins" and "walk *in* sins" find their remedy in being "made alive with Christ" (συνεζωοποίησεν τῷ Χριστῷ), "raised with [Christ]" (συνήγειρεν), and "seated with [Christ]" (συνεκάθισεν), all of which occurs "*in* Christ Jesus" (ἐν Χριστῷ Ἰησοῦ, 2:5–6). Each of these salvific blessings is made possible through the resurrection and exaltation of Jesus Christ (1:20), in whom humans must invest faith (2:8) and to whom they must be united, by the Spirit (2:18, 22), in order to participate in Christ's heavenly rule.[21] Indeed, it is only through this mystical union with the Messiah that believers are "created *in* Christ Jesus [κτισθέντες ἐν Χριστῷ Ἰησοῦ] for good works which God prepared beforehand, that [they] should walk *in* them [ἵνα ἐν αὐτοῖς περιπατήσωμεν]" (2:10). The remedy to an existence in the sphere of sins, therefore, is found in being relocated into the exalted sphere of Christ Jesus, where new creation is actuated and the power to walk in the sphere of good works is made available.

Sin and Its Remedy in Ephesians 2:1–10	
Before/Below	After/Above
Dead (2:1, 5)	Alive (2:5); raised up (2:6); seated (2:6)
In/by/because of transgressions and sins (2:1)	By/because of grace (2:5, 7, 8)
Walk in sins (2:1–2)	In Christ Jesus (2:6, 7); walk in good works (2:10)

5:2; Col 2:6).

20. Larkin labels the syntactical function of ἐν as "sphere" and adds, "Extending the figure of a way of life as 'walking' (περιεπατήσατε), [ἐν] gives the environment in which it is pursued" (*Ephesians*, 28). Eadie, *Ephesians*, 124: "The ἐν marks out the sphere or walk which they usually and continually trod, for in this sleep of death there is a strange somnambulism." Hoehner, *Ephesians*, 309: "The preposition ἐν emphasizes the sphere of the walk." Cf. John Paul Heil, *Ephesians: Empowerment to Walk in Love for the Unity of All in Christ* (SBL 13; Atlanta: Society of Biblical Literature, 2007), 95.

21. Cf. Joshua W. Jipp, "Sharing in the Heavenly Rule of Christ the King: Paul's Participatory Language in Ephesians," in *"In Christ" in Paul: Explorations in Paul's Theology of Union and Participation* (eds. M. J. Thate et al.; Grand Rapids: Eerdmans, 2018), 253–79.

| The age of this world (2:2) | The coming ages (2:7) |
| Children of wrath (2:3) | New creation (2:10) |

This locative or spherical account of sin in Colossians and Ephesians, though not common, is not entirely out of step with the rest of the Pauline corpus. Indeed, it finds support from noteworthy parallels in the undisputed letters. For example, in Romans Paul cautions believers against "remaining in sin" for the purpose of exploiting God's grace (ἐπιμένωμεν τῇ ἁμαρτίᾳ, ἵνα ἡ χάρις πλεονάσῃ;), warning of the absurdity of having "died to sin" while continuing to "live in it" (οἵτινες ἀπεθάνομεν τῇ ἁμαρτίᾳ, πῶς ἔτι ζήσομεν ἐν αὐτῇ; Rom 6:1-2).[22] Likewise, in 1 Cor 15:17 the apostle underscores the centrality of Jesus's resurrection for Christian hope, concluding that "if Christ has not been raised, your faith is futile and you are still *in your sins* [ἔτι ἐστὲ ἐν ταῖς ἁμαρτίαις ὑμῶν]." In both Romans and 1 Corinthians, Paul is portraying sin(s), much like he does in Colossians and Ephesians, as a sphere of existence, with additional connotations attached to each verse.[23] The notion of sin as realm of power, then, is not common in the undisputed letters, yet neither is it unprecedented.

Sin as Habitus

What should we make of the *realm* of sin and its relationship to sin as *infraction*? What model most effectively explains how Paul conceptualizes these two notions of sin in Colossians and Ephesians?[24] We find

---

22. James D. G. Dunn, *Romans 1-8* (WBC 38a; Dallas: Word, 1988), 306: "the verb can have the force of '"remain in the sphere of."' Douglas J. Moo, *Romans* (NICNT: Grand Rapids: Eerdmans, 1996), 358: "'Living in sin' is best taken as describing a 'lifestyle' of sin—a habitual practice of sin, such that one's life could be said to be characterized by that sin rather than by the righteousness God requires. Such habitual sin, 'remaining in sin' (v. 1), 'living in sin' (v. 2), is not possible, as a constant situation, for the one who has truly experienced the transfer out from under the domain, or tyranny, of sin. Sin's power is broken for the believer, and this *must* be evident in practice."

23. In Romans, to "remain" and "live *in sin*" is to have one's life dominated by the cosmic power of sin. As Dunn explains, "the phrase ['in sin'] is most likely equivalent to 'remain under the lordship of sin' ([Rom] 5:21; 6:14)" (*Romans 1-8*, 306). In 1 Corinthians, to be "in sins," as Roy E. Ciampa and Brian S. Rosner explain, implies that an individual is "culpable for [sins] and standing under divine judgment" (*The First Letter to the Corinthians* [PNTC; Grand Rapids: Eerdmans, 2010], 757).

24. Paul himself suggests that these two notions of sins are interrelated since in both Colossians and Ephesians the phrase "the forgiveness of sins/trespasses" appears in apposition to the notion of "redemption" (Col 1:14; Eph 1:7).

explanatory assistance from the theoretical resources of sociology, particularly Pierre Bourdieu's concept of *habitus* and its relationship to *practice*. Bourdieu defines a habitus as "a system of lasting, transposable dispositions which, integrating past experiences, functions at every moment as a *matrix of perceptions, appreciations, and actions* and makes possible the achievement of infinitely diversified tasks."[25] Put differently, a habitus is "a subjective but not individual system of internalized structures, schemes of perception, conception, and action common to all members of the same group or class and constituting the precondition for all objectification and apperception."[26] A habitus, in other words, is a frame of reference, a shared epistemological vantage point, that programs reality and engenders practice for a particularly situated demographic. Thus, a habitus is a "generative principle" responsible for producing all of one's thoughts, behaviors, speech patterns, mannerisms, sensibilities, expressions, and tastes.[27]

Yet, according to Bourdieu, habitus is not the product of a single person; it is socially constructed, conditioned, and operated. The habitus is programmed in accordance with one's *field*, which consists of a network of agents that are, as Richard Jenkins summarizes, "structured internally in terms of power relations"—"a social arena within which struggles or manoeuvres take place over specific resources or stakes and access to them."[28] The conditions and experiences of the various persons within the field generate the habitus, which is shared by the field's participants, becomes ingrained in their mental structures, and manifests in their bodily practices, often unconsciously. The embodiment of habitus, which Bourdieu calls *body hexis*,[29] is shaped by and reflects one's field and inhabited space—it is "the appropriating by the world of a body thus enabled to appropriate the world."[30] Thus, body hexis is a significant expression of enculturation, but it is also a principal means of field construction.

Due to the interplay between field, habitus, and body, it is hardly surprising that for Bourdieu the habitus both governs and is governed by

---

25. Pierre Bourdieu, *Outline of a Theory of Practice* (trans. R. Nice; Cambridge: Cambridge University Press, 1977), 72–95, at 82–83.

26. Bourdieu, *Outline of a Theory of Practice*, 86.

27. Bourdieu, *Outline of a Theory of Practice*, 78.

28. Richard Jenkins, *Pierre Bourdieu* (New York: Routledge, 1992), 85, 84.

29. Bourdieu, *Outline of a Theory of Practice*, 87, 93–94.

30. Bourdieu, *Outline of a Theory of Practice*, 89.

practices. It must be understood, however, that the habitus limits practices without determining them.

> As an acquired system of generative schemes, the *habitus* makes possible the free production of all the thoughts, perceptions and actions inherent in the particular conditions of its production—and only those. Through the *habitus*, the structure of which it is the product governs practice, not along the paths of a mechanical determinism, but within the constraints and limits initially set on its inventions. . . . Because the *habitus* is an infinite capacity for generating products—thoughts, perceptions, expressions and actions—whose limits are set by the historically and socially situated conditions of its production, the conditioned and conditional freedom it provides is as remote from creation of unpredictable novelty as it is from the simply mechanical reproduction of the original conditioning.[31]

Seeking in this way to avoid determinism and free agency, Bourdieu maintains that the habitus produces what he calls "regulated improvisations," yet these practices themselves also reinforce the habitus by shaping the conditions (the field) that generate it.[32] The habitus functions as a force standing between the field and human volition. Thus, the habitus is, as Bourdieu calls it, "history turned into nature."[33]

The concept of habitus is useful to Paul's sin discourse because it helps to explain the how and why of practices by pointing beyond individual human agency, yet also without attributing causality to external structures. That appears to be precisely what Paul is doing when invoking the notion of being "in sin(s)." In Colossians and Ephesians, Paul views sins as performative (as *practice*), though on a deeper level sins are also a mode of existence or scheme of living (a *habitus*) calibrated by sinful practices. When a person walks or lives "in sin," their patterns of thought, affections, and behaviors have become attuned to ethical vices that produce a disposition of vice, which then perpetuates sinful activity. Understood in this way, the unbeliever who in Pauline (emic) terms walks or lives *in sins* operates in Bourdieuan (etic) terms by a *habitus of sin*.[34]

31. Pierre Bourdieu, *The Logic of Practice* (trans. R. Nice; Stanford: Stanford University Press, 1990), 55.
32. Bourdieu, *Outline of a Theory of Practice*, 78. Cf. Bourdieu, *Logic of Practice*, 57.
33. Bourdieu, *Outline of a Theory of Practice*, 78.
34. John M. G. Barclay refers to the "*habitus* of sin" as well as the "force-field of sin and death" ("Under Grace: The Christ-Gift and the Construction of a Christian *Habitus*,"

The associated concepts in Bourdieu's logic of practice (field and body hexis) are also present in the Pauline letters, particularly in Eph 2:2–3. There, Paul identifies three powers that collectively constrain unbelievers. The first of these powers is *the world*. Paul indicates that his audience formerly walked in sins "according to the age of this world" (κατὰ τὸν αἰῶνα τοῦ κόσμου τούτου, 2:2b). The preposition κατά sometimes denotes conformity to a norm, though in this context it suggests control (cf. Rom 8:4–5).[35] Likewise, ὁ αἰών here follows typical Pauline usage in denoting temporality (Eph 1:21; 2:7; 3:9, 11, 21), referring as it does to the present evil age (cf. Gal 1:4). The addition of ὁ κόσμος, on the other hand, supplies a spatial dimension to the construction, signifying not only the unredeemed "turf" affected by cosmic sin but also the toxic ethos of the present world order.[36] Together, τὸν αἰῶνα τοῦ κόσμου τούτου refers to the totality of fallen reality that has existed from the entrance of cosmic sin and death to the day of eschatological redemption. In this sense, the world serves as the *field* that generates the habitus of sin. This destructive cosmic order negatively affects and controls humanity by promulgating a culture or disposition of self-interest and discord, resulting in rebellious practices. As Lincoln explains, unbelieving humanity's "sinful activities were simply in line with the norms and values of a spatio-temporal complex wholly hostile to God."[37]

The age of this world is closely related to, though distinguishable from, the second power Paul identifies—*the devil (demonic beings)*. Unbelievers walk, Paul asserts, "according to the ruler of the domain of the air" (κατὰ τὸν ἄρχοντα τῆς ἐξουσίας τοῦ ἀέρος, 2:2c). Paul has already announced in Ephesians that Christ conquered and was seated above "every rule and authority and power and lordship" (πάσης ἀρχῆς καὶ ἐξουσίας καὶ δυνάμεως καὶ κυριότητος, 1:21), and later he will warn his readers to stand strongly opposed to such potentates (6:12). In the latter passage, these powers are said to consist neither of flesh nor blood; rather, they are "spiritual forces

---

in *Apocalyptic Paul: Cosmos and Anthropos in Romans* [ed. B. R. Gaventa; Waco, TX: Baylor University Press, 2013], 59–76, at 71 and 75).

35. Ernest Best, *Ephesians* (ICC; Edinburgh: T. & T. Clark, 1998), 202; Clinton E. Arnold, *Ephesians* (ZECNT; Grand Rapids: Zondervan, 2010), 130.

36. Edward Adams, *Constructing the World: A Study of Paul's Cosmological Language* (SNTW; Edinburgh: T. & T. Clark, 2000), 241: "In apocalyptic discourse, 'this world' is a spatio-temporal reality. It embraces human beings but comprehends the non-human world as well."

37. Lincoln, *Ephesians*, 95.

of evil" that inhabit "the heavenlies" (τὰ πνευματικὰ τῆς πονηρίας ἐν τοῖς ἐπουρανίοις, 6:12). Their leader, however, is identified as "the devil" (ὁ διάβολος, 6:11), who is likely the ruler Paul identifies in 2:2. His "domain" (ἐξουσία) is identified as "the air" (ὁ ἀήρ), the "realm in which forces hostile to humans dwell."[38] Yet Paul maintains that the devil (together with his demonic band of underlings) is even now operating *in* and *among* the sons of disobedience (τοῦ πνεύματος τοῦ νῦν ἐνεργοῦντος ἐν τοῖς υἱοῖς τῆς ἀπειθείας, 2:2), controlling them principally by diluting their minds (Eph 4:17–19) and dividing communities (4:26–27). In this way, the devil functions as an agent within the field of the world whose own practices contribute to the habitus of sin.[39]

Paul identifies the third power associated with sin in 2:3—*the flesh*. By noting the flesh, Paul moves from external forces (the world and the devil, i.e., the field) to the internal powers that plague humanity. He asserts that "we all lived once in the passions of our flesh [ἐν ταῖς ἐπιθυμίαις τῆς σαρκὸς ἡμῶν], doing the desires of the flesh and of the thoughts [ποιοῦντες τὰ θελήματα τῆς σαρκὸς καὶ τῶν διανοιῶν], and we were by nature children of wrath, as also were the rest." When Paul speaks of "the passions of *our* flesh," the possessive pronoun ἡμῶν indicates that the flesh has invaded and now inhabits each person. This initial use of σάρξ, then, refers to the human's general rebellious disposition, and the flesh's *passions*—one's own appetites for pleasure and self-gratification—are produced by this wayward orientation and are at odds with God's moral standard. Thus, to live "in the passions of our flesh" is essentially the same as to live "in sin"—Paul is once again referring to the unbeliever's *habitus* of sin, just as "*doing* the desires of the flesh and of the thoughts" refers to sinful *practices* generated by the unbeliever's habitus.[40]

---

38. Fowl, *Ephesians*, 69. See, however, that demonic forces are also said to be located "in the heavenlies" (ἐν τοῖς ἐπουρανίοις, 3:10; 6:12). Cf. M. Jeff Brannon, *The Heavenlies in Ephesians: A Lexical, Exegetical, and Conceptual Analysis* (LNTS 447; London: T. & T. Clark, 2011).

39. In Colossians, Paul identifies these same two powers (the world and demonic beings) that stand opposed to humanity, though he uses different terminology. In Col 1:14, Paul refers to the age of this world as the "dominion of darkness" (τῆς ἐξουσίας τοῦ σκότους, 1:13), which is the realm inhabited by the evil suprahuman powers he refers to as "thrones," "lordships," "rules," and "authorities" (θρόνοι εἴτε κυριότητες εἴτε ἀρχαὶ εἴτε ἐξουσίαι, 1:19; cf. 2:10, 15). Paul announces that believers have been "rescued" (ῥύομαι) and "transferred" (μεθίστημι) from this evil domain into a new *field*, the kingdom of God's beloved son, Jesus Christ (1:13).

40. Best, *Ephesians*, 210: "in v. 3a 'flesh' must apply to the whole of human existence,

Paul, however, diagnoses the problem in still greater detail, using similar terms to paint a fuller portrait concerning the genesis of sinful practices. Paul explains the former lifestyle of unbelievers as involving sinful activity, and in so doing shares that such practices are the product of "the desires of the flesh and of the thoughts." The coupling of "flesh" with "thoughts" makes clear that the second use of σάρξ in 2:3 has a different sense from the first—"flesh" now refers to the unredeemed corporeal substance of the person. Thus, by referring to "the desires of the flesh and of the thoughts," Paul locates the root of sinful practices within the body (cf. Rom 6:12; 7:5) and within one's disposition (cf. Eph 4:17–19).[41] For this reason Paul laments that he, the Ephesians, and the rest of humanity were children of wrath *by nature* (3:3), for their culpability before God is grounded in "their deepest instincts, by virtue of their birth as humans."[42] The similarities here with the concept of habitus are striking. Just as the habitus, according to Bourdieu, is ingrained in both the body (i.e., body hexis) and mental structures, so according to Paul the unbeliever's pattern of life and moral practices are directed by both deep-seated bodily appetites and corrupt moral reasoning.[43]

Conclusion

This essay has analyzed Paul's sin language in Colossians and Ephesians and observed two complementary conceptualizations at play. "Trespasses," "sins," and various synonyms refer in the first place to moral-religious infractions that cause estrangement from God and are responsible for inciting divine wrath. But "sins" is also a sphere of existence, which unbelieving

---

indicating a life lived apart from God, or, in less religious terms, a life governed by human (cf 2:11; 6:5 for this translation of σάρξ) desires whose main aim is self-expression."

41. Paul conveys a similar anthropology in Colossians, where Paul's readers are inclined to pursue purity through law observance and other ascetic practices. But while such ordinances have a reputation for wisdom (λόγον μὲν ἔχοντα σοφίας, Col 2:23) and anticipate (as a "shadow") what has now been climactically revealed in the person and work of Jesus Christ (2:17), Paul declares that they themselves are of no real value for satisfying or guarding oneself against the indulgence of *the flesh* (οὐκ ἐν τιμῇ τινι πρὸς πλησμονὴν τῆς σαρκός, 2:23; cf. 2:18). The implication is that violating God's ordinances remains inevitable, not so much because of the overwhelming burden of the ordinances themselves, but because of the susceptibility of the person to their self-interested bodily appetites (cf. 2:11, 13).

42. Fowl, *Ephesians*, 71.

43. Cf. Sarah Harding, *Paul's Eschatological Anthropology: The Dynamics of Human Transformation* (Minneapolis: Fortress 2015), 135–53.

humanity inhabits and which effectively traps them within a mode of behavior characterized by vice and disobedience. Sin language in Colossians and Ephesians, therefore, is polyvalent, projecting distinct ways of conceiving the human plight. Even so, for both conceptions the remedy to sins is the person and work of Jesus Christ, whose death not only affects forgiveness of sins but also transfers the human into the sphere of Christ Jesus, wherein the believer is able to operate in accordance with the life-giving power of the new creation.

This essay has also observed how these two ways of defining sin are analogous to the notions of *habitus* and *practice* outlined by Pierre Bourdieu, whose theory of practice provides a helpful model for configuring the relationship between sins as infractions (practices) and sins as a sphere of power (habitus). It is important to note that there is very little difference between the spherical concept (or habitus) of sin in Colossians and Ephesians and Paul's diagnosis elsewhere of humanity being "under sin" (Rom 3:9; 7:14; Gal 3:22)—both discourses portray sin as an enslaving power. That being so, we must reject Andrew Lincoln's assertion that "the notion of sin as a power or force is missing from Ephesians."[44] Karl Barth is on slightly surer ground when in his lectures on Ephesians he says that "the slavery of humans is related to sin; their sins have *either* landed them in prison *or* constitute the prisons themselves."[45] Yet both of Barth's accounts appear to be correct: sins are the cause of imprisonment *and* the prison in which the sinner is confined. They are, as Barth observes, "the chains which hold him," such that "[a]nything that the creature can do will simply perpetuate his own παραπτώματα, forge additional chains, deepen his bondage, and prolong his servitude."[46] Sins as infractions and sphere of power, then, are interrelated plights in need of divine resolution. But thanks be to Christ, "in whom we have redemption, the forgiveness of sin" (Col 1:14; cf. Eph 1:7).

---

44. Lincoln, *Ephesians*, 29.
45. Barth, *Epistle to the Ephesians*, 105 (original emphasis).
46. Barth, *Epistle to the Ephesians*, 105.

9

"But I Never Intended . . .": Implicit Hamartiology in the Thessalonian Correspondence

Andy Johnson

WRITING AN ESSAY ON Paul's understanding of holiness/sanctification or eschatological matters would require a significant amount of attention to be paid to the Thessalonian correspondence.[1] In contrast, on the face of it at least, these letters might barely deserve mention when explicating the apostle's understanding of sin.[2] This is quite understandable given that, with the exception of Paul's use of the term ἁμαρτίαι (sins) in 1 Thess 2:16, they contain none of the typical terms Paul uses for sin or transgression.[3] Moreover, nowhere in them does Paul explicitly mention the audience's past or present sins, or any guilt or forgiveness associated with them, nor is there the sort of vice list that one might see in other letters (e.g., Rom 1:29-31;

---

1. For my reasons for assuming Pauline authorship of 2 Thessalonians, see Andy Johnson, *1 and 2 Thessalonians* (THNTC; Grand Rapids: Eerdmans, 2016), 6-8.

2. In his almost fifty-page exposition devoted to this task in *The Theology of Paul the Apostle*, James D. G. Dunn refers to passages in 1 and 2 Thessalonians four times, none of which figure prominently (*The Theology of Paul the Apostle* [Grand Rapids: Eerdmans, 1998], 79-127).

3. For example, none of the following appear in these letters: ἁμάρτημα (sin, transgression); παράπτωμα (trespass, sin) παράβασις (transgression); ἁμαρτάνω (the verbal form, "to sin").

"BUT I NEVER INTENDED..." 131

1 Cor 5:10-11; 6:9-10; Gal 5:19-21).⁴ There are, however, some intriguing connections—both terminological and thematic—between these letters and Paul's description of life "in Adam" under the cosmic power of Sin in Romans. The purpose of this essay is to flesh out these connections and thereby make more explicit the implicit hamartiological assumptions in 1 and 2 Thessalonians.

A cluster of sin-related terms in Rom 6:12-23 (ἀκαθαρσία, ἀνομία, ἀδικία), where Paul contrasts the characteristics of being under Sin's cosmic power with the consequences of being liberated from it, appear in the Thessalonian correspondence: impurity (ἀκαθαρσία in 1 Thess 4:7); lawlessness (ἀνομία in 2 Thess 2:3, 7); injustice/wrongdoing (ἀδικία in 2 Thess 2:10, 12). Together with Paul's lone use of the word ἁμαρτία in 1 Thess 2:16, these terminological connections with Rom 6:12-23 suggest that we focus on 1 Thess 2:13-16, 1 Thess 4:3-8, and 2 Thess 2:3-12. The essay, then, will proceed as follows. I will begin with a brief summary of the relevant aspects of Paul's argument in Romans regarding Sin's cosmic power and life "in Adam." Then, in the main section I will discuss the three passages referred to above, fleshing out their connections with Paul's argument in Romans regarding Sin's cosmic power and life "in Adam." Since 1 Thess 2:13-16 and 2 Thess 2:3-12 have to do with sins and the way Sin works outside the Christian community, I will discuss them first. A discussion of 1 Thess 4:3-8 focusing on the continuing threat of sinful behavior to those in Christ will close this main section of the essay. I will conclude by offering brief reflections on some of the implicit hamartiological assumptions at work in these letters.

Romans, Sin, and Life "in Adam"

Paul only explicitly uses the phrase "in Adam" to describe a death-bound sphere in 1 Cor 15:22 ("in Adam all die"). Yet the phrase succinctly summarizes his description of the human condition, beginning in Rom 1:18, in which humans presently experience a foretaste of God's judgment day

4. Paul does, however, describe the typical honor seeking, exploitative behavior of the charlatan orators with whom he contrasts himself and his companions by using language from his vice list in Rom 1:29-31: πλάνη in 1 Thess 2:3 (cf. Rom 1:27); δόλος in 1 Thess 2:3 (cf. Rom 1:29); πλεονεξία in 1 Thess 2:5 (cf. Rom 1:29). No doubt, Paul considers such behavior as sinful. The same could be said about the lack of self-control, with drunkenness as one of its manifestations, exhibited by the "children of darkness" (1 Thess 5:6-7).

wrath (ὀργή) which God is revealing against "all the idolatry/impiety [ἀσέβεια] and injustice/wrongdoing [ἀδικία] of those who suppress the truth [ἀλήθεια] with injustice/wrongdoing [ἀδικίᾳ]." This experience of present wrath takes the form of God "giving up" humanity to the consequences of their own destructive choices, the first of which is to refuse God's lordship by engaging in idolatry. The ultimate consequence of humanity's destructive choices is a debased mind that can no longer even discern God's will (1:28), so that they not only practice every kind of injustice/wrongdoing (πάσῃ ἀδικίᾳ) as well as a whole host of vices (1:29–31), they also applaud those who do so (1:32). Although this latter passage is sometimes read as simply a (somewhat caricatured) portrayal of the typical gentile situation—and it clearly echoes typical Jewish critiques of gentiles—Paul's allusion to the golden calf incident (1:23; cf. Ps 106:19–20) and his ensuing argument in 2:1—3:20 suggest that 1:18 is the beginning of his description of the human predicament of both Jews and gentiles as a whole.[5] Since, on the basis of his argument from 1:18—3:8, Paul concludes that all, both Jews and Greeks, are "under Sin" (ὑφ᾽ ἁμαρτίαν) in 3:9, we may infer that Sin as a cosmic power ushering in death for all after Adam (5:12; cf. 1 Cor 15:22) is at work precisely in this human predicament.[6] Beginning in Rom 1:18, then, Paul offers an extended description of life in the death-bound sphere of Adam which is ruled over by the cosmic power of Sin.

When referring to some of the consequences of being delivered from this death-bound sphere ruled by the Sin's cosmic power, Paul uses sin-related terminology in Rom 6:12–23 that we will see again in 2 Thess 2:3–12 and 1 Thess 4:3–8.

> [13]No longer present your members to Sin [τῇ ἁμαρτίᾳ] as weapons of injustice/wrongdoing [ἀδικίας] but present yourselves to God as ones raised to new life from the dead and your members as weapons of saving justice [δικαιοσύνης] to God.... [18]Now having been freed from Sin [τῆς ἁμαρτίας], you all have been enslaved to [God's] saving justice.... [19b]For just as you all presented your members as slaves to impurity [ἀκαθαρσίᾳ] resulting in [καί] lawlessness leading to more lawlessness [τῇ ἀνομίᾳ εἰς τὴν ἀνομίαν],

---

5. Cf. Michael J. Gorman, *Inhabiting the Cruciform God: Kenosis, Justification, and Theosis in Paul's Narrative Soteriology* (Grand Rapids: Eerdmans, 2009), 50–51.

6. Leander E. Keck notes similar connections (*Romans* [ANTC; Nashville: Abingdon, 2005], 95).

so now present yourselves as slaves to [God's] saving justice [τῇ δικαιοσύνῃ] leading to holiness/sanctification.[7]

This passage implies that the death-bound sphere of Adam ruled over by the cosmic power of Sin is characterized by ἀδικία, ἀκαθαρσία, and exponential ἀνομία. In this context, impurity (ἀκαθαρσία) is closely associated with lawlessness (ἀνομία),[8] and both are related to an enslaved pattern of life of being "weapons of injustice/wrongdoing [ἀδικίας]" in the hands of Sin, all of which is characteristic of those "in Adam." We may begin to recognize this conceptuality of life "in Adam" under Sin's cosmic rule at work in the Thessalonian correspondence by teasing out the implications of 1 Thess 2:14–16, the only place where Paul uses the word sin (ἁμαρτία) in these letters.

Implicit Hamartiological Assumptions at Work in the Thessalonian Correspondence

1 Thessalonians 2:14–16

In 1 Thess 2:13 Paul gives thanks that the Thessalonians received God's message/gospel as the truth that is continuing to work among (or even by means of) them as they exercise believing allegiance in Thessalonica. He then continues in vv. 14–16:[9]

> [14]This is evident, brothers and sisters, in the way that you yourselves became imitators of the churches of God who are in Judea in Christ Jesus because you yourselves also suffered the same things by your own compatriots just as they themselves also [suffered] by the Judeans[10] [15]who killed both the Lord Jesus and the prophets

---

7. Unless otherwise noted, all Scripture translations are my own.

8. I translate the καί in v. 19b as expressing result because here ἀνομία appears to describe the pattern of life that results when one becomes a slave to impurity (ἀκαθαρσία).

9. I treat these verses in more detail in my *1 and 2 Thessalonians*, 72–81. Their caustic tone, their use by some in Anti-Jewish or Anti-Semitic ways, and their apparent tension with what Paul says about Israel later in Rom 9–11 have led some interpreters—without supporting manuscript evidence—to propose that all or part of vv. 13–16 is a post-Pauline interpolation (see esp. B. A. Pearson, "1 Thessalonians 2:13–16: A Deutero-Pauline Interpretation," *HTR* 64 [1971] 79–94). I give my reasons for rejecting this proposal in *1 and 2 Thessalonians*, 75.

10. I translate Ἰουδαίων as "Judeans" and avoid placing a comma after the word to signal that the following actions should be understood as being restricted to a specific

and persecuted us. They are not pleasing to God and oppose all people ¹⁶by hindering us from speaking to the gentiles in order that they might be saved. The result of this is that they are constantly filling up the cup of their sins [ἁμαρτίας] to the brim. But [God's] wrath [ἡ ὀργή] has come upon [ἔφθασεν] them unto the end [εἰς τέλος].

In this context, Paul uses the word "sins" to characterize actions that, from his perspective, are in direct, even violent, opposition to God's saving mission. The effect of these Judean Jews' opposition to all people by hindering Paul's mission to the gentiles[11] is their continuing to "fill up the cup of their sins to the brim." When combined with their "killing of the Lord Jesus and the prophets," their ongoing actions constitute "the final straw," the bringing of their sins to a fulfilled state.[12]

That sins such as these are somehow connected with God's wrath is clear, but Paul's use of the aorist indicative, ἔφθασεν, in v. 16c muddies the waters. The verb could be a "prophetic aorist" (a future event of experiencing God's eschatological wrath that is so certain that it can be spoken of as already having happened)[13] or could refer to a traumatic past event or events (in Judea?) which Paul understands as God's eschatological wrath already beginning to overtake those to whom he is referring.[14] Alternatively, one might appeal to Paul's language in Rom 1:18-32 indicating that God's judgment day wrath can be anticipated and a foretaste of it experienced in the present when God "gives up" human beings like these Judeans to

---

group of first-century Judean Jews who violently opposed Jesus and his early Jewish followers. Hence, Paul's polemical description does not refer to "Jews" in general, is clearly hyperbolical, and is somewhat typical of first-century intra-Jewish polemic (on which, see my 1 and 2 Thessalonians, 76-78; cf. esp. Frank D. Gilliard, "The Problem of the Antisemitic Comma Between 1 Thessalonians 2.14 and 15," NTS 35 (1989) 481-502; Idem, "Paul and the Killing of the Prophets in 1 Thess. 2:15," NovT 36 [1994] 259-70.

11. Later in Romans, Paul connects Israel's own final salvation with the success of his gentile mission (Rom 11:25-32). On that logic, any group opposing his salvific mission among the gentiles could be described as "opposed to all people," *i.e., opposed to Jews and gentiles* (cf. Gilliard, "Antisemitic Comma," 500).

12. My rendering of Paul's awkward combination of ἀναπληρῶσαι ("to fill up/complete") and πάντοτε ("always/at all times"), "constantly filling up the cup of their sins to the brim," attempts to convey that while their sinful actions may continue, their effects have reached a state of fulfillment in the sense that "the damage is already done."

13. E.g., Gordon D. Fee, *The First and Second Letters to the Thessalonians* (NICNT; Grand Rapids: Eerdmans, 2009), 102.

14. E.g., Markus Bockmuehl, "1 Thessalonians 2:14-16 and the Church in Jerusalem," *TynBul* 52 (2001) 25-28.

the consequences of their own choices, the effect of which is to "suppress the truth by means of injustice/wrongdoing" (Rom 1:18). Their actions "have evoked (in the past), and manifest (in the present), a foretaste of God's wrath that awaits its consummation in the future judgment because God has now given them up to the consequences of their own destructive choices,"[15] and—at least as long as they persist in such sinful actions[16]— God will continue doing so until the end.[17]

In this context, Paul is speaking *from his current perspective* of being a persecuted participant in God's mission. However, there is little doubt that, *from the perspective of these specific Judean Jews*, the actions Paul is castigating are anything but sinful. In fact, like Saul the persecutor (1 Cor 15:9; Phil 3:6) and Phinehas his precursor (Num 25:1–15; Ps 106:28–31), these Jews may perhaps be characterized as "seeking to establish their own righteousness/covenant faithfulness [δικαιοσύνη]" (Rom 10:3), by demonstrating their loyalty to God in opposing those they believe to be God's enemies. What Paul now calls "sins," these Judean Jews would not have considered a transgression of God's Torah when they engaged in these actions. Rather, their actions probably emerged from an intention to be radically faithful to God and Torah, rather than to willingly commit an action contrary to God's will. One might see this as a confirmation of Paul's argument in Rom 7 that Torah itself can be taken over by Sin's cosmic power and used as an instrument that ultimately brings death when it was intended to lead to life (Rom 7:4–12). Hence, actions committed with the intention of keeping Torah (or for that matter, obeying Christian Scripture!) may actually be sins against the God who gave it if such actions result in impeding God's salvific, life-giving intentions for the world. When that happens, those "in Adam" who *consciously* imagine themselves to be aligned with God are *unconsciously* a "weapon of injustice" in the hands of Sin's cosmic power (Rom 6:13a).[18]

---

15. Johnson, *1 and 2 Thessalonians*, 80. This interpretation has the advantage of maintaining the more usual sense of the aorist without resorting to speculations about particular events in Judea.

16. Paul's caustic language here indicates that he probably expects these Judean Jews to suffer the eschatological consummation of the wrath they are currently experiencing. But his own life as a persecutor of the Church, an "enemy of [God's] good news" (cf. Rom 11:28) to whom God extended grace, should leave open the possibility that they too may finally be included in "all Israel" who will be saved (cf. Rom 11:26).

17. Taking εἰς τέλος in a temporal sense.

18. Cf. Matthew Croasmun, *The Emergence of Sin: The Cosmic Tyrant in Romans* (Oxford: Oxford University Press, 2017), 128–33.

Hence, human intentionality cannot be the primary arbiter as to what constitutes a sinful action. In this case, what distinguishes the actions Paul describes as "sins" is that such actions—regardless of intent—impede God's salvific, life-giving mission for the world. These actions literally cause death for those whom God chose as instruments of that mission and ultimately bring God's eschatological wrath/destruction to its consummation on the (unrepentant) perpetrators.

2 Thessalonians 2:3–12

The enslaved pattern of life under Sin's cosmic power is the antithesis of what Adam/humanity was intended to be and its pinnacle is personified by the "man of lawlessness [ἀνομίας]" in 2 Thess 2:3–12.[19] As such, 2 Thess 2:3–12 can be characterized as describing the pinnacle of life "in Adam," i.e., Adam *in extremis*. In Paul's letters, lawlessness (ἀνομία) is a sinful pattern of activity exhibiting complete disregard for God's intent for human life or the well-being of others. The phrase "man of lawlessness (ἀνομίας)" in 2 Thess 2:3 is a way of describing a person in whom such chaotic action opposing God and God's will for human flourishing comes to its fullest expression.[20]

While Paul depicts this man as a single human figure,[21] the pattern of his actions echoes a (barely) caricatured story of humanity attempting to go beyond its creaturely status and step into God's place of sovereignty. This story begins in the garden (Gen 2–3), goes through the tower of Babel (Gen 11:1–9), and then finds expression in several paradigmatic kings in the OT (e.g., Isa 14:3–23 LXX, esp. vv. 13–14; Dan 11:21–45, esp. v. 36 OG).[22] The long-recognized triangular connections between Gen 2–3, Ezek 28:1–19 LXX, and 2 Thess 2:3–12 are most relevant for our purposes here.[23] In Ezek

---

19. In this section, I am adapting material from my *1 and 2 Thessalonians* (179–200, 271–87) and "Paul's 'Anti-Christology' in 2 Thessalonians 2:3–12 in Canonical Context," *JTI* 8 (2014) 125–43.

20. Cf. Abraham Malherbe, *The Letters to the Thessalonians* (AYBC; New York: Doubleday, 2000), 419.

21. Most probably as a present or future Roman emperor (Johnson, *1 and 2 Thessalonians*, 187–89).

22. In their own contexts, neither Gen 2–3 nor 11:1–9 need be read as emphasizing human arrogance. But their intertextual connections with these prophetic texts suggest that they probably were read this way very early on.

23. These connections are both thematic and terminological in that Ezekiel depicts

28:1–19, we see a paradigmatic king who represents humanity when its false understanding of reality[24] is manifested in an idolatrous arrogance that attempts to overcome its creaturely bounds and share in the honor due only to the creator God. Such idolatrous arrogance is inevitably accompanied by acts of injustice. In Pauline terms, this Ezekiel text upon which Paul may be drawing in 2 Thess 2:3–12 paradigmatically portrays a heightened form of life "in Adam," clearly characterized by the idolatry/impiety (ἀσέβεια) and injustice/wrongdoing (ἀδικία) against which God's current wrath is being revealed (Rom 1:18).

But, if Paul is indeed drawing on this Ezekiel text, he ups the ante in 2 Thess 2:3–12 where he depicts the pinnacle of this pattern of life "in Adam"—Adam *in extremis*—in the "man of lawlessness," particularly in his actions in vv. 3–4.

> [3]No one should deceive you all in any way because [that Day will not come] unless the rebellion comes first and the man of lawlessness [ἀνομίας] is revealed, the son destined for destruction, [4]the one who opposes and exalts himself above every so-called god or object of worship [σέβασμα], [finally] resulting in his seating himself in the inner sanctuary of God's temple in order to create the impression that he is a god.

In terms of impiety or idolatrous arrogance, Paul's description of this man of lawlessness in 2 Thess 2:4 pushes this pattern beyond its OT precursors or the historical figures (e.g., Antiochus, Pompey, and Caligula) through which these OT examples are refracted. Second Temple Jews might associate language like "I myself am a god" and "I dwell in the dwelling of a god" (Ezek 28:2, 9) with the claims and actions of Antiochus, Pompey, and Caligula. But Paul's man of lawlessness exalts himself *above* every so-called god or object of worship[25] and embodies this claim by entering the

---

God explicitly taunting the king of Tyre with a mock lamentation *as if he were Adam in the garden* (Ezek 28:12–13a) overstepping his creaturely bounds. Decrying this king's claim to divinity (Ezek 28:2, 9; cf. 2 Thess 2:4b), God also castigates the injustice (ἀδικία; Ezek 28:15, 18; cf. 2 Thess 2:10, 12) and lawlessness (ἀνομία; Ezek 28:16; cf. 2 Thess 2:3, 8) that accompany his impiety, all of which bring him to destruction (ἀπώλεια; Ezek 28:19; cf. 2 Thess 2:3).

24. The crime of Tyre's prince is not simply arrogance but a "culpably false understanding of reality" (Robert W. Jenson, *Ezekiel* [BTCB; Grand Rapids: Brazos, 2009], 219).

25. Even Daniel's arrogant king (patterned after Antiochus) goes on to honor/acknowledge a strong/foreign god (Dan 11:38–39 LXX/OG).

inner sanctuary of the Jerusalem temple and seating himself there on what was presumed to be God's own throne, effectively announcing that he, not Israel's God, is creation's King/Lord.[26] This is the pinnacle of the idolatrous trajectory of disobedience initiated in the garden, the story of humanity's grasping for equality with God and refusing to be God's representative king on God's own terms. Such a portrayal of a human being publicly signifying that he intends to displace Israel's God as king over creation arrogantly blurs the line between Creator and creature, thereby vividly acting out humanity's "exchange of the truth of God for *the lie* [τῷ ψεύδει]" that creature rather than the Creator is worthy of being worshiped and served (Rom 1:25). This, then, is indeed the pinnacle of life "in Adam," Adam *in extremis*.

But those under Sin's cosmic power who themselves live "in Adam" cannot see "the lie" for the deception that it is. They can only evaluate such a man by the common-sense categories of a culture sculpted by Sin's cosmic power, a culture in which it is "obvious" that raw, exploitative power is not revelatory of "lawlessness" per se, but of kingship and divinity. So, when Paul describes the royal welcoming parade (παρουσία) of the "lawless one,"[27] including the deception and injustice that inevitably accompanies his arrogant idolatry, it is not surprising that they ultimately wind up offering believing allegiance to "the lie" he embodies:

> [9]The "royal coming" of the lawless one is in line with Satan's working with all power, with both signs and wonders that serve the lie, [10]and with every deception which engenders [acts of] injustice/wrongdoing [ἀδικίας] among those who are perishing because they did not receive the love for the truth in order that they might be saved. [11]And because of this, God is going to send to them a deluding influence resulting in their offering believing allegiance to the lie [τῷ ψεύδει]. [12]The result of this is that all who do not offer believing allegiance to the truth but delight in injustice [ἀδικίᾳ] will be judged/condemned. (2 Thess 2:9–12)

The royal coming of this false king is backed by Satan and primarily characterized by power, the fundamental characteristic of common-sense conceptions of kingship in the Greco-Roman world. Most probably such power is manifest by this lawless one in the form of "signs and wonders"

---

26. I defend this reading of τὸν ναὸν τοῦ θεοῦ in v. 4b in my *1 and 2 Thessalonians*, 187–88.

27. The where and when of this παρουσία is unclear, but most likely it is assumed to occur after the events of vv. 3–4.

experienced by those who acclaim him as divine king as beneficial/salvific, i.e., as bringing peace, security and prosperity[28]—albeit at the expense of bringing violence, chaos, and economic deprivation to others. Under the cosmic power of Sin that fuels the common sense of their culture, those who are perishing "in Adam" welcome this promising, yet deceptive, display of power that seems to benefit them but winds up also engendering acts of injustice/wrongdoing—whether or not they recognize them as such—among them.[29]

The reason they are deceived,[30] Paul says, is that "they did not receive the love for the truth in order that they might be saved" (v. 10b). This implies that they, like those now in the Thessalonian church (1 Thess 2:13), will have had some opportunity to receive that love for the truth—probably in the form of hearing the gospel narrated by, and/or seeing it embodied in, the church—but rejected its implications for their lives. That is, they had heard the good news that the "living and true God" raised his crucified Son, made him the true divine King of the cosmos, and now calls all to turn from their idolatry and offer allegiance to him. But unlike those in the Thessalonian church (1 Thess 1:9), they had acted in accordance with their culture's common-sense, Sin-sculpted assumptions that a crucified Jew as divine King of creation was utter foolishness (cf. 1 Cor 1:18, 23) and they had refused to turn away from their idolatry.[31] *Because of this prior decision*, Paul says in v. 11 that "God sends them a deluding influence so that they might offer believing allegiance [πιστεῦσαι] to the lie [τῷ ψεύδει]," i.e., the implied (false) claim of sovereignty over creation signaled by the deceptive actions of the man of lawlessness in the Temple that blur the distinction between creature and Creator. This is *the* originating lie in the garden (cf. John 8:44) continuing to shape those "in Adam" who, as Paul says in Rom

---

28. It was a common imperial claim that Rome and its emperors were bearers of such salvific benefits (James R. Harrison, *Paul and the Imperial Authorities at Thessalonica and Rome: A Study in the Conflict of Ideology* [WUNT 273; Tübingen: Mohr Siebeck, 2011], 63–65).

29. Here I am translating ἀδικίας in v. 10 as an objective genitive, i.e., deception whose object(ive) is to stimulate injustice/wrongdoing.

30. Alternatively, v. 10b may be taken as giving the reason for their perishing as in the NIV. But since their perishing goes hand in hand with their being deceived, one need not choose between these two alternatives.

31. Admittedly, neither here nor elsewhere does Paul give a definitive and clear answer as to why the Spirit-enabled proclamation and embodiment of the gospel convinced some to turn to God but did not convince others.

1:25, "exchange the truth of God for *the lie* [τῷ ψεύδει], that is, they worship and serve the creature rather than the creator."

God's sending them a "deluding influence" that seemingly increases the effectiveness of Sin's deceptive power is disconcerting for many interpreters (including me!). However, it is not an unfamiliar pattern in Scripture whereby God responds to people's prior actions in ways that further the effects of the destructive life pattern which they have, in some sense, chosen for themselves.[32] We have already seen this pattern in Rom 1:18–32 where God "gave up" humanity to the chaotic consequences (1:24) for which they had already voted with their actions in vv. 19–23. This Romans pattern suggests that God's sending those who are perishing a "deluding influence" is in essence a manifestation of his current wrath that "hands them over" to "the lie" embodied by this man of lawlessness, the lie for which they will have voted with their prior choice not to receive the love of the truth (cf. "suppressing the truth," Rom 1:18), i.e., the truth that the creator God has made the crucified and risen Jesus the true divine King of creation and calls all to allegiance to him. The final result[33] of all this will be that all "who do not offer believing allegiance to that truth but delight [εὐδοκήσαντες] in injustice [ἀδικίᾳ]" will be judged/condemned (v. 12; cf. Rom 1:29).

Even though Paul probably intends the language to have a broader reference, the persecuted Thessalonian community would likely hear his language regarding those "who do not offer believing allegiance to that truth but delight [εὐδοκήσαντες] in injustice [ἀδικίᾳ]" as a fitting description of those persecuting them because of their witness to the truth.[34] Of course, these persecutors would not describe themselves in this way. Rather, they would more likely understand their actions through the lens of their own common-sense cultural categories as giving a troublesome group threatening cultural cohesion the justice they deserve. With their culpably false understanding of reality which they have refused to have corrected by the lens

---

32. E.g., God's sending an "evil spirit" upon Saul (18:10; 19:9) *after* his disobedience in 1 Sam 15 resulting in Saul's increasingly destructive behavior; God's response to his people's prior actions, which themselves have a stupefying effect, by pouring out a spirit of stupor upon them (Isa 29:9–10).

33. Taking ἵνα in v. 12a as expressing result not purpose.

34. Paul describes their persecutors in 2 Thess 1:8 as "those who do not acknowledge God and those who are not obeying the good news about our Lord Jesus." While they have been exposed to knowledge of God through the church's life/witness to the good news about Jesus, creation's true Lord, they have refused to render believing allegiance to him by confessing his lordship and sharing in his fidelity to Israel's God (for this way of reading 2 Thess 1:8, see my *1 and 2 Thessalonians*, 170–72).

of the gospel, they are simply reflecting the life pattern of being "in Adam" with an impaired ability to discern God's will. They remain unaware that they are essentially weapons of injustice under Sin's cosmic power who give honor and allegiance to a human who is the pinnacle of their own enslaved and lawless life "in Adam." As in the case of the Judean Jews, engaging in sinful actions while under Sin's cosmic power does not require consciousness of one's enslavement or consciousness that one's actions are "sinful."

1 Thessalonians 4:3–8

When they heard the good news proclaimed and saw it embodied in the lives of Paul and his companions, the Thessalonians had turned away from their enslaving idolatry—their life "in Adam" under the cosmic power of Sin—to be enslaved to (δουλεύειν) the living God (1 Thess 1:9).[35] To give it persuasive and liberating power, not only did this gospel proclamation take the empowering presence of the Holy Spirit acting upon its hearers; it required a concrete, Spirit-enabled, re-embodiment of its essence by its proclaimers (1 Thess 1:5, 2:1–12).[36]

Throughout the first half of 1 Thessalonians, Paul unequivocally affirms their fidelity (πίστις) to God,[37] until 1 Thess 3:10b where he expresses his desire to "make complete [καταρτίσαι] the things lacking in your faithfulness [πίστεως]." The verb, καταρτίζω, is often used in educational contexts referring to a teacher completing a student's training to enable the student to live as a fully functioning adult (cf. Luke 6:40).[38] Hence, given these gentiles' relatively recent conversion and its accompanying new value system, "the things lacking in your faithfulness" are probably not things involving *intentional* disloyalty to God, but rather *a lack in the Thessalonians' ability to discern* how their πίστις should be embodied in the varied circumstances that might confront them in ancient Mediterranean society. Having turned from their idolatry, freed from the cosmic power of Sin, they

---

35. Cf. the liberative movement from being slaves of Sin/impurity to being slaves of God/obedience/saving justice in Rom 6:12–23.

36. See comments on 1 Thess 1:5 and 2:5–12 in my *1 and 2 Thessalonians*, 46–47, 63–72.

37. Paul uses πίστις in the sense of faithfulness/loyalty in 1 Thess 1:3, 8, 3:2, 5, 6, 7, 10 and possibly in 5:8 and in 2 Thess 1:3, 4, 11. On the use of πίστις in Paul's letters, see now Nijay Gupta, *Paul and the Language of Faith* (Grand Rapids: Eerdmans, 2020).

38. Gene L. Green, *The Letters to the Thessalonians* (PNTC; Grand Rapids: Eerdmans, 2002), 174; similarly, Malherbe, *Letters*, 205.

still had to undergo a radical resocialization in a community whose moral life was to be characterized by a cruciform pattern of fidelity to God and self-giving love for others. This move from life "in Adam" to life "in Christ" would have required no less than a "sanctification of their imaginations,"[39] a transformative process of unlearning one way of making sense of their world and relearning another. In such a process, those recently liberated from Sin's cosmic power had to begin learning what constituted an individual act of sin.

In 4:1–8, Paul begins to address the need to strengthen the Thessalonians' ability to discern how their πίστις should be embodied in sexual matters. He warns them about possible[40] threats to their fidelity to God arising from certain assumptions about sexual activity that would have been understood as common sense in their culture. In non-Jewish, Greco-Roman society at large (apart from some moral philosophers like Musonius Rufus), the idea that free males had the right to various forms of sexual relations outside of marriage would have been socially "hardwired" into the imaginations of most. Hence, in vv. 3–8, Paul reminds this recently converted gentile audience that any such activity would compromise their identity as God's holy people.

The syntactical structure and exact meaning of the clauses containing prohibitions in vv. 3b–6a (particularly that of v. 4) are debated, but all appear to be closely related and have to do with sexual matters. The first admonition (i.e., to abstain from sexual immorality in 3b) is made more specific by the second admonition in vv. 4–5, which I understand as Paul's counseling the males in the audience to learn how to exercise control over their own penis.[41] The last clause (not to wrong or exploit your brother or sister in this matter in 6b) explicates the effect of failing to follow Paul's admonition in vv. 4–5. The fact that Paul equates engaging in the specific sexual activity prohibited in vv. 4–5 as wronging or exploiting one's "brother/

39. On which see my "The Sanctification of the Imagination in 1 Thessalonians," in *Holiness and Ecclesiology in the New Testament* (ed. K. Brower and A. Johnson; Grand Rapids: Eerdmans, 2007), 275–92.

40. The "threatening tone" of vv. 6–8 notwithstanding, Paul does *not* imply that some in the audience are *currently engaging* in the practices he warns them against in 4:3–8 (contra Green, *Letters*, 184, 186–87, 200). Rather, he depicts the Thessalonians as *currently* conducting themselves in a way that is "pleasing to God" (vv. 1–2). Cf. Malherbe, *Letters*, 220.

41. For a full discussion of the main interpretive options regarding this disputed verse, see Jay E. Smith, "1 Thessalonians 4:4: Breaking the Impasse," *BBR* 11 (2001) 65–105. For a defense of the view I am taking here, see my *1 and 2 Thessalonians*, 108–12.

sister" (τὸν ἀδελφόν, v. 6) makes it likely that these particular admonitions are directed primarily toward warding off potential intra-communal sexual practices where some (free males in particular) in the community, under the influence of the common-sense assumptions previously "hardwired" into their imaginations, might self-indulgently treat others as simply objects for gratifying their sexual desires without necessarily understanding such an action as sinful.

Such exploitative behavior would be the opposite of the holiness to which this audience is called since it would reflect anything but the cruciform character of the holy God explicated by Christ in Paul's "master story" in Phil 2:6-8.[42] Instead it would reflect life among "the gentiles who do not acknowledge God" (4:5), i.e., life "in Adam" among those who have not "turned to God from idols to be enslaved to the living and true God." Like the God of Israel, when his people's actions violate his holy character (cf. Ezek 36:16-21), Paul reminds the Thessalonians that the *cruciform* Lord, to whom the church owes its existence, will avenge activity within the corporate life of this people that violates his own character.

Paul goes on to associate these exploitative sexual actions with ἀκαθαρσία, a term that we have already noted he associates with sin elsewhere.[43] Although ἀκαθαρσία (impurity) generally refers to some form of ritual impurity in the OT, even there its meaning was being extended to include the polluting effects of idolatry (e.g., Ezek 36:25b, 29a) and other offensive practices including sexual immorality (e.g., Ezek 22:10-16). For Paul the ἀκαθαρσία that is expressed by, and results from, sinful sexual activity seems to retain some of its OT character as a dynamic, contagious force that can infiltrate, pollute, and damage entire relational networks (see, e.g., 1 Cor 5).[44] That it can be enslaving as well is implied by the language of 1 Cor 6:12 where, according to Paul, having sex with prostitutes can put one under the control of one's own sex drive. Engaging in such activity would essentially plunge the recently liberated Thessalonians back into the

---

42. On which see Michael J. Gorman, "'Although/Because, he was in the Form of God': The Theological Significance of Paul's Master Story (Phil 2:6-11)," *JTI* 1 (2007) 147-69.

43. Paul occasionally uses ἀκαθαρσία with non-sexual nuances (e.g., 1 Thess 2:3), but more often uses it in contexts having to do with sexual immorality (e.g., Rom 1:24; 2 Cor 12:21; Gal 5:19-20; cf. Eph 4:19, 5:3; Col 3:5).

44. Anyone who has seen the rippling effects of the damage done to relationships in multiple directions at once when improper sexual behavior is discovered in a tight-knit, local church will share a sense of Paul's concern.

sphere of life "in Adam" in which they used to present their "members as slaves to ἀκαθαρσία" (Rom 6:19b).

Once it is clear to these recently converted gentiles that this sort of sexual activity compromises their fidelity to God by violating the character of the cruciform Lord, to willingly engage in such activity would expose one to the same eschatological vengeance (ἐκδίκησις) as those refusing to acknowledge God and obey the good news about Jesus (2 Thess 1:8).[45] Such a conscious, intentional act of sin would be a rejection of enslavement to God (1 Thess 4:8) and could re-enslave the person who initiates the sexual encounter to Sin's cosmic power, all the while re-exposing the whole community to its polluting, death-dealing effects. However, this need not happen since, as Paul assures the community, God "is [continually] giving [διδόντα] his Holy Spirit into you all" (4:8).[46] Hence, with God's *Holy* Spirit now continuously transforming their imaginations and energizing every part of their bodies (even their sexual organs), they need not be enslaved to what they now know full well to be *sinful* cultural patterns of πορνεία that would make their bodies vehicles for the contagious, enslaving effects of impurity (ἀκαθαρσία).

Having been socialized into a culture whose common-sense patterns of thinking and behaving are sculpted by Sin's cosmic power, those who become enslaved to the living and true God must learn what constitutes a sinful act *after* being liberated from Sin's cosmic power. They must be taught what it means to "walk worthily of the God who continues calling [them] into his own kingdom and glory/honor" (1 Thess 2:12). Under the lordship of a cruciform Lord, any act that violates that Lord's own character is an act of sin[47] and willingly engaging in such actions invites eschatological punishment, along with the potential of being re-enslaved to Sin's cosmic power and re-exposing the whole ecclesia to its death-dealing effects. God, however, is faithful to grant the ongoing gift of the Holy Spirit to enable those "in Christ" not to willingly engage in acts they now know to be sins and thus not to be swept back into Sin's cosmic, enslaving power. But

---

45. Especially given its rarity in Paul as an eschatological referent, the language of the Lord being an avenger (ἔκδικος) in 1 Thess 4:6 and inflicting vengeance (ἐκδίκησις) in 2 Thess 1:8 suggests this sort of connection between the two passages.

46. The present tense participle, διδόντα, signals an ongoing supplying of the Spirit (cf. Gal 3:5) "into" this community, not simply a one-time gift of the Spirit.

47. Other such actions referred to in these letters that might possibly be regarded as sinful based on this criterion include repaying evil for evil (1 Thess 5:12) and exploiting the community's resources by refusing to work (1 Thess 5:14; 2 Thess 3:6–16).

given the depth of the effects of Sin's sculpting power on the imaginations of those formerly under its enslaving power, those now enslaved to the living and true God must remain open to learning which of their unconscious patterns of thinking and behaving actually violate the cruciform Lord's own character. That is, they must remain open to the Spirit's continuing—and often painful—work in sanctifying their imaginations.

Concluding Reflections

Fleshing out the connections between the Thessalonian correspondence and Paul's argument in Romans regarding Sin's cosmic power and life "in Adam" has enabled us to see more clearly some of the implicit hamartiological assumptions in 1 and 2 Thessalonians. It has become clear, for example, that human intentionality cannot be the primary arbiter as to what constitutes a sinful action against the "living and true God" who raised his Son from the dead (1 Thess 1:9–10). Since their common-sense patterns of thinking and behaving are so sculpted by Sin's cosmic power, those "in Adam" may imagine their actions as just—even underwritten by divine approval—when they are actually sins against the true God. Regardless of intent, actions that impede God's salvific, life-giving mission for the world are sins that further Sin's cosmic reign of death. Hence, engaging in sinful actions while under Sin's cosmic power does not require consciousness of one's enslavement or consciousness that one's actions are "sinful."

The fact that Torah itself—and by extension, Christian Scripture—can be taken over by Sin's cosmic power and used as an instrument that ultimately brings death to those to whom it was intended to lead to life (Rom 7:4–12) highlights the inadequacy of making human intentionality the primary arbiter of what constitutes sin. Actions committed with the intention of keeping Torah or obeying Christian Scripture may be sins against the God who gave Torah/Christian Scripture when such actions result in impeding God's salvific, life-giving intentions for the world and/or violate the cruciform character of creation's Lord, Jesus. One might think here of members of lynch mobs across the US during the lynching era. Although *consciously* imagining themselves to be aligned with the Christian God by using Scripture to support white supremacy, they were *unconsciously* "weapons of injustice" in the hands of Sin's cosmic power (Rom 6:13a). Under the protection of civil law—itself an instrument of Sin's cosmic power—and Christian Scripture interpreted as supporting their cause,[48] they saw themselves as only giving a troublesome group of people the justice they deserved.

All this illustrates just how effective Sin is in sculpting the personal and social imaginations of those under its cosmic power. For those "in Adam," Sin sculpts sinful assumptions that become physically embedded in the neural network of a person's brain and socially embeds each person within a network of relationships so that these assumptions become common sense. This is why those who become enslaved to the living and true God must learn what constitutes a sinful act *after* being liberated from Sin's cosmic power. The Spirit must bring about a sanctification of one's imagination so that one's very neural network is physically "rewired" in more cruciform ways,[49] enabling one to recognize unconscious patterns of thinking and behaving that violate the cruciform Lord's own character. In other words, to recognize what constitutes a sinful act against the "living and true God" who raised his Son from the dead requires intentional openness to the ongoing sanctifying work of the Spirit who also provides the enabling power not to willingly engage in such actions.

---

48. Cf. Croasmun, *Emergence*, 127–33.

49. Cf. Paul Markham, *Rewired: Exploring Religious Conversion* (Eugene: Wipf & Stock, 2007).

10

Re-Ordering the Household: Misalignment and Realignment to God's οἰκονομία in 1 Timothy

GEORGE M. WIELAND

THE FIRST LETTER TO Timothy, in common with 2 Timothy, Titus, and other letters whose authorship is disputed, is often approached with an agenda of comparison with the undisputed Pauline letters. Given that the scholarly consensus for much of the last century has been that the three "Pastoral Epistles" represent an attempt some time after Paul's death to enlist his name and authority in the interests of a particular strand of post-Pauline Christianity,[1] it is natural that the degree of conformity to or divergence from the Paul whom we know from those letters whose authenticity is less in dispute should be a matter of interest and debate. A reading driven by such questions, however, runs the risk of distorting the theological, ecclesial, missional, and other contours that might emerge should the letters be approached on their own terms. Similarly, the prior decision that the two letters addressed to Timothy together with the one addressed to Titus should be treated as a corpus sharing a single provenance, perspective, and

---

1. Luke T. Johnson comments, "The term 'debate' is surely too strong for the present situation, which is closer to a fixed academic consensus" (*The First and Second Letters to Timothy* [AYBC 35a; New York: Doubleday, 2001], 55). He goes on, however, to propose a re-examination of that majority opinion in the introductory section of his commentary ("III. Assessing the Authorship of the Pastoral Letters," 55–90).

purpose impedes the attempt to hear any distinctive voice that might be discerned should the letters be considered separately. Happily, recent work on the letters exhibits a greater attentiveness to individual characteristics of each.[2] In agreement with this tendency, the approach of this study will be to examine one of the three letters, known to us as the First Letter of Paul to Timothy, largely on its own terms. We shall note its professed occasion and purpose and ask where the topic of sin and its remedy might be treated or discerned, and what perspectives and prescriptions emerge.

Discussion of sin in the writings and theology of Paul has suffered markedly from the tendency to privilege the so-called *Hauptbriefe* over all other letters in the Pauline corpus as the evidence from which an account of Pauline theology may be constructed. As Simon Gathercole remarks,

> [S]cholars routinely argue that Paul does not really have much interest in 'sins'—that is to say, 'particular infractions of God's will'. On this view Paul has bigger fish to fry, namely the sinful condition of Adamic humanity, the flesh, and the hostile powers of death, the Law and Sin with a capital 'S'.[3]

This way of speaking about sin, however, is found almost exclusively in just one letter, Romans. Furthermore, within that letter it belongs principally to the sustained argument of one section, Rom 5:12—8:3. James Dunn reports the "extraordinary intensity of usage" represented by the fact that of the sixty-four occurrences of the noun ἁμαρτία in the Pauline corpus, forty-eight are found in Romans, and, of those, forty-one in 5:12—8:3.[4] He also acknowledges that "the striking personification of 'sin' in Romans is almost equally as unusual in the rest of the Pauline corpus, where the plural usage ('sins') predominates," apart only from 1 Cor 15:56, and Gal

---

2. See, e.g., the brief discussion in I. Howard Marshall, *The Pastoral Epistles* (ICC; Edinburgh: T. & T. Clark, 1999), 1–2, and the interpretation offered by James W. Aageson, *Paul, the Pastoral Epistles, and the Early Church* (Peabody: Hendrickson, 2008), passim. See also George M. Wieland, *The Significance of Salvation: A Study of Salvation Language in the Pastoral Epistles* (Milton Keynes: Paternoster, 2006), 265–66. William A. Richards, *Difference and Distance in Post-Pauline Christianity: An Epistolary Analysis of the Pastoral Epistles* (SBL 44; New York: Peter Lang, 2002), goes further in positing "three separate texts, from three different hands, set at three different points along the road from Paul" (240).

3. Simon Gathercole, "'Sins' in Paul," *NTS* 64 (2018) 143–61, 143.

4. James D. G. Dunn, *The Theology of Paul the Apostle* (Grand Rapids: Eerdmans, 1998), 111.

2:17 and 3:22.[5] It is nonetheless this particular treatment of sin as a personified power that Dunn goes on to expound as the characteristically Pauline understanding of sin.[6] Important though it undoubtedly is, however, this portrayal of sin as a power over against the power of the gospel that Paul develops in Romans is by no means the only way in which sin is referred to and discussed even in the undisputed letters of Paul. Before elevating it to the status of the definitive Pauline account of sin, it is appropriate to ask whether there are specific social or occasional considerations that might explain the highly distinctive discussion of sin at that point in the argument of Romans.[7] Of the Pauline corpus as a whole, Gathercole argues, "Paul is not only or predominantly concerned about Sin, singular with a capital S."[8] As we turn to the examination of 1 Timothy, it is with the recognition that, for Paul, it is not only Sin but sins that call for a divine remedy.

The occasion and purpose of the letter known to us as the First Letter of Paul to Timothy is set out as follows:

> I urge you, as I did when I was on my way to Macedonia, to remain in Ephesus so that you may instruct certain people not to teach any different doctrine, and not to occupy themselves with myths and endless genealogies that promote speculations rather than the divine training that is known by faith. (1 Tim 1:3-4)

According to Gordon Fee, "everything in the letter has to do with 1:3."[9] Whatever it has to say about sin and its remedy must be heard against that background of the threat to the community of teaching considered by the author to be damaging and the requirement to confront those perpetrating it.

In this letter the terms ἁμαρτάνω and cognates appear with relative frequency.[10] The verb ἁμαρτάνω (to sin) appears once (5:20), the noun

5. Dunn, *Theology of Paul*, 111.

6. Dunn, *Theology of Paul*, 111-14.

7. See, e.g., T. L. Carter, *Paul and the Power of Sin: Redefining 'Beyond the Pale'* (SNTSMS 115; Cambridge: Cambridge University Press, 2004), who seeks to understand Paul's sin language (principally in Romans) within the social context of Jewish-gentile relations in the church: "In placing all humanity under the power of sin, Paul was primarily concerned to establish that the Torah-observant Jew had no advantage over the law-free Gentile" (4).

8. Gathercole, "Sins," 161.

9. Gordon D. Fee, *1 and 2 Timothy, Titus* (NIBC 13; Peabody: Hendrickson, 1988), 7.

10. The five occurrences are far fewer than in Romans (60) or 1 Corinthians (12) but equal with Galatians and more than are found in any other letter attributed to Paul.

ἁμαρτία (sin) twice (5:22, 24), and the substantive ἁμαρτωλός (sinner) twice (1:9, 15).[11] There is also one occurrence of the noun παράβασις (transgression, 2:14). These must not be assumed to exhaust the presence and treatment of the idea of sin in this letter, but they do represent data that must be taken into account in an investigation of the understanding of sin and the role it plays in the letter's conceptual framework and argument. Accordingly, they provide a convenient starting point.

Sinners as Lawbreakers (1:9-11)

The term ἁμαρτωλός appears in 1 Tim 1:9 paired with ἀσεβής, yielding the phrase, "ungodly and sinner(s)" (NASB). The same pairing occurs frequently in LXX Psalms (1:1, 5; 11:31; cf. 57:11) and other Wisdom literature (Prov 11:31; Sir 12:6; 41:5), and once in the Prophets (Ezek 33:8). In the New Testament, besides 1 Tim 1:9, it is found in 1 Pet 4:18 and Jude 15. The two terms complement and explicate each other, to the extent that the pairing might be regarded as a hendiadys: the "sinner" is ungodly, deficient in relation to God, and indifferent or hostile to the way of God.

The broader setting for the term ἁμαρτωλός in 1:9-11 is a "vice list," one of several utilized in the New Testament letters.[12] Though these do exhibit similarities to catalogues of wrongdoing in the Hellenistic environment,[13] there is sufficient distinctiveness in both content and form for each of them to be regarded as constructed or at least intentionally deployed to serve the author's particular purposes.[14] In this instance the topic under consideration is the Law. Those teachers who were deviating from the healthy instruction that the letter commends wished to be regarded as νομοδιδάσκαλοι ("teachers of the Law"). The reference later in the letter

---

11. Of this vocabulary we find only one occurrence in 2 Timothy (ἁμαρτία, 3:6) and, in Titus, one each of ἁμαρτάνω (3:11) and ἁμαρτωλός (3:2).

12. Neil J. McEleney, "The Vice Lists of the Pastoral Epistles," *CBQ* 36 (1974) 203-19, identifies 1 Tim 1:9-10; 6:4-5; 2 Tim 3:2-5; Titus 3:3. Philip H. Towner, *The Letters to Timothy and Titus* (NICNT; Grand Rapids, MI: Eerdmans, 2006), includes 1 Tim 3:3 (139). They are prevalent both in the letters of Paul (see C. G. Kruse, "Virtues and Vices," in *Dictionary of Paul and His Letters* [eds. G. Hawthorne et al.; Downers Grove, IL: IVP Academic, 1993], 962-63), and in other NT letters (see D. G. Reid, "Virtues and Vices," in *Dictionary of the Later New Testament and Its Developments* [eds. R. P. Martin and P. H. Davids; Downers Grove, IL: IVP Academic, 1997], 1190-94).

13. Kruse, "Virtues and Vices," 962-63.

14. See McEleney, "Vice Lists," 216-17.

to those who "forbid marriage and demand abstinence from foods" (4:3) suggests that their teaching might have exhibited an ascetic and legalistic tendency. In this context, the function of the vice list seems to be to indicate the inappropriateness of such laying down of the law for a community founded on faith in Christ. The list here comprises fourteen specific items together with a general category, all of them set in contradistinction to the one positive characterization, the δίκαιος (1:9), representing the righteous person whose ways please God.[15] This aligns with the wicked/righteous dichotomy that is prevalent in much of the OT Wisdom literature.[16] Although the placing of the term ἁμαρτωλός in the list does not afford it any particular prominence, W. Günther's evaluation of the range of such vocabulary is pertinent: "All the other concepts and synonyms are overshadowed by *hamartia* and are to be understood in the light of this concept."[17]

The structure of this catalogue of sinners displays some correspondence to that of the Decalogue, in that sinfulness that offends against God (first three pairs of characteristics) is followed by offences against other people.[18] Interestingly, however, those negative behaviors are said to be contrary not only to the Law but also to Paul's gospel (1:11). The rhetorical function of the vice list is not to set the Law over against the gospel but rather to indicate that, while it has a role in addressing "extreme lawbreakers,"[19] the Law is not the appropriate emphasis when teaching the "righteous" (δίκαιος, 1:9) in order to nurture the health of the church. In the broader context of this opening section of the letter, a preoccupation with esoteric topics that serve only to stir up fruitless speculation is contrasted to the teaching appropriate to a community of faith whose life is in accord with God's οἰκονομία (1:4). In the world-affirming perspective of this letter,[20] this οἰκονομία may be understood as more than, though including, "God's plan of salvation."[21] It is "God's way of ordering things,"[22]

15. [νόμος... κεῖται] ἀνόμοις δὲ καὶ ἀνυποτάκτοις, ἀσεβέσι καὶ ἁμαρτωλοῖς, ἀνοσίοις καὶ βεβήλοις, πατρολῴαις καὶ μητρολῴαις, ἀνδροφόνοις, πόρνοις, ἀρσενοκοίταις, ἀνδραποδισταῖς, ψεύσταις, ἐπιόρκοις, καὶ εἴ τι ἕτερον τῇ ὑγιαινούσῃ διδασκαλίᾳ ἀντίκειται.

16. See, e.g., Pss 1 and 37; Prov 10–12; Eccl 3:17, etc.

17. W. Günther, "Sin," *NIDNTT*, 3:577–87, 579.

18. Towner, *Letters*, 125.

19. Towner, *Letters*, 124.

20. See, e.g., 2:1–4; 4:1–5.

21. See discussion in Marshall, *Pastoral Epistles*, 367–68.

22. Johnson, *First and Second Letters to Timothy*, 164.

both in the church (God's οἶκός, 3:15) and the world. This aligns with the OT perspective as described by Mark Boda that views sin as "an offense against a divinely ordered norm."[23]

What, then, is the sin-related problem for which a remedy must be found? In this instance the issue to be addressed is not directly the committing of the sins whose perpetrators are listed in 1:9–11, but rather the activity of those teachers in the church who are stirring up contentious speculation and laying down the law. They are not at this point described as sinners, but the polemic against them is rigorous. Their teaching is labeled heterodox (1:3), its effects are exposed as damaging (1:4), they are said to have deviated from the οἰκονομία θεοῦ to futile talk (1:4–6), they are accused of self-serving motives (1:7), and there is perhaps an implied association of those law-teachers with the vices that the Law is intended to regulate. All of this serves to position them over against Paul's God-entrusted gospel, and the healthy teaching that conforms to it (1:10b–11). The medical connotation of "healthy" (ὑγιαίνω, to be in health) in the characterization of teaching that conforms to the gospel (1:10–11) is significant. Such teaching addresses the sickness that was afflicting the community. So what is the remedy? At its most basic level it is simply that those who are promulgating corrosive, unhealthy teaching should be persuaded to stop, and return to health: to the kind of instruction that is in conformity with Paul's gospel and God's way of ordering the world, and that cultivates love, purity, good conscience, and sincere faith (1:5).

Remedy for Sinful People (1:12–17)

The next occurrence of the substantive ἁμαρτωλός is in the context of one of five "trustworthy sayings" identified by the formula πιστὸς ὁ λόγος that are found in the letters to Timothy and Titus.[24] The saying here affirms that the purpose of Christ's coming into the world was to save ἁμαρτωλοί (1:15).[25] It is Christ's historical appearing (1:15) and continuing activity in showing mercy, judging faithful, empowering, and bestowing grace

---

23. Mark J. Boda, *A Severe Mercy: Sin and Its Remedy in the Old Testament* (Winona Lake, IN: Eisenbrauns, 2009), 11.

24. The formula appears in some form in 1 Tim 1:15; 3:1; 4:9; 2 Tim 2:11; Titus 3:8. See Marshall, *Pastoral Epistles*, 326–30, Excursus 9: "The trustworthy sayings."

25. Echoing the dominical saying, "I have come not to call the righteous, but sinners" (Matt 9:13; pars. Mark 2:17; Luke 5:32).

(1:12–14) that is the remedy for the sinner's alienation from the life and service of God in the past, present, and future. Although this general soteriological significance is by no means excluded, the saying functions here in a very particular way in relation to the topos of rectifying the behavior of teachers who are damaging the church. It is Paul himself who exemplifies the ἁμαρτωλοί who are the objects of Christ's saving; indeed, he is πρῶτος ("foremost") among them.[26] So determined was his opposition to God's ordering of the world as it is realized in Christ, the gospel, and the church that he could be fitly characterized as βλάσφημος καὶ διώκτης καὶ ὑβριστής ("a blasphemer and a persecutor and a man of violence," 1:13). The remedy for this sinful condition was the outpouring of Christ's mercy and grace, generating in Paul faith and love in the place of unbelief and hostility, and placing the erstwhile enemy of God, now trusted and empowered, in the service of the one whom he had opposed (1:12–16).[27]

Christ's dealing with Paul thereby serves as a prototype (ὑποτύπωσις, 1:16) of how Christ's saving operates.[28] It brings an unbeliever (1:13) to faith and into eternal life (1:16–17),[29] but more specifically within the argument of 1:3–20 it transforms the opponent into the faithful servant of Christ and the gospel (1:12–13, 11). From the lips of the blasphemer (1:13) issues exultant praise (1:17). Having begun with a depiction of the damaging teaching of people who have deviated from pure love, good conscience, and authentic faith (1:3–7), this section of the letter concludes with pathways to its remedy. The servant, Timothy, must avoid such sinful deviation in his own ministry by maintaining faith and a good conscience (1:18–19). As for those who, according to the characterization in this section, are already sinners, opponents of God and the gospel, Christ's limitless patience offers hope (1:16). Educative and restorative discipline, even in the extreme form of whatever is meant by being "turned over to Satan" (1:20), might reorient those blasphemers into the path of faithful ministry now exemplified by the former blasphemer (1:13). It is within this paraenetic

26. On preferring "foremost-in-degree" to "first-in-a-series" here see discussion in Wieland, *Significance of Salvation*, 40.

27. M. Wolter, "Paulus, der berkehrte Gottesfeind. Zum Verständnis von 1.Tim. 1:13," *NovT* 31 (1989) 48–66, makes the case that Paul is presented here as a stereotypical figure, the θεομάχος ("enemy of God").

28. Taking what is exemplified to be Christ's saving rather than Paul the saved sinner, in agreement with Johnson, *First and Second Letters to Timothy*, 181.

29. The ζωὴ αἰώνιος which faith in Christ envisions is connected by the ensuing doxology to the imperishable life of God (1:16–17).

movement that the explanation that Paul had been shown mercy because he had sinned in ignorance (ὅτι ἀγνοῶν ἐποίησα ἐν ἀπιστίᾳ, 1:13) should be understood. There may well be a reflection here of the OT distinction between intentional and unintentional sins (e.g., Num 15:22-31). If that is the case, however, its purpose is not to protect Paul's reputation by pleading ignorance as a mitigating factor in his wrongdoing.[30] Rather, it could have in view the opportunity that is being extended to the heterodox teachers to recognize the inadequacy of their present state of knowledge and embark on a pathway—marked out by Paul himself—to restoration and fruitful ministry through receiving new learning (ἵνα παιδευθῶσι, 1:20).

Remedy for a Sinful World (2:1-8)

In this section prayer is urged for all people, and particularly for those who rule, on the basis of God's desire to save and Christ's mediation. Sin is not mentioned explicitly but the divine provision of saving and ransom may be assumed to address the *Unheil* and alienation that sin produces. The specific content of the saving envisaged in 2:2 is ἵνα ἤρεμον καὶ ἡσύχιον βίον διάγωμεν ἐν πάσῃ εὐσεβείᾳ καὶ σεμνότητι, which suggests that divine ordering of the world to which sin is opposed.[31] The marked emphasis on "everyone" (ὑπὲρ πάντων ἀνθρώπων, 2:1; ὃς πάντας ἀνθρώπους θέλει σωθῆναι, 2:4; ἀντίλυτρον ὑπὲρ πάντων, 2:6; cf. ἐν παντὶ τόπῳ, 2:8) signals a universalizing impulse that accords with Paul's role as "teacher of the gentiles" (2:7). Specifically, Paul's teaching was to be "in faith and truth" (2:7), corresponding to the coming to know the truth that, in 2:4, explicates the idea of being saved.[32] Since the gentiles collectively could be considered sinners simply by their not having the Law that gave them access to God's way of ordering the world,[33] teaching them would in itself constitute, on one level, a remedy for sin.

30. So Fred D. Gealy and Morgan P. Noyes, "The First and Second Epistles to Timothy and the Epistle to Titus: Introduction and Exegesis," in *The Interpreter's Bible* (vol. 11; Nashville: Abingdon, 1955), 341-551: "Paul is gently shielded from the impact of his pre-Christian wickedness by the attributing of it to unbelief as a result of ignorance" (389). But cf. Marshall: "The sinfulness of the pre-enlightened apostle's persecution of the church is not downplayed here in the least—on the contrary it serves to heighten the response of wonder and thankfulness at the experience of grace" (*Pastoral Epistles*, 393).

31. See above on 1:9-11.

32. This reading is argued in Wieland, *Significance of Salvation*, 55-56.

33. See Günther, "Sin," 579; K. H. Rengstorf, "ἁμαρτωλός," in *TDNT*, 1:317-33, 326.

The remedy for lack of knowledge could only be effective salvifically, however, because of the divine remedy for the alienation of all humanity accomplished by the self-giving of Christ (2:5-6). Again, universality is stressed: one God and savior (2:3, 5), one mediator (2:5-6), and in the affirmation that Christ's self-giving was ὑπὲρ πάντων (2:6) rather than, as in the Markan form of the *Hingabemotiv*, ἀντὶ πολλῶν (Mark 10:45). The rare term ἀντίλυτρον (2:6) certainly carries priestly and sacrificial connotations, though the precise significance of the ἀντί- compound is much discussed. Colin Brown suggests, "a ransom which has been completely paid, an atonement that has been effected."[34] The idea of substitution—not only on behalf of (ὑπέρ) but in the place of (ἀντί) is plausible.[35] This redemption that addresses the plight of all, and specifically the gentiles in their state of sin without the Law, is the content of τὸ μαρτύριον καιροῖς ἰδίοις, the eschatological witness to the nations for which Paul is commissioned (2:6).[36] Here as in 1:12-17 we have found testimony (in the form of traditional material) to the divine remedy for the sinful state of people and nations effected in the historic Christ event alongside an affirmation of the role of teaching and training in remedying sinful behavior.

Deception, Transgression, and Their Remedy (2:9-15)

In 2:9-15, where the author addresses issues concerning women in the Christian community, we discover again the twin elements of a salvation-historical remedy for sin together with a strong interest in the role of teaching both in causing and in remedying sinful behavior. There is no occurrence of ἁμαρτάνω, ἁμαρτία, or cognates in this passage, but the noun παράβασις, "transgression," appears in relation to Eve in the unusual construction ἐν παραβάσει γέγονεν (2:14), which might be rendered, "entered into (a state of) transgression."[37] With regard to the detrimental influence of heterodox

---

Cf. "gentile sinners," Gal 2:15.

34. C. Brown, "λύτρον," *NIDNTT*, 3:189-200, 197.

35. See discussion in William D. Mounce, *Pastoral Epistles* (WBC 46; Nashville: Thomas Nelson, 2000), 89-90; Towner, *Letters*, 183-85.

36. A similar cluster of ideas, including the one God who redeems, the forgiveness of sins and the gathering of the nations, is found in Isa 43-44. The possibility that the Isaiah passage influences 1 Tim 2:1-7 is noted in Wieland, *Significance of Salvation*, 67-68, and developed fruitfully by Peter D. Brown, "The Use of Ransom Language in 1 Timothy 2:1-7 and Titus 2:11-14" (PhD diss., Catholic University of America, 2014), 118-24.

37. This use γέγονεν is unique in biblical Greek, but there is a faint resonance with

teaching, a particular threat might have been the targeting of women and their households by proponents of esoteric but fruitless speculations (cf. 2 Tim 3:6-7). Such a problem would be compounded should women, under that sort of influence, attempt to assume the place of teaching and leading in their households and in the Christian assembly and use it to disseminate the heterodox message. The account of the deception and consequent sin of Adam and Eve in Gen 3 provides the material from which the author's paraenesis is developed. Eve was deceived, and as a result found herself in a state of transgression, with dire consequences. Those women who were in danger of being enticed by heterodox teachers should also beware of being deceived and drawn away from the teaching and way of life that conformed to the gospel as it had been entrusted to Paul, and they should certainly not be influencing others in that sinful direction.

The practical remedy for this sinful state lies also in the realm of teaching, in two ways. First, women are to learn (μανθανέτω, 2:11). The radical nature of that command is often missed in the very different cultural contexts in which the text is read today. Preservation from sinful deception comes through being established in the truth. Secondly, those prone to deviate into unhealthy teaching, whether the primary perpetrators (1:3) or, as here, the women of the community who in that context seemed particularly vulnerable to it are to have their teaching activity restricted (2:12), at least until necessary corrective learning has taken place (2:11? Cf. 1:20).

The passage moves from the practical remedy for the unhealthy teaching that diverges from the gospel to the remedy for the state of sin in which the world lies. Continuing in the manner of a haggadic discourse on the Genesis account of Eve's deception,[38] saving is affirmed, in an allusive reference to Gen 3:15-16: σωθήσεται δὲ διὰ τῆς τεκνογονίας (2:15). Commentators have seen a range of possible meanings in this enigmatic statement, from a salvation-historical reference to Mary's bearing of the Christ child as Savior of the world to a pragmatic insistence that the women of the Ephesian church should find their salvation from the ascetic prescriptions of the heterodox teachers (4:3; cf. 5:14-15) in settling down to a domestic role.[39] It is plausible that there could be both an indication of a salvation-

---

Gen 3:22 LXX, where God says of Adam that γέγονεν ὡς εἷς ἐξ ἡμῶν. Also unique is the expression ἐν παραβάσει, but ἐν ἀνομίαις and ἐν ἁμαρτίαις are found in parallel in Ps 50:7 LXX.

38. See A. T. Hanson, *The Pastoral Epistles* (NCBC; London: Marshall, Morgan & Scott, 1982), 72, and *Studies in the Pastoral Epistles* (London: SPCK, 1968), 65-77.

39. See discussion of options in Marshall, *Pastoral Epistles*, 468-70.

historical reading of Gen 3:15, whereby Eve's childbearing sets in motion the succession of childbearings from which would ultimately come the messiah, and the paraenetic effect of affirming motherhood as a sphere within which Christian salvation might be fully experienced.

At this point there is a shift from the singular subject of the verb σωθήσεται to the plural verb of the conditional clause, ἐὰν μείνωσιν ἐν πίστει καὶ ἀγάπῃ καὶ ἁγιασμῷ μετὰ σωφροσύνης (2:15b). Somewhat obscured by the chapter division, the statement is followed by another πιστὸς ὁ λόγος formula, which could be taken to refer back rather than forward.[40] If so, then we are dealing with traditional material that has been woven into the discussion. Though syntactically awkward, the plural μείνωσιν has the effect of widening the focus from "Eve," "the woman," and "she" to women in general, to whom, as much as to men, might be applied the "faithful word" that "those will be saved who remain in faith, love, and holiness."[41] The addition of "with propriety" returns to the practical remedying of disordered (and therefore sin-tainted) behavior with which this section began (2:9-10).

The Sins of Elders? (5:17-25)

Other than in the passages considered above the terms ἁμαρτάνω and ἁμαρτία occur in this letter only in a section mostly concerned with how Timothy is to act in regard to church elders. He is to rebuke those who "persist in sin" (present participle τοὺς ἁμαρτάνοντας, 5:20), avoid participating in the sins (ἁμαρτίαι) of others (5:22), and remember that the sins (ἁμαρτίαι) of some people are obvious while the sins of others may only become apparent at the judgment (5:24). It is commonly assumed that "those who persist in sin" are themselves elders. Mounce comments that, "Many of the problems in Ephesus originated with the elders, their heretical teaching and their sinful behavior."[42] In this pericope, however, the concern is first to give due honor to elders who serve well (5:17), and then to protect elders from accusations that cannot be verified (5:18). Behind the instruction in 5:20 stands the Deuteronomic law concerning witnesses (Deut

---

40. In agreement with Frances Young, *The Theology of the Pastoral Letters* (NTT; Cambridge: Cambridge University Press, 1994), 56-57, who suggests that all those sayings have soteriological content.

41. This reading is argued more fully in Wieland, *Significance of Salvation*, 69-84.

42. Mounce, *Pastoral Epistles*, 321.

19:15-22). The correspondences are striking, particularly with LXX. Two or three witnesses are required for an accusation to be entertained (Deut 19:15//1 Tim 5:19); if an individual brings an accusation, both accuser and accused must appear before the Lord and the community's leaders (Deut 19:16-17//1 Tim 5:21a); should the accusation be found to be false, the accuser is to be punished (Deut 19:18-19//1 Tim 5:20?); the outcome will be that "the rest shall hear and be afraid," and the evil of bearing false witness shall be purged from the community (Deut 19.20: οἱ ἐπίλοιποι ἀκούσαντες φοβηθήσονται//1 Tim 5:20: οἱ λοιποὶ φόβον ἔχωσιν); the judges are not to be swayed by partiality in dealing with the malicious accuser (Deut 19:21//1 Tim 5:21b).[43]

This background is the more plausible given the reference to Deut 25:41 in the immediate context, in 1 Tim 5:18. The sins in view here, then, are not the heretical teaching or immoral behavior of certain elders but the sin of bearing false witness (Exod 20:16). The remedy prescribed is public rebuke, not only to correct the perpetrators but to root out such destructive behavior from the community (5:20).

Although separated by the advice about drinking wine, the two references to ἁμαρτίαι that follow have in view the same context of Timothy's community leadership. He is told not to share in the sins of others (5:22) by "laying on hands" too quickly, and cautioned that sins are not always obvious before the time of judgment (5:24). If, as most commentators assume, the laying on of hands represents here the appointing of new elders (cf. what seems to be a commissioning of Timothy himself in 4:14),[44] then to share in others' sins would be to bear part of the responsibility for sins of those whom Timothy had appointed to leadership, either past sins that might have disqualified them from leadership or sins committed once they became leaders.[45] The act of laying on hands could, however, have other significance. In the case of an accusation of blasphemy recounted in Lev 24:10-23, Moses gathered the people and required all who were testifying to the guilt of the accused to lay their hands on his head (ἐπιθήσουσιν ... τὰς χεῖρας αὐτῶν ἐπὶ τὴν κεφαλὴν αὐτου, Lev 24:13 LXX), thus passing

---

43. Towner notes the verbal correspondences, but on balance considers the persistent sinners in 5:20 to be a reference to the elders (*Letters*, 371-72). Frances Young, however, without referring to Deuteronomy in this instance, finds it plausible in the light of early church history that "those who persist in sin" are those who challenge the *presbyteroi* who preserve the tradition (*Theology*, 106-7).

44. Options are discussed in Marshall, *Pastoral Epistles*, 620-22.

45. Towner, *Letters*, 375.

judgment that would then be enacted by the community. Both context and terminology would fit well as background to the instructions to Timothy on how to deal with accusations against elders. As well as censuring any who bring unsubstantiated accusations (5:20) he himself is not to be hasty in adding his condemnation by laying hands on the accused (5:22).

The intertestamental story of Susanna offers another example of false testimony and accusation (Sus 41, 43, 55, 59, 61), although in this case elders are the perpetrators not the victims. Two elders conspired to seduce the beautiful and virtuous Susanna. She spurned their advances and the furious elders accused her of adultery with someone else. When the people gathered for the case to be heard and Susanna was called, her two accusers "laid their hands on her head" (ἔθηκαν τὰς χεῖρας ἐπὶ τὴν κεφαλὴν αὐτῆς, Sus 34).[46] The death sentence was passed. Susanna was rescued by the sudden intervention of the young Daniel, who refused to participate in the execution, declaring himself καθαρός (clean, pure) of the woman's blood (Sus 46). The two elders were called back, and Daniel warned the first that his former sins had now caught up with him (νῦν ἥκασιν αἱ ἁμαρτίαι σου ἃς ἐποίεις τὸ πρότερον, Sus 52). As the two were cross-examined, an angel of the Lord was standing by to ensure justice and execute God's judgment (Sus 55, 59). Those elements are all present in the instructions to Timothy concerning accusations against elders: accusations that might be suspect (5:19), the presence of angels to ensure justice (5:21), laying on hands (5:22), which could involve participating in sins (of false witness) initiated by others (5:22), staying pure by refusing to participate in unjust judgment (5:22), and the assurance that sins, though hidden for a time, will in the end come to judgment (5:24).

Sin as Misalignment to God's Way of Ordering the World

This brief investigation of passages in 1 Timothy where particular vocabulary suggests an interest in sin has yielded the contours of the letter's perspective on sin and its remedy. Sin is whatever opposes or steps out of alignment with God's οἰκονομία (1:4), expressed to some extent in the Law but more fully in the gospel (1:8, 11). The remedy is both in God's saving realized in Christ and in the promulgation of healthy teaching. Oriented

---

46. Rahlf's LXX includes both an older version that survived in Syriac, and Theodotion's translation dating from the second century CE. The version quoted here is Theodotian's.

by that perspective, we are able to summarize, drawing more widely on the content of the letter.

The remedy for the misalignment of the world is provided through the coming of Christ Jesus into the world (1:15; 2:15), his priestly sacrifice and mediation (2:5-6), his future manifestation (6:13-15), and, meantime, the continuing operation of his mercy and grace (1:12-16). As this is believed and received, people such as Paul and other servants are rightly aligned to God's οἰκονομία and take their place in the witness to the nations (2:6b-7; 3:16) that will bring them in turn into well-ordered life in enjoyment of God's saving rule over creation (4:4-5), the world (2:1-2) and the church (3:14-15). This life now is oriented towards and will lead into a sharing of the eternal life of God (1:16-17; 6:16, 17-19).

For sin's damage to be repaired, however, the work of teaching is critical. Healthy teaching is to be offered tirelessly, damaging teaching is to be countered, and those who promote it are to be dealt with. Sin's remedy in the form of the gospel that declares and orients towards God's good ordering of the world and its future hope has been entrusted to Paul (1:11), and now to Timothy (the παραθήκη, 6:20). He is to guard it, both for the church and for himself.

Index of Modern Authors

Aageson, James W., 148
Abbott, T. K., 120
Achtemeier, Paul J., 50
Adams, Edward, 126
Anderson, Gary, 8

Barclay, John M. G., 15, 19, 20, 56, 57, 73, 96, 112, 125
Bartchy, S. Scott, 18
Barrett, C. K., 53, 90
Barth, Karl, 31, 64, 65, 66, 67, 68, 80, 114, 129
Barth, Markus, 118
Becker, Jürgen, 101, 111, 113
Belleville, Linda L., 88
Best, Ernest, 116, 126, 127
Biddle, Mark E., 102, 110
Bieringer, Reimund, 82, 88, 92, 95
Bird, Michael, 111
Bockmuehl, Markus, 134
Boda, Mark, 7-8, 152
Boer, Martinus C. de, 17, 19, 23, 24, 28, 54, 55, 70
Bourdieu, Pierre, 124, 125, 126, 129
Brand, Miriam, 13
Branick, Vincent P., 95
Brannon, M. Jeff, 127
Breytenbach, Cilliers, 76, 90
Brooke, George J., 85
Brown, Alexandra R., 68, 71
Brown, C., 155
Brown, Derek R., 39
Brown, Peter D., 155
Brown, William Laban, 63, 64, 65
Bruce, F. F., 121

Bultmann, Rudolf, 24, 26, 27, 53, 61
Bunyan, John, 34-35
Burton, Ernest deWitt, 108

Caird, G. B., 100
Calvin, John, 69, 70, 90
Carter, T. L., 149
Ciampa, Roy E., 61, 123
Clayton, Philip, 78
Coakley, John, 67
Collins, Raymond F., 88
Conradie, E. M., 67
Cowper, William, 64, 65, 66, 67, 80
Croasmun, Matthew. 15, 17, 18-19, 24, 27, 28, 37, 61, 62, 66, 78, 79, 85, 135, 146

Das, A. Andrew, 59, 106
Davids, P. H., 150
Denny, James, 53
deSilva, David A., 100, 101, 102, 103, 105, 106, 110
Dunn, J. D. G., 101, 108, 116, 119, 120, 123, 130, 148, 149

Eadie, John, 118, 122
Eastman, Susan Grove, 15, 17, 19, 27, 28, 30, 50, 51, 68, 69, 70, 71, 79, 85, 89
Engberg-Pederson, Troels, 56, 57, 109

Fee, Gordon D., 56, 134, 149
Fitzmyer, Joseph A., 15, 52, 55, 56, 59, 93
Ford, David F., 81

INDEX OF MODERN AUTHORS

Foster, Paul, 119
Fowl, Stephen E., 118, 127, 128
Fung, Ronald, 110

Garlington, Don, 61
Gathercole, Simon, 15, 17, 34, 55, 57, 69, 70, 75, 76, 92, 97, 101, 103, 107, 108, 117, 118, 148, 149
Gaventa, Beverly Roberts, 15, 17, 26, 34, 35, 38, 50, 66, 70, 71, 79, 126
Gealy, Fred D., 154
Gilliard, Frank D., 134
Gorman, Michael, 108, 110, 132, 143
Green, Clifford, 66
Green, Gene L., 141, 142
Günther, W., 151, 154
Gupta, Nijay, 141

Hanson, A. T., 156
Harding, Sarah, 34, 128
Harris, Murray J., 56
Harrison, James R., 139
Hays, Richard, 57, 76
Heil, John Paul, 121, 122
Hoehner, Harold W., 118, 122
Hooker, Morna, 57, 58, 89, 96, 97
Hurst, L. D., 100

Jenkins, Richard, 124
Jewett, Robert, 58
Jipp, Joshua W., 122
Johnson, Andy, 130, 135
Johnson, Luke T., 147, 151, 153
Johnson, S. Lewis, Jr., 52, 56, 61

Käsemann, Ernst 23, 27, 30, 53, 59, 60, 61
Keck, Leander E., 132
Kendall, Guy, 2
King, Martin Luther Jr., 64
Kooten, George H. van, 85
Kruse, C. G., 150

Laato, Antti, 58, 59
Lam, Joseph, 6-8
Larkin, William J., 119, 122
Levison, John R., 53
Lightfoot, J. B., 121

Lincoln, Andrew T., 114, 118, 126, 129
Little, Joyce A., 50
Lohse, Eduard, 116
Longenecker, Bruce W., 37, 39, 47, 49
Longenecker, Richard N., 52
Lyonnet, Stanislas, 84

Malherbe, Abraham, 136, 142
Markham, Paul, 146
Marshall, I. Howard, 148, 151, 152, 154, 158
Martin, Dale B., 85
Martin, Ralph P., 88, 150
Martyn, J. Louis, 27, 31, 32, 50, 51, 55, 69, 70, 110
Matera, Frank J., 93
McEleney, Neil J., 150
McKnight, Scot, 120
Meiser, Martin, 54, 55
Merkle, Benjamin L., 118
Meyer, Paul W., 72
Mininger, Marcus A., 15, 16, 17, 21, 22, 25
Moo, Douglas, 52, 53, 61, 62, 123
Moule, C. F. D., 56
Mounce, William D., 155, 157
Muddiman, John, 119

Nathan, Emmanuel, 85
Newton, John, 64
Nickelsburg, G. W. E., 11
Noyes, Morgan P., 154
Nygren, Anders, 50

Ogereau, Julien M., 116

Pannenberg, Wolfhart, 71
Pao, David W., 120
Porter, Stanley E., 60

Räisänen Heikki, 50
Reid, D. G., 150
Richards, William A., 148
Reno, R. R., 110
Roberts, Erin, 73, 86
Robinson, H. Wheeler, 60
Rogerson, J. W., 60
Rodd, Cyril S., 60

Rosner, Brian S., 61, 123
Rutledge, Fleming, 118

Sabourin, Léopold, 88
Sanders, E. P., 101
Schäfer, Peter, 53
Shauf, Scott, 110
Schleiermacher, Friedrich, 67
Schmeller, Thomas, 82, 91
Schnelle, Udo, 21, 24
Schreiner, Thomas R., 52, 56, 61
Shedd, Russell Phillip, 60
Shum, Shui-Lun, 58
Seifrid, Mark, 110
Siker, Jeffrey, 67
Smith, Jay E., 142
Stegman, Thomas, 88
Stendahl, Krister, 75, 76
Stone, M. E., 11

Tack, Laura, 94
Tamez, Elsa, 68
Thrall, Margaret E., 56, 84, 87, 88, 93
Timmins, Will N., 28
Thiselton, Anthony C., 61, 74

Tolkien, J. R. R., 68, 72
Tonstad, Sigve, 46
Towner, Philip H., 150, 151, 155, 158

Vegge, Ivar, 82

Wagner, Ross J., 58, 59
Wallace, Daniel B., 119
Walsh, Brian, 40
Wedderburn, A. J. M., 24
Wieland, George M., 148, 153, 154, 155, 157
Weiland, Sperna, 67
Westerholm, Stephen, 51, 52, 53, 62
Wilson, R. McL., 120
Wink, Walter, 40, 45
Wolter, M., 153
Wright, N. T., 96, 112

Young, Frances, 81, 157, 158

Zahn, Theodor, 52
Zeisler, John, 53
Ziegler, Philip, 27, 40

Index of Ancient Documents

Old Testament

Genesis

2–3	136
2:16–17	22
2:17	20, 24
3	156
3:3–4	20
3:9	106
3:11	22
3:15–16	156
3:15	38, 157
3:19	20, 24
3:22	156
4:7	7, 12
11:1–9	136
12:3	106
18:18	106
18:20	6

Exodus

20:16	158

Leviticus

18:3–4	119, 121
24:10–23	158
24:13	158

Numbers

15:22–31	154
25:1–15	135

Deuteronomy

6:5–6	26
19:15–22	157–58
19:15	158
19:16–17	158
19:18–19	158
19:20	158
19:21	158
25:41	158

1 Samuel

18:10	140
19:9	140

Job

1:5	8

Psalms

1	151
1:1	150
1:5	150
11:31	150
31:1–2	92
31:1	91
31:2	92
32:1–2	75
35:2	26
36	26
37	151
50:7	156
51:9	7

Psalms (continued)

57:11	150
106:19–20	132
106:28–31	135
111:9	94

Proverbs

10–12	151
11:31	150
13:22	8
20:9	7

Ecclesiastes

3:17	151

Isaiah

14:3–23	136
14:13–14	136
29:9–10	140
40–55	57, 59
43–44	155
43:25	7, 92
44:3	106
50:08	58
52:7	59
52:15	59
53	57, 58, 59, 75, 76
53:1	59
53:4	75
53:6	7, 59
53:11–12	59
53:11	58
59:20	75

Jeremiah

18:11	7
31:34	92

Ezekiel

11:19–20	106
18:31	106
22:10–16	143
28:1–19	136–37
28:2	137
28:9	137
28:12–13a	137
28:15	137
28:16	137
28:18	137
28:19	137
33:8	150
36:16–21	143
36:25b	143
36:26–27	106
36:29a	143

Daniel

11:21–45	136
11:36	136
11:38–39	137

New Testament

Matthew

9:13	152
24:45	61
24:47	61
25:21	61
25:23	61

Mark

2:17	152
3:27	45
10:45	155
14:36	47

Luke

5:32	152
6:40	141

John

8:12	121
8:44	139

Romans

1-8	36, 123
1-4	34
1-3	35, 52
1	25
1:4	46, 48
1:5	47
1:16-17	46
1:18—3:20	15
1:18-3:8	132
1:18-32	34, 49, 62, 134, 140
1:18-20	55
1:18	15, 23, 25, 34, 35, 131, 132, 135, 137, 140
1:19-23	23, 140
1:19-20	25
1:20-21	52
1:20	31, 35
1:21-28	55
1:23	25, 132
1:24	15, 25, 35, 140, 143
1:25	25, 138, 139-40
1:26	25, 35
1:27	131
1:28	25, 35, 132
1:29-31	25, 40, 84, 130, 131, 132
1:29	15, 39, 84, 131, 140
1:32	25, 52, 132
2:1—3:20	132
2:4	21
2:5-11	49
2:5	25, 35
2:7-10	15
2:8	15, 25
2:9	35
2:12-16	49
2:12	14, 17, 22, 34
2:14-15	15, 108
2:23	15, 107
2:24	22
2:26-29	15
3:3-7	46
3:5-8	35
3:5	15, 25
3:7	14
3:8	16, 35
3:9	13, 14, 15, 16, 18, 22, 26, 34, 35, 36, 38, 41, 49, 129, 132
3:10	18
3:11-18	18, 49
3:18	26
3:19	51
3:20	14, 16, 21, 22
3:21-26	46
3:21	49
3:22	46
3:23	14, 17, 18, 23, 34, 49, 110
3:24	31
3:25-26	46
3:25	14, 17, 23, 34, 49
4:3	92
4:5	15, 92
4:7-8	13, 34, 49, 92
4:7	14, 15, 75, 91
4:8	14, 16, 92, 101
4:15	15, 22, 25, 107
4:17	47
4:17b	20
4:18-21	47
4:24-25	47
4:25	23, 34, 46, 57, 58, 75, 107
5-8	16, 20, 24, 27, 28, 36, 41, 50, 51, 52, 53, 54, 62, 70, 71
5-7	49, 52
5-6	13, 29
5	37, 93
5:1	29, 36
5:2	31
5:5	47, 52
5:6-10	27
5:6-8	45
5:6	15, 27, 28
5:8	14, 17, 28, 29
5:9-10	93
5:9	25, 29
5:10	28, 29
5:11	36
5:12—8:3	148
5:12-21	19, 20, 24, 25, 36, 37, 48, 51, 52, 60, 61, 62
5:12-18	90
5:12-16	36
5:12	14, 16, 17, 18, 24, 47, 52, 53, 54, 55, 56, 60, 61, 132

Romans (continued)

5:12a	23, 36, 54
5:12b	38, 52, 54, 55
5:12d	23, 24
5:13–14	22, 27
5:13	14, 19
5:13b	101
5:14	14, 15, 16, 22, 23, 49, 55, 107
5:15–21	29, 49
5:15–19	54, 56, 58, 59
5:15	15, 51, 56, 107
5:16	14, 15, 23, 49, 56, 107
5:17	15, 19, 56, 107
5:18	15, 56, 107, 107
5:19	14, 17, 23, 38, 46, 51, 52, 58, 61
5:20–21	50, 51, 62
5:20	14, 15, 21, 23, 36, 101, 107
5:21	14, 16, 19, 30, 31, 36, 38, 39, 40, 47, 107, 123
6–8	19
6	17, 20, 29, 46, 48
6:1–4	120
6:1–2	123
6:1	14, 22, 50
6:1b	30
6:2	14, 29, 30, 50
6:3–13	50
6:4	20, 30, 50
6:5	20, 30
6:6–8	110
6:6	14, 16, 28, 29, 30, 49
6:7	14, 30, 50
6:8	31
6:9	19, 20, 29, 30, 49, 50
6:10	14, 30
6:11	20, 29, 30, 31, 119
6:12–23	130, 132–133, 141
6:12	14, 16, 20, 28, 29, 30, 36, 49, 128
6:13–14	31
6:13	14, 15, 16, 29, 31
6:13a	135, 145
6:14–15	22, 30, 31, 36
6:14	14, 16, 49, 50, 123
6:15	14, 17, 50
6:16–23	51
6:16	14, 16, 19, 31, 101
6:17	14, 17
6:18	14, 30, 31, 49, 50, 101
6:19	15, 16, 28, 29, 31, 50
6:19b	144
6:20	14, 17, 30, 31, 101
6:21	19
6:22	14, 30, 31
6:23	14, 20, 31, 36
7	17, 21, 22, 26, 27, 28, 36, 39, 40, 43, 72, 135
7:1–6	50
7:2–3	50
7:3	30
7:4–12	135, 145
7:4	50
7:5	14, 16, 19, 21, 28, 29, 128
7:6	29, 50
7:7	14, 50
7:8	14, 16, 21, 29, 39
7:8–11	21
7:8–10	21
7:9–11	19
7:9–10	27
7:9	14, 22, 26
7:10	21
7:11	14, 27
7:12	21, 36
7:13	14, 19
7:14–25	50
7:14	14, 17, 21, 22, 28, 36, 129
7:16–17	17
7:17	14, 28
7:18	28
7:18b	17
7:20	14, 17
7:22	21
7:23	14, 19
7:24–25	36
7:24	19, 20, 28, 36
7:25	14, 36, 43
8	28
8:2	14, 30
8:3	14, 21, 29, 46, 88, 89
8:3a	22
8:4–5	126
8:4	28, 47
8:5	43
8:6	19
8:7	28

8:8	28	1:23	139
8:10–11	19	1:24	94
8:10	14, 16, 20, 29, 30, 31	1:27–31	80
8:11	28	1:30	68, 93, 96
8:12–13	28	2:1	77
8:12	20	2:6–16	77, 78
8:13	16, 20, 31	2:6	68
8:14	31	2:9	77
8:15	47	2:10	77
8:19–23	52	3:16	77
8:21	30	5	71, 143
8:23	20	5:5	77
8:29	110	5:8	67
8:32	46, 48, 58	5:10–11	131
8:33	58	5:10	97
8:39	36	5:11	84
9–11	133	6	75, 77
9:14	15	6:7–8	66
9:22	25	6:9–10	84, 131
10:3	134	6:11	68
10:17	59	6:12–20	83
11	46	6:12	143
11:11	15, 107	6:13	74
11:12	15, 107	6:18	14, 66, 74, 83
11:25–32	134	6:19	83
11:26	15, 135	7	73, 75
11:27	14, 34, 75	7:25–35	74
11:28	135	7:28	14, 73
12:19–21	45	7:31	67, 72
12:19	25	7:36	14, 73
13:4–5	25	8	74, 75, 77
13:8–10	47	8:11–12	75
13:13	84	8:12	13, 14, 74
14:1—15:6	47	10	71
14:23	13, 14, 16, 101	10:11	66, 72, 78
15:1–6	47	11:7	110
15:7–13	45, 47	13	92
15:8	46	13:1	68
15:15–19	57	13:5	92
15:20	59	13:6	15
16:20	38, 39, 40, 45	15	19, 20, 37, 71, 72
16:26	47	15:3	13, 14, 68, 69, 75, 76, 100
		15:7	14
		15:8–10	103
1 Corinthians		15:9	135
1–2	68	15:10	27
1	71, 77	15:17	75, 76, 123
1:18	67, 139	15:21–22	20, 24

1 Corinthians (continued)

15:22	60, 67, 71, 131, 132
15:24–26	45
15:25–26	72
15:26	78
15:27–28	45
15:28	78
15:32–34	77
15:34	14, 80
15:35–44	20
15:54	78
15:50–57	28
15:54–56	72
15:56	14, 148

2 Corinthians

1–9	82
1:5	81
1:19–20	95
1:22	81
2	91, 92
2:5–11	91
2:5	91
2:7	91, 92
2:10	91
3:1—4:15	94
3	94
3:9	94, 107
3:18	94, 98, 110
4:4	110
4:6	110
5	87, 92, 94, 96
5:2	56
5:5	81
5:4	56
5:10	85
5:14–21	90, 92
5:14–20	87, 89, 94
5:14–15	89
5:14	89
5:15	88, 89, 98
5:15b	95
5:16–21	89
5:16–20	89
5:16	90
5:17	89, 93
5:18–21	82, 88, 93
5:18–20	89
5:18	94
5:19	15, 23, 75, 81, 84, 90, 92, 107
5:19b	90, 92, 95
5:20	89, 92, 94
5:20d	98
5:21	29, 72, 76, 82, 83, 84, 85, 87, 89, 90, 91, 92, 93, 94, 95, 96, 98
5:21b	90, 95
6:7	82, 95
6:14—7:1	84, 85, 96
6:14–21	82
6:14–16	85
6:14	15, 84
6:16	85
7	91
7:1	85
7:2	84
7:9–10	21
7:12	84, 91
8	81
8:2	81
8:9	96, 98
9	94
9:5	84
9:8	98
9:9–10	95
9:9	94
11:7	14, 83, 86, 87
11:27	101
12:11	21
12:13	15, 84, 87, 91, 92
12:17–18	84
12:20	84
12:21	15, 83, 84, 143
13:2	83
13:7	85
13:21	97

Galatians

1:3–4	100, 113
1:4	13, 14, 75, 100, 103, 108, 110, 126
1:13–16	103
1:15	103
2:11	103
2:13	104

2:14	104	6:1	15, 107
2:15-21	107	6:7-8	107, 109, 112
2:15	13, 14, 103, 155	6:8a	101
2:16	106	6:14	102, 109, 111, 112
2:17	14, 103, 104, 148-49	6:15	110
2:18	103, 104		
2:19-21	57		

Ephesians

2:19	30, 111		
2:20	103, 110, 113	1:7	23, 116, 117, 118, 123, 129
2:21	100, 107	1:20	122
3:2-5	103, 111	1:21	126
3:5	144	2	45, 121
3:8	106	2:1-10	122
3:9	106	2:1-2	122
3:13-14	103, 109, 111	2:1	23, 115, 116, 117, 118, 121, 122, 123
3:13	88, 89, 110, 113		
3:14	106	2:2-3	126
3:19-25	109	2:2	119, 121, 123, 127
3:19	15, 105, 107	2:2b	126
3:21	21, 108, 110	2:2c	126
3:22	13, 14, 15, 16, 18, 70, 105, 129, 148-49	2:3	117, 123, 127, 128
		2:5-6	122
3:23-25	105	2:5	23, 119, 22
3:23	22	2:6	122
3:28	102, 113	2:7	122, 123, 126
4:1-11	105	2:8	122
4:3	112, 113	2:10	122, 123
4:4-5	22, 109	2:11-18	118
4:6-7	111	2:11	128
4:9-10	104	2:14	117
4:19	110, 113	2:15	116
4:21	22	2:16	117
4:24-26	105	2:17	117
5:1	111	2:18	117, 122
5:3-4	100	2:22	122
5:5	108	3:3	128
5:13-25	103, 106	3:9	126
5:13-14	111	3:10	47, 127
5:16	111	3:11	126
5:18	22	3:21	126
5:19-21	84, 101, 108-9, 131	4:1	121
5:19-20	109, 111, 143	4:17—5:20	116
5:19	15, 101	4:17-19	127
5:21	101	4:17-18	128
5:22-24	111, 113	4:18	117
5:22-23	109	4:19	143
5:24	101, 109, 111, 112	4:26-27	127
5:25	112	4:26	115

Ephesians (continued)

4:30	118
4:32	92, 118
5:2	117, 122
5:3	143
5:5	117
5:6	116, 117, 118
5:8	117
5:14	117
6:5	128
6:11	127
6:12	37, 126, 127

Philippians

2:6–11	29, 89, 143
2:6–8	143
2:10	45
2:11	45
2:12–14	57
3:6	103, 135
3:8–11	110
3:12	56
4:10	55

Colossians

1:13	117, 127
1:14	115, 116, 118, 123, 127, 129
1:15–20	45
1:19–20	45
1:19	127
1:20	117, 118
1:21	116, 119, 120
1:22	117, 118
2:2	122
2:6	120, 121
2:10	127
2:11	128
2:13	23, 92, 115, 116, 117, 118, 119, 121, 128
2:14	116
2:15	127
2:17	128
2:18	128
2:20	116, 120
2:23	128

3	121
3:1	121
3:2	119, 121
3:3	121
3:5	116, 120, 121, 143
3:5a	119
3:5b	119
3:6	116, 117, 118, 119, 120
3:6b	120
3:7	119, 120, 121, 122
3:8–9	116
3:8	120
3:9	116, 120, 121
3:10	121
3:12–14	121
3:13	92, 118

1 Thessalonians

1:3	141
1:5	141
1:8	141
1:9–10	145
1:9	139, 141
2:1–12	141
2:3	15, 131, 143
2:5–12	141
2:5	131
2:12	144
2:13–16	131, 133
2:13	133, 139
2:14–16	133–134
2:14	134
2:15	134
2:16	14, 130, 131
2:16c	134
3:2	141
3:5	141
3:6	141
3:7	141
3:10	141
3:10b	141
4:1–8	142
4:3–8	131, 132, 141, 142
4:3b–6a	142
4:3b	142
4:4–5	142
4:4	142

4:5	143	1:11	151, 153, 159, 160
4:6–8	142	1:12–17	152, 155
4:6	143	1:12–16	153, 160
4:6b	142	1:12–14	153
4:7	15, 131	1:12–13	153
4:8	144	1:13	153, 154
5:6–7	131	1:15	150, 152, 160
5:8	141	1:16–17	153, 160
5:12	144	1:16	153
5:14	144	1:17	153
		1:18–19	153
		1:20	153, 154, 156

2 Thessalonians

		2:1–8	154
1:3	141	2:1–7	155
1:4	141	2:1–4	151
1:8	140, 144	2:1–2	160
1:11	141	2:1	154
2:3–12	131, 132, 136, 137	2:2	154
2:3–4	137, 138	2:3	155
2:3	131, 136, 137	2:4	154
2:4	137	2:5–6	155, 160
2:4b	137, 138	2:5	155
2:7	131	2:6	154, 155
2:8	137	2:6b–7	160
2:9–12	138	2:7	154
2:10	131, 137, 139	2:8	154
2:10b	139	2:9–15	155
2:11	139	2:9–10	157
2:12	131, 137, 140	2:11	156
2:12a	140	2:12	156
3:6–16	144	2:14	150, 155
		2:15	156, 160

1 Timothy

		2:15b	157
		3:1	152
1:3–20	153	3:3	150
1:3–7	153	3:14–15	160
1:3–4	149	3:15	152
1:3	149, 152, 156	3:16	160
1:4–6	152	4:1–5	151
1:4	151, 152, 159	4:4–5	160
1:5	152	4:3	151, 156
1:7	152	4:9	152
1:8	159	4:14	158
1:9–11	150, 152, 154	5:14–15	156
1:9–10	150	5:17–25	157
1:9	150, 151	5:17	157
1:10–11	152	5:18	157, 158
1:10b–11	152	5:19	158, 159

1 Timothy *(continued)*

5:20	149, 157, 158, 159
5:21	159
5:21a	158
5:21b	158
5:22	150, 157, 158, 159
5:24	150, 157, 158, 159
6:4–5	150
6:13–15	160
6:16	160
6:17–18	160
6:20	160

2 Timothy

2:11	152
3:2–5	150
3:2	150
3:6–7	156
3:6	150
3:11	150

Titus

1:4	61
2:11–14	155
3:3	150
3:8	152

1 Peter

4:18	150

2 Peter

1:8	61

Jude

15	150

Apocrypha

4 Ezra

3:7–11	25
3:7	54
7:116–119	25
7:118–20	54

Tobit

3:1–5	8
3:3	8
3:4–5	9

Wisdom of Solomon

1:4	9
10:1	23
10:13	9
11:15–16	9
12:2	9
15:2	9

Ecclesiasticus

2:11	9
3:3	9
3:14	9
3:30	9
5:4–5	9
5:6–7	9
12:6	150
14:1	9
15:14–17	54
21:2a	9
21:2b–c	9
25;24	54
28:1	9
41:5	150

Baruch

1:18	119

Susanna

34	159
41	159
43	159
46	159
52	159
55	159
59	159
61	159

Index of Ancient Documents

1 Maccabees

1:10	9
2:44	9
2:48	9
2:62	9

Pseudepigrapha

2 Baruch

23:4	24, 54
48:42–47	25
54:14	25
54:15	24, 25
54:19	25, 54
56:6	24

Life of Adam and Eve

7.1	53
8.2	53
13.8	54

Psalms of Solomon

14	9, 10
14:1–5	10
14:6–9	10
14:6b–7	10
14:6	10
14:9a	10
14:10	10

Testament of Judah

19:1–2	10
19:2	10
19:3	10
19:4	10

Testament of Issachar

7:1	11
7:2–3	11
7:5	11
7:6	11
7:7	11

Josephus

Antiquities	11

Philo of Alexandria

On Flight and Finding	12
On Sobriety	12
Special Laws	12
That the Worse is Wont to Attack the Better	12

Greco-Roman Writings

Aristotle

Nicomachean Ethics	2
Politics	3

Arrian

Anabasis	5–6

Greek Papyri

BGU 3 846	2
BGU 4 1141	2

Herodotus

Histories	3

Plutarch

On Moral Virtue	5

Polybius

Histories	3–5

Strabo

Geography	5

Patristics Writings
Augustine
"Nature and Grace"   27

www.ingramcontent.com/pod-product-compliance
Lightning Source LLC
Chambersburg PA
CBHW031433150426
43191CB00006B/492